BYRON EUBANKS

The Academy and the Possibility of Belief

Essays on Intellectual and Spiritual Life

Critical Education and Ethics

Editors

Barry Kanpol, *St. Joseph's University*
Fred Yeo, *Southeast Missouri State University*

The Academy and the Possibility of Belief: Essays on Intellectual and
   Spiritual Life
   *Mary Louise Buley-Meissner, Mary McCaslin Thompson, and
   Elizabeth Bachrach Tan (eds.)*

Issues and Trends in Critical Pedagogy
   Barry Kanpol

Teachers Talking Back and Breaking Bread
   Barry Kanpol

Forthcoming

Dialogic Virtues: Negotiating Diversity in Multicultural Education
   Eric Bain-Selbo

The Ethics of Critical Pedagogy: The Need for a Moral
   Compact in Educational Reform
   Barry Kanpol and Fred Yeo

JOY as a Metaphor of Convergence: A Phenomenological and
   Aesthetic Investigation of Social and Educational Change
   Delores D. Liston

Demarcating the Borders
   Carlos Tejada, Corrine Martinez, and Zeus Leonardo

From Otherness to Cultural Democracy
   Suzanne SooHoo

Teaching as a Spiritual Activity: A Classroom as a
   Place of Darkness and Mystery
   Carol Zinn

The Academy and the Possibility of Belief

Essays on Intellectual and Spiritual Life

edited by

Mary Louise Buley-Meissner
University of Wisconsin-Milwaukee

Mary McCaslin Thompson
Anoka Ramsey Community College

Elizabeth Bachrach Tan
University of Massachusetts-Amherst

HAMPTON PRESS, INC.
CRESSKILL, NEW JERSEY

Printed in the United States of America

Library of Congress Cataloging-in-Publication Data

The academy and the possibility of belief : essays on intellectual and spiritual life/ edited by Mary Louise Buley-Meissner, Mary McCaslin Thompson, Elizabeth Bachrach Tan.
    p. cm. -- (Critical education and ethics)
    Includes bibliographical references and indexes.
    ISBN 1-58283-220-2 -- ISBN 1-57273-221-0 (pbk)
    1. Education, Higher--Aims and objectives. 2. Spirituality--Study and teaching (Higher) I. Buley-Meissner, Mary Louise. II. Thompson, Mary McCaslin. III. Tan, Elizabeth Bachrach. IV. Series

LB2324.A27 1999
378'01--dc21   99-047996

Hampton Press, Inc.
23 Broadway
Cresskill, NJ 07626

To my Milwaukee family, whose sense of humor and appreciation of the present moment have kept me going through the long winters of this project.
MLBM

* * * * *

For Christopher, who bears Christ to me.
MMT

* * * * *

To Peter Elbow, with appreciation for his encouragement during the early stages of this project.
To my husband, Barrie Tan, with love and gratitude for his unwavering support and remarkable enthusiasm for integrating his spiritual and intellectual commitments.
EBT

Contents

Series Foreword

Barry Kanpol
St. Joseph's University
Fred Yeo
Southeast Missouri State University

As we contemplate the rapidly approaching 21st century, with its promises of new technologies, cyber-realities, new subjectivities, and cultural demands for new responses to old transcendent questions, American schooling is increasingly defined by arthritic traditionalisms of standardized assessment and testing, school and teacher accountabilities, models of exacerbated efficiency and tracking, and ever more strident state and federal calls for more of the same. The lack of vision in and out of the U.S. educational establishment continues to underwrite the spread of the "savage inequalities" that Kozol (1991) found so disparaging in inner-city schools, even to those in hitherto secluded suburbia. Mired in their increasingly narrow traditional practices and corporate market logic, U.S. schools and their government factotums trumpet national reports that herald increasing failure and simultaneously increasing reliance on syllogisms that wipe away democratic and humanistic possibilities. U.S. education faces the potentialities of the future with the instruments of the past.

With this in mind, it is no small claim that U.S. schooling is representative and simultaneously constitutive of the race, class, and gender disparities illustrative and symptomatic of the larger U.S. society. As an ideologic alternative to both the mainstream's and Right's configurations of education and society, critical theory and its practitioners have long argued that for schools to thrive and be more democratic, inroads must be made to challenge the overt and hidden assumptions that frame U.S. education. Critical theorists argue that we live in an age where there is an illusion of education and the actuality of profound democratic decline (McLaren, 1991). Progressive multiculturalists such as Banks (1991) and critical multiculturalists such as Nieto (1995), Giroux (1992), and Sleeter and McLaren (1995) have attempted theoretically to identify a critical and politically just pedagogy framed within postmodern understandings of difference and borders of cultural identity to challenge dominant forms of alienation, oppression, and marginalization.

Critical theory has, however, its own contradictions and failures. Although challenging theoretically dominant social, cultural, and educational paradigms, these authors' insights have sadly effected little societal transformation on the way out of the growing despair of poverty, the melanoma of racism (West, 1993), and the general malaise that attends a social system characterized as misanthropic and segregated by class, race, and gender. Critical theorists argue vociferously for U.S. schools to secure a more democratic and egalitarian community. However, they rarely speak in a unified fashion to effect a program for social or political change and are seemingly at a loss for answers as to "how to fix things up." Mired in the postmodern quandary, they do not want to be labeled as *technocratic strategists, essentialists*, or *pragmatic,* so they offer no clear plan or normative framework to guide the changes they advocate. In many senses, despite the validity of their critique, critical theorists have become stymied by an intolerance of praxis.

The foregoing, as a pedagogically theoretical, practical, and professional realization, has prompted us and others (e.g., Purpel and Shapiro, 1995) to view what has become known as the postmodernist critique with increasing cynicism and a growing concern that the questions we are asking may well be the wrong ones. The influences of postmodernism on critical theory, although insightful, have acted to splinter transformative possibilities resulting in a dizzying array of balkanized positions and interpretations among radical educational theorists. Yet, what would represent a unifying possibility for the current disarray of the Left, a "politics of meaning" for education?

In response, and central to our purpose, a few theorists on the Left, notably those grounded in some form of liberation theology or holism, have argued that both the mainstream and the Left crises are not just political or economic, but are at their heart moral and spiritual. Specifically, West (1993) has argued that the need for change is fueled by what he has termed a "human quest"—a reconceptualization of the democratic and ethical implications of a spiritual conception of what it is to be human in an era often labeled as being represented by a failure of conscience. Although the political Left has powerfully argued about the demise of political democracy and social equity (Giroux, 1992; McLaren, 1991) and education's place in that, others have critiqued the Left for its cynicism and nihilism (Habermas, 1987; Purpel and Shapiro, 1995; West, 1993). We argue that the Left's ineffectualness is due to a failure to ground political critique in moral possibility. In our opinion, the struggle of the academic educational Left, particularly one that is rooted within the postmodern, is bereft of the language of the ethical or the moral—the human language of hope that must frame any obscure discourse of change, possibility and justice. The educational mainstream and Right have forgotten that democracy is about change and the Left has failed to understand that it is also about hope, the moral and the spiritual—what some have termed as *prophetic education.*

Instead of writing about an agenda of commitment to community, the Left, conforming to a postmodern sensibility, has parlayed, one might suggest even trapped, itself into fragmentation; a politics of division, exclusion, separation, and irrelevance. The critical endeavor has become an end in itself, and in our sentiment, lacks the moral and ethical certitude of commitment to a humane and democratic vision of social justice based on a notion of human compassion, hope, and even spirituality—all of which form the foundation of human imagining that life can be better, fairer, more just.

Although we acknowledge that this argument has and is being asserted in education by a few critical theorists, it is either framed within generalized social concerns or is targeted at mainstream suburban schools. Even the most trenchant of arguments posed by the Left are aimed at general education, often reifying the social in a political critique. Lost amidst this discussion are those schools most in need of transformative possibilities—urban and inner-city school sites and their attendant communities. Admittedly, critical theorists and researchers in education have attempted some description and theorizing on the systemics and dehumanization of inner-city education; on the need to reconstruct both the social and ideologic paradigms of how we understand education in general; and on the need to incorporate educationally configured postmodern understandings of issues such as difference, identity, ethnicity, race, gender, marginalization, the "other," and so on.

Yet, it seems that each of these still misses being able to mobilize, stir, motivate their respective audience and the greater public to effect change. In some cases, these writers have unintentionally obfuscated potential practical frameworks for transformative change within the esoterica of theory. In others, although advocating social transformation, the practicalities of effecting such change in schools has been lost within an essentially political menu. It is our argument that in order to effect a re-democratization of the social and the educational in this country, a fusion or synthesis must occur between insights offered by critical theory, postmodernism, and liberation spiritualism. More specifically, we believe the response to the issue of balkanization or the irrelevance caused by theories of fractionalization should be to ask and address the heretofore unasked questions; that is, to seek possibilities for radical transformation within a moral and spiritual framework where a critical argument is subsumed in an ethical one. Put differently, it is time for critical theorists and pedagogists to pose the eminently practical and ultimately ethical question of what constitutes the "good society."

With this in mind, the aim and purpose of this series is to bridge the gap between the educational Left, as embodied within postmodern criticality, and the prophetic or spiritual tradition within all its multiplicities. This series is

derived of a concern for a morally and spiritually driven vision that has to date
been severely underplayed in, if not outright missing from, the literature of educational critique and has thereby left it to the religious Right to parlay its trun-
cated orthodoxy into the nation's political, educational, and social discourse.
Within this series, we provide a forum to investigate the parameters of a morally grounded prophetic and democratic platform intended to fulfill the critical
theorists' ideas of the possibilities of educational and social change in general;
change that must be morally, ethically, and spiritually grounded in a transcendent and subjective critique, hope, and humanity.

REFERENCES

Banks, James A. *Teaching Strategies for Ethnic Studies* (5th ed.). Boston: Allyn &
Bacon, 1991.
Giroux, Henry. *Border Crossings: Cultural Workers and the Politics of Education.* New
York: Routledge, 1992.
Habermas, J. *The Philosophic Discourse of Modernity.* Cambridge, MA: MIT Press,
1987.
Kozol, Jonathan. *Savage Inequalities; Children in America's Schools.* New York: Crown
Publishers, 1991.
McLaren, Peter. "Critical Pedagogy: Constructing an Arch of Social Dreaming and a
Doorway to Hope." *Journal of Education, 173* (1991).
Nieto, Sonia. *Affirming Diversity: The Sociopolitical Context of Multicultural Education*
(2nd ed.). New York: Longman, 1995.
Purpel, David, and Svi Shapiro. *Beyond Liberation and Excellence: Towards a New
Public Discourse for Education.* New York: Routledge, 1995.
Sleeter, Christine, and Peter McLaren. (Eds.). *Multicultural Education, Critical
Pedagogy and the Politics of Discourse.* Albany: SUNY Press, 1995.
West, Cornel. *Race Matters.* Boston, MA: Beacon Press, 1993.

Acknowledgments

We thank Barbara Bernstein, our general editor at Hampton Press, for her initial and consistent support of this project. From the beginning, Fred Yeo and Barry Kanpol, our series editors, have had complete confidence in the value of this collection. We always will be grateful for their commitment to careful inquiry into the ethical and moral dimensions of critical education. We thank our contributors for writing here out of personal and professional conviction. Their dedication to teaching and learning has brought this book to life. Finally, we thank Daniel Meissner, without whose help this project would have been impossible to complete.

1

Introduction

Mary Louise Buley-Meissner

Mary McCaslin Thompson

Elizabeth Bachrach Tan

In this book, we not only acknowledge the important work being done by teachers and students, but we also recognize the singularity, integrity, and complexity of their lives. At a time when theory has explained how all of us are constructed and produced by society, culture, and discourse, we hope to return attention to the rich reality of lives shaped by the interrelationship of mind and spirit, intellect and imagination, reason and feeling, immanence and transcendence. Toward that end, we challenge predominant intellectual assumptions that open discussion of spirituality should be silenced rather than encouraged; that religious beliefs should be discarded rather than examined or deepened; that "higher" education in particular means moving beyond faith to reason. As Ernest Boyer (a former president of the Carnegie Foundation for the Advancement of Teaching) has observed:

> Educating students in a multicultural world means affirming the sacredness of every individual, celebrating the uniqueness of every culture, and acknowledging . . . the distinctiveness that makes us who we are. . . . In our deeply divided world, students also must begin to understand that while we are unique, we do share many things in common. (1992, p. 4)

Many educators today share Boyer's concern that we must respect our students' individuality and recognize their commonalities. Aware that approximately 80%

of first-year college and university students indicate some form of religious preference ("Fact File," 1992), we encourage educators to reconsider the spiritual dimensions of students' diversity.

Perhaps more so than any other educators, English teachers must attend carefully to the complexities of students' development in self-expression, communication of ideas, and comprehension of views different from their own. In language and literature courses, we often work closely with students from widely varying religious backgrounds, whose self-expectations, intellectual interests, and social interactions are influenced by their faith communities. For example, it may not be unusual at a large university for an introductory class to include Puerto Rican and Cuban Catholics, African Americans and Mexican American Baptists, a Russian Jew, an East European Lutheran, an Indian American Hindu, Korean and Hmong Buddhists. Other teachers may find that most of their students are more homogeneous in their backgrounds. However, even if only a few students in a class identify themselves as different from the rest in their religious upbringing, their ideas can challenge everyone's sense of what is reasonable, ethical, or justifiable. In our classrooms—as in the civic community to which we all belong—cross-cultural communication takes place through identification much more than persuasion. Achieving a deeper understanding of each other's lives becomes possible only through practicing "the discipline of displacement," Palmer's (1983) term for imagining what the world looks like from perspectives other than our own (pp. 115–16). And more often than not, what the world looks like is informed (especially in the etymological sense of being animated or inspired) by spirituality.

In fact, our motivation for developing this book can be found in a question asked by co-editor Tan five years ago: "How can English teachers—and other educators in the humanities—extend their discussions of students' diverse identifications to include more careful consideration of students' spirituality?" Many students in undergraduate and graduate programs have been embarrassed, scorned, or shamed when they have acknowledged in class their religious backgrounds or faith traditions. The implicit (sometimes explicit) message from their teachers has been clear: To be educated means to be educated out of beliefs affirmed by church, temple, synagogue, or sacred circle. To be educated means to become an intellectual skeptic, an independent thinker whose judgments are based on material reason and logical analysis. Attempting to meet the demands of the university, students frequently assume the distanced critical stance essential to academic inquiry. They take on the roles of well-disciplined rationalists as they try to speak and write standard academic discourse. With varying degrees of success, they learn to disassociate themselves from the objects of their study. But outside of class, they often raise troubling questions about the means and ends of that education. Why should the life of the mind and the life of the spirit be separated? Why does higher education so often result in self-doubt rather than self-knowledge? A central concern emerges: If pluralism, diversity, and inclusiveness are guiding concepts of educational reform, why are students so often silenced into intellectual conformity?

   This collection originated in response to such questions. Our initial aim was to break the enormous silence on spirituality by opening up more opportunities (pedagogical, theoretical, institutional) for thoughtful inquiry into the sources, forms, and consequences of students' world views. This led us to develop a roundtable on "The Academy and the Possibility of Belief" for the 1993 Conference on College Composition and Communication (CCCC). Our efforts were motivated by our experience with undergraduates, graduate students, and colleagues, which had affirmed the accuracy of Henry Louis Gates' (1992) observation: "There is no tolerance without respect—and no respect without knowledge" (p. 37). Frequently, well-meaning skeptics had cautioned us that it would be better not to discuss such a controversial subject as spirituality at all. However, we realized that to remain silent would be to maintain an antagonistic attitude; as Maria Harris (1987) puts it, "Ignorance is never neutral" (p. 100). The roundtable discussion therefore emphasized that the plurality of student identities in higher education deserves affirmative recognition; participants included ourselves, Mary Rose O'Reilley, Robin Brown, and Michael Jon Olson. That discussion—and our interaction with the audience—raised questions and themes that guided the development of this book.

   We decided to keep "The Academy and the Possibility of Belief" as the title for this collection to indicate our concern with the complexities of truths other than the strictly rational or abstractly theoretical. In using the word *belief*, we highlight our interest in perspectives evolved through the creative interrelationship of mind and spirit; deeply held feelings affirmed by spiritual fellowship; self-knowledge and social values derived from membership in faith communities. At the roundtable, audience interest and involvement in these issues convinced us that teachers as well as students often struggle with questions of identity and integrity, particularly teachers who lead the "divided lives" described by Parker Palmer (1983). In our work, many of us practice intellectual skepticism and apply the principles of antifoundationalism; in our lives outside the academy, we belong to mosques, temples, synagogues, churches, and meeting houses of many kinds. The truths most significant in our lives—sometimes realized in moments of grace or revelation, sometimes achieved through lifelong struggles between faith and doubt—often are truths that cannot be voiced in the academy. At risk of being dismissed as unprofessional, teachers too are silenced into conformity. Like our students, many of us have tried to separate what is inextricably connected: the formation of our selves and our knowledge of the world. Perhaps that is what prompted one member of the roundtable audience to remark: "This is the first time I've been able to discuss spirituality in a professional setting. You should try to reach a wider audience with these ideas. Teachers need to have the complexity of their own lives—as well as their students'—affirmed."

   Indeed, this collection has come together at a time when many are realizing that a wider audience interested in spirituality exists, for religious movements have not disappeared from U.S. cultural life as some predicted would happen. In *Fire From Heaven*, theologian Harvey Cox (1995) concedes that his predictions in the 1960s about the eventual disappearance of religion from the public square were faulty. In fact, he now sees a global resurgence of religious interest and involvement:

> A religious renaissance of sorts is under way all over the globe. Religions that some theologians thought had been stunted by western materialism or suffocated by totalitarian repression have regained a whole new vigor. Buddhism and Hinduism, Christianity and Judaism, Islam and Shinto, and many smaller sects are once again alive and well. . . . We are definitely in a period of renewed religious vitality, another "great awakening" if you will, with all the promise and peril religious revivals always bring with them, but this time on a world scale. (p. xvi)

Journalists are also noticing, as Cox does, the increasing visibility of various religions and spiritualities. At any moment in the past few years, one could look to the media for coverage of religious issues in the United States and abroad; however, the press typically focuses on the unusual or the sensational: the Branch Davidians in Waco, Texas; religious/ethnic conflicts in Bosnia and the Middle East; Libya's $1 million offer to the Nation of Islam; Sinead O'Connor ripping apart a picture of Pope John Paul II on late-night TV; Scientology's celebrity membership; the vote to ordain women in the Anglican church; best-seller Gregorian chant CDs; angels, angels, angels; New Age channelers; baby boomers returning to God; religion online; Jihad; Fatwa; the bombing of mosques and temples in India; the burning of African American churches.

Of course, the scandalous, the violent, and the bizarre in the world of religion receive perennial attention, upstaged only periodically by an archaeological discovery or momentous gathering. Still, what the media recognizes, language and literature programs almost always ignore: Religion and spirituality compose an integral dimension of human experience in contemporary life.

New developments, however, are starting to occur: We are entering a period when academics are reexamining the interrelationships between personal faith and intellectual life. Numerous books and articles have begun to challenge viewpoints that dismiss or deride the value of religious inquiry for professors, scholars, and students. Quite a number of beginning and revamped subscription journals and newsstand magazines now address spiritual concerns, often including articles and essays written by intellectuals and university educators: *First Things, Tikkun, Common Boundary, Parabola, Tricycle: The Buddhist Review, Lilith, Image: A Journal of the Arts and Religion, Religion and American Culture, The Quest, Commentary, Weavings, The Oxford Review.* Older journals and magazines with religious emphases continue to find active reading audiences as well: *America, Cross Currents, Soundings, Sojourners, Christianity Today, The Christian Century, Commentary.* And, in all of the aforementioned periodicals, it is not uncommon to find bylines of humanities and science professors from both small liberal arts colleges and large research universities. Most of the voices are not whining in the wilderness. Most do not present visions of return to halcyon conditions when clergy tended the gardens of learning, and Christian ideals were the normative values and the assumed best virtues for all. Instead, the writers object to prevalent assumptions that religious belief is incongruous and incompatible with intelligent, advanced education.

Although there appears to be a reinvigorated discussion taking place, we also recognize that in some quarters the discussion never abated, and that in others there has been strong resistance to acknowledging that spirituality and the intellectual life are not necessarily antithetical. Many recent books focus on an educational context that has increasingly marginalized religious studies and professionals with outspoken or acknowledged religious identifications. Some writers—David Gill (1997) in *Should God Get Tenure?: Essays on Religion and Higher Education*, James Tunstead Burtchaell (1998) in *The Dying of the Light: The Disengagement of Colleges and Universities From Their Christian Churches*, George Marsden (1994) in *The Soul of the University*, Warren Nord (1995) in *Religion and American Education: Rethinking a National Dilemma*, Page Smith (1990) in *Killing the Spirit: Higher Education in America*, and Mark Schwehn (1993) in *Exiles from Eden: Religion and the Academic Vocation in America*—consider historical developments that have transformed teaching universities into research institutions that emphasize mind over spirit (and body), research and grant writing over teaching, and professional training over character development. These scholars suggest that learning environments have become inhospitable to religious studies and religiously informed perspectives for a number of reasons: professionalization of the academic vocation, divestiture of clerical control of colleges, increasing influence and funding by government and business. Changing views of the mission of universities as well as the widespread appeal of agnosticism, relativism, scientific empiricism, and social constructivism have created classroom conditions in which religious ideals are questioned suspiciously or antagonistically. When religious views are considered, most writers claim that skepticism has become the primary (typically only) accepted intellectual posture for serious investigations.

As many of us are all too aware, antagonism toward religious peoples and ideas on college campuses is apparent, not only because of skepticism, but also because of bigotry. Anti-Semitic rhetoric and vandalism continue to be reported; anti-Islamic attitudes and discourse continue to emerge. Another aspect of this situation, although more subtle and less violent, has also begun to be noticed: discrimination at the institutional level of academe. Researchers such as Robert Wuthnow (1990), a sociologist and the director of the Center for the Study of American Religion at Princeton University, contend that religious people in higher education experience anti-religious bias and ostracism.

Wuthnow's observations find support from two scholars in English departments—Roy Battenhouse (1987) and Robert Detweiler (1991). Both have written about contentious remarks made by Jonathan Culler (1986), a previous president of the Modern Language Association (MLA). First in an essay published in *Profession*, an annual MLA journal, and later in a chapter in his book *Framing the Sign: Criticism and Its Institutions*, Culler has viewed a renewed interest in religious issues by literary scholars as disconcertingly sympathetic, and he has urged a staunch refusal of religious viewpoints. Associating all religions with superstition, Culler encourages literary critics to employ a "critical demysticatory force on the cultural pieties of a nation" (p. 30) because he finds "seldom anyone who actively attacks religion" (p. 31). Culler's desire to liberate academics from silent skepticism so that we can de-mythologize and de-legitimize all religions, serves as one more example of how strong the current can run against religious ideas.

Detweiler, while decrying the extreme hostile position that Culler assumes, also challenges Culler for being, simply put, wrong:

> I am astonished by Culler's total dismissal of religion in academe. . . . What is happening, in my experience, is just the opposite of what Culler thinks and says is happening. Religious studies departments have emerged, are emerging, that comprehend religion as a cultural, social, political, psychological, historical, and linguistic phenomenon that demands investigation. Their attitudes and approaches are critical, self-critical, comparative, and professional. They examine, in fact, the kind of biased and naive attitudes toward religion expressed by such as Culler as part of the purview of their study. They are becoming, more and more, amalgams of Christians, Jews, Muslims, Hindus, and a variety of other traditions; yet even to put it that way is misleading, for many of the faculty of religion departments these days are not necessarily believers in the traditions that they teach. . . . (p. 64)

Here, Detweiler points to religion departments as positive examples of intellectual-spiritual interchange. However, George Marsden, a professor at The Divinity School, Duke University, thinks differently. He argues:

> Despite the presence of many religion departments and a few university divinity schools . . . there is a definite bias against any perceptible religiously informed perspectives getting a hearing in the university classroom. Despite the claims of the contemporary universities to stand above all for openness, tolerance, academic freedom, and equal rights . . . my impression is that considerable numbers of instructors in religious studies programs . . . hope that their students will come to think as they do, so a goal in teaching becomes, in effect, to undermine the traditional religious faith of their students. (pp. 33–34, 36)

As Wuthnow, Detweiler, and Marsden search for conditions within the academy that create what D.G. Hart (1992) describes as a "deep bewilderment in American higher education about how religion should be taught and studied" (p. 197), Stephen Carter (1993), a Yale law professor, points to influences beyond the university. In Carter's now famous *The Culture of Disbelief*, he demonstrates how ingrained the trivialization of belief has become within U.S. society. His critique challenges as it exposes subtle and blatant negations of religious devotion within contemporary life. One of Carter's central arguments enjoins us to realize how important religion is to people and yet

> in our sensible zeal to keep religion from dominating our politics, we have created a political and legal culture that presses the religiously faithful to be other than themselves, to act publicly, and sometimes privately as well, as though their faith does not matter to them. (p. 1)

Many of the difficulties that Wuthnow and others see within the university reflect what Carter asserts are tensions within North American society as a whole. He writes: "our culture has come to belittle religious devotion, to humiliate believers, and even if indirectly, to discourage religion as a serious activity" (p. 16).

Academics in religion departments have already well defined the concerns and difficulties attached to the inclusion of religious perspectives and studies that have not been fully recognized or articulated in English and composition departments. Robert Cummings Neville (1993), in his presidential address to the American Academy of Religion (AAR), summarizes the contentions that some contributors to this book aim to identify: "The feeling of many people . . . particularly those who themselves are committed to the practice of religion, [is] that they are not welcome in the Academy" (pp. 185–86). Judith Berling (1993), in her own presidential address to the AAR, describes some of the cultural assumptions that generate an uneasiness about religious discourse in the academy and promote the unwelcome environment that Neville acknowledges. Some of the assumptions she recognizes include:

> all statements concerning religion are statements for a particular religious position . . . hearing about a position other than one's own might undermine faith, challenge belief, and seduce one away from certainty . . . the legal separation of church and state relegates religion to a private realm, unfit for public discourse . . . statements about religion, since they are suited only for a particular and discrete religious community, cannot contribute to the public good . . . different religious positions can meet only as competing systems in a one-up, one-down winner-takes-all encounter. (pp. 1-2)

The difficulties that Neville and Berling say "religionists" (scholars of theology and religious studies) must wrangle with are what many of the writers in this collection seek to work out. For, if conditions of bias against religiously informed viewpoints exist within religion departments and society at large, it is not surprising that language and literature programs offer little room or accommodation for serious or respectful dialogue about contemporary spirituality. Chris Anderson (1989), in "The Description of an Embarrassment: When Students Write about Religion," describes a teaching assistant's reaction to a student's paper about

God: disdainful, uneasy, embarrassed. He reveals that he is as bothered about the student's religious rhetoric as is the teaching assistant, but he argues that although current views of language generally reject the transcendent, it is important for teachers and theorists to avoid being "absolutist in their antiabsolutism" and to "be open to the possibility of religious discourse" (p. 13).

Before this collection, little discussion has taken place as to what it means to be open to the possibilities of religious discourse within the work and culture environments of language studies. Charting new territory, the contributors in this collection explore ways to think, write, and teach—receptively, critically, hospitably—about the interplay between intellectual and religious pursuits, for themselves and for their students at universities in different parts of the United States. They seek ways to wrestle with the perplexities and, in the words of Schwehn (1993), to "reconceive the linkages between religious and public life, between higher learning and religious commitment" (p. 196).

Indeed, our contributors' backgrounds show that spirituality itself can be complex, open to new insights, and ever changing: a process of lifelong learning. As intellectuals, our contributors are accomplished in analysis and argument. They are skillful researchers in their fields. They know how to ask difficult, probing questions. Yet they also affirm the power of spirituality in clarifying their vision of what is most important in their lives both inside and outside the academy. The subtitle of this book, "Essays on Intellectual and Spiritual Life," indicates our central concern with teachers' and students' attempts to interrelate—even to integrate—dimensions of experience that enrich all of our lives: intellectual inquiry and spiritual insight, rational analysis and creative imagination, skepticism about the completeness of knowledge in any field, faith in the fullness of truth we are pursuing. We hope this book enables our readers to re-imagine the academy as a place where the possibility of belief is taken seriously, where our sense of truth illuminates our advancement of knowledge.

The writers included here offer a range of insights and experiences affirming that this vision is not only possible, but is real and present. Generally speaking, they take one of two approaches in arguing for the interrelationship of spirituality, pedagogy, and knowledge. The first is by means of experiential and theological knowledge: Sollod, Carlton and Emmons, Chappell, Lindholm, Miller, and Handelman (in that order) investigate the extension of personal belief into the classroom or curriculum. The second approach is to defend belief on philosophical premises: O'Donnell, Brummett, Swearingen, Brown and Olson, and Spellmeyer explain how the warrant for belief comes from within the academy's own thinking.

For all these writers, integrity means that the complexity of the human faith experience is recognized, that faith is a kind of knowledge, and that faith accords respect, especially in the particularity of the individual's encounter with it.

Writers in the first group make explicit the practical implications of their efforts to integrate spiritual and intellectual commitments. Integrity, they tell us, demands the acknowledgment not only of others' belief, but of our own.

It demands that we take our belief seriously, studying the traditions we value and experimenting with ways to teach from these traditions. Robert Sollod's important piece, first printed in the *Chronicle of Higher Education* and reprinted here as our opening chapter, addresses the problem of failing to take spiritual commitments seriously. In ignoring the influence of belief in intellectual formation, he argues, the academy has created only a "hollow curriculum." Restoration to wholeness is possible, however, affirm mother and daughter co-authors Karen Carlton and Chalon Emmons. Their chapter explains ways that Carlton's practice and study of Catholic mysticism and Emmons' of Buddhist mysticism shape their conceptions of students, of texts, and of teaching.

Virginia Chappell describes how the commitment she has made to living her Christianity through "the work [she] is sent out to do every day"—the teaching of writing—makes that work both rich and demanding. For her, teaching requires practicing an "active receptivity" to the ideas her students struggle to make clear. Despite the challenge it can be to continually attend to each student, each essay, and each conference, her faith provides her a hope persistent enough to lead others with the patience that learning demands. For Jan Lindholm, this patience extends to listening to that expression many teachers find uncomfortable to hear: students' articulation of personal faith. She asserts that when learning and teaching are motivated by love, the difficulties inherent in trying to express belief in an academic context are mitigated, and she proposes ways to respond to such writing with grace and respect.

To varying extents, each chapter here reveals its author's process of bringing personal and professional insight together. Two writers, Hildy Miller and Susan Handelman, share their efforts to achieve this integration and then take us beyond personal history to show how they have related their commitments to theoretical approaches in the discipline of English. Miller identifies her experience with feminist political and theological circles as the starting point for implementing feminist theory and pedagogy in her work. She explains how feminist critical theory, literature, and goddess spirituality have made it possible for her to transform students' writing and learning experiences. By validating nonrationalist ways of knowing, these discourses make room for knowing that is experiential and spiritual. Handelman, in her essay reprinted here from *Cross Currents*, also connects personal experience and critical investigation. She shows how her relationship to Judaism directs the reconsideration of her teaching and scholarship. In explaining the Jewish conception of faith, *emunah*, as a skill that needs training and nurturing, she finds a parallel between education and religion. Handelman explores the implications of Jewish midrash, a method of inquiry into the meaning of Scripture, for contemporary literary criticism. In so doing, she locates an intellectual place for faith in the academy.

Although these chapters from the first part of the collection are useful to readers who hope to learn something practical, they also encourage us to persist in our own commitments, even while persisting is not simple or safe.

Because belief calls into question accepted tenets of knowledge and discourse, a believer in our midst confounds the perceptions that academia holds of itself. In the second part of the collection, Kevin O'Donnell, Barry Brummett, Jan Swearingen, Robin Brown and Michael Jon Olson, and Kurt Spellmeyer investigate the ideologies that shape these perceptions, asking why some knowledge counts in the academy while some does not. Their answers demonstrate the possibility of belief by showing, in widely varying ways, that belief is itself a legitimate way of knowing. Kevin O'Donnell, for example, critiques the preeminence in English studies of antifoundationalism—a philosophy that ignores and suppresses the power of belief—by uncovering its inherent contradictions. In delineating fundamental parallels between the antifoundationalists, chiefly Richard Rorty and Ralph Waldo Emerson, O'Donnell shows how belief can be accommodated and even celebrated without privileging a foundational position. He suggests that antifoundationalists, with Emerson's example, can reconsider the role of belief. Brummett also argues against any simple response to the problem of belief. He asserts a "rhetorical epistemology," an understanding that it is by persuasion that we come to know, and we come to believe, as well. His chapter takes the speech classroom as a "representative anecdote" of how the academy can accommodate spiritual knowing.

Swearingen continues this vein of discussion by arguing that an "expanded repertoire of ways of knowing" is now necessary if the academy is to continue the realignment of models of thinking and identity initiated with the multicultural movement. The ability "to read with the eyes of faith," she argues, is essential to the lives of many thinkers and learners. Brown and Olson would agree; identifying themselves as "religiously uncommitted," they nonetheless argue for the validity of spiritual discourse as a way of articulating knowledge. What suppresses this articulation, they reveal, are forces emerging out of the power dynamics of our research institutions. Their theoretical exposition of these dynamics defends inquiry and expression of the spiritual. Spellmeyer recalls James Agee's identification of education as liberator turned oppressor to critique the impact of the "semiotic turn" in contemporary critical theory. Spellmeyer shows that to read Agee now is to understand how far the discourses of postmodernism and poststructuralism have permitted us to distance ourselves from "the real," the embodied and holistic experience of living as humans in the world. Although academic life seems often to call for the separation of knowing and being, the contributors in this collection call us to question the validity of such division. They encourage a reintegration of the ways we know and a revision of what counts as knowledge.

The contributors to this collection enact a public forum for ideas and concerns that many of us have often considered privately. Each chapter relates in interesting ways to those that precede and follow it, and we intend by this arrangement to involve our readers in the conversation as well. The result is the possibility that we might begin to bring together what the contemporary academy would often have us hold apart.

Working on this book for the past five years—with Elizabeth in Massachusetts, Mary in Minnesota, and Mary Louise in Wisconsin—we have logged hundreds of hours in telephone calls to discuss themes, drafts, revisions, and other editorial responsibilities. These years have been busy and fulfilling, challenging each of us to balance the demands of our professional and personal lives: Elizabeth completed her dissertation on contemporary spiritual narratives, Mary gave birth to a daughter (her first child), and Mary Louise taught in China through a Fulbright award. Belief has been integral to our sense of purpose and commitment in bringing together the theories, practices, and possibilities described here. We hope our readers' classrooms and communities will be enriched by many of the insights discovered here.

REFERENCES

Anderson, Chris. "The Description of an Embarrassment: When Students Write about Religion." *ADE Bulletin, 94* (1989): 12–15.

Battenhouse, Roy. "Anti-Religion in Academia." *Christianity and Literature, 37* (1987): 7–22.

Berling, Judith A. "Is Conversation About Religion Possible? (And What Can Religionists Do to Promote It?)." *Journal of the American Academy of Religion, 61* (1993): 1-22.

Boyer, Ernest L. "Curriculum, Culture, and Social Cohesion." *Leadership Abstracts, 5.9* (Nov. 1992): 4–5.

Burtchaell, James Tunstead. *The Dying of the Light: The Disengagement of Colleges and Universities From Their Christian Churches*. Grand Rapids: Eerdmans, 1988.

Carter, Stephen L. *The Culture of Disbelief: How American Law and Politics Trivialize Religious Devotion*. New York: Basic Books, 1993.

Cox, Harvey. *Fire from Heaven: The Rise of Pentecostal Spirituality and the Reshaping of Religion in the Twenty-first Century*. Reading, MA: Addison-Wesley, 1995.

Culler, Jonathan. "Comparative Literature and the Pieties." *Profession* (1986): 30-32.

————. "Political Criticism: Confronting Religion." *Framing the Sign: Criticism and Its Institutions*. Norman: University of Oklahoma Press, 1988. 69-82.

Detweiler, Robert. "Vexing the Text: The Politics of Literary-Religious Interpretation." *Christianity and Literature, 41* (1991): 61-69.

"Fact File: This Year's College Freshmen: Attitudes and Characteristics." *Chronicle of Higher Education, 22* (January 1992): A34-36.

Gates, Henry Louis, Jr. "Pluralism and Its Discontents." *Profession* (1992): 35-38.

Gill, David, ed. *Should God Get Tenure?: Essays on Religion and Higher Education*. Grand Rapids: Eerdmans, 1997.

Harris, Maria. *Teaching and the Religious Imagination*. San Francisco: Harper San Francisco, 1987.

Hart, D. G. "Faith and Learning in the Age of the University: The Academic Ministry of Daniel Coit Gilman." *The Secularization of the Academy*. Ed. George M. Marsden and Bradley J. Longfield. New York: Oxford University Press, 1992. 107-45.

Marsden, George M. *The Soul of the American University.* New York: Oxford University Press, 1994.

_____ . "The Soul of the American University: An Historical Overview." *The Secularization of the Academy.* Ed. George M. Marsden and Bradley J. Longfield. New York: Oxford University Press, 1992. 9-45.

Neville, Robert Cummings. "Religious Studies and Theological Studies." *Journal of the American Academy of Religion 61* (1993): 185-200.

Nord, Warren. *Religion and American Education: Rethinking a National Dilemma.* Chapel Hill: University of North Carolina Press, 1995.

Palmer, Parker. *To Know as We Are Known: A Spirituality of Education.* San Francisco: HarperCollins, 1983.

Smith, Page. *Higher Education in America: Killing the Spirit.* New York: Viking Penguin, 1990.

Schwehn, Mark R. *Exiles from Eden: Religion and the Academic Vocation in America.* New York: Oxford University Press, 1993.

Wuthnow, Robert. "Living the Question—Evangelical Christianity and Critical Thought." *Cross Currents, 40* (1990): 160-75.

2

The Hollow Curriculum *

Robert N. Sollod
Cleveland State University

The past decade in academe has seen widespread controversy over curricular reform. We have explored many of the deeply rooted, core assumptions that have guided past decisions about which subjects should be emphasized in the curriculum and how they should be approached. Yet I have found myself repeatedly disappointed by the lack of significant discussion concerning the place of religion and spirituality in colleges' curricula and in the lives of educated persons.

I do not mean to suggest that universities should indoctrinate students with specific viewpoints or approaches to life; that is not their proper function. But American universities now largely ignore religion and spirituality, rather than considering what aspects of religious and spiritual teachings should enter the curriculum and how those subjects should be taught. The curricula that most undergraduates study do little to rectify the fact that many Americans are ignorant of religious and spiritual teachings, of their significance in the history of this and other civilizations, and of their significance in contemporary society. Omitting this major facet of human experience and thought contributes to a continuing shallowness and imbalance in much of university life today.

Let us take the current discussions of multiculturalism as one example. It is hardly arguable that an educated person should approach life with knowledge of several cultures or patterns of experience. Appreciation and understanding of human diversity are worthy educational ideals. Should such an appreciation exclude the religious and spiritually based concepts of reality that are the backbone upon which entire cultures have been based?

---

*This chapter was originally published in *The Chronicle of Higher Education,* March 18, 1992. Reprinted with permission.

Multiculturalism that does not include appreciation of the deepest visions of reality reminds me of the travelogues that I saw in the cinema as a child—full of details of quaint and somewhat mysterious behavior that evoked some superficial empathy but no real, in-depth understanding. Implicit in a multicultural approach that ignores spiritual factors is a kind of critical and patronizing attitude. It assumes that we can understand and evaluate the experiences of other cultures without comprehension of their deepest beliefs.

Incomprehensibly, traditionalists who oppose adding multicultural content to the curriculum also ignore the religious and theological bases of the Western civilization that they seek to defend. Today's advocates of Western traditionalism focus, for the most part, on conveying a type of rationalism that is only a single strain in Western thought. Their approach does not demonstrate sufficient awareness of the contributions of Western religions and spirituality to philosophy and literature, to moral and legal codes, to the development of governmental and political institutions, and to the mores of our society.

Nor is the lack of attention to religion and spirituality new. I recall taking undergraduate philosophy classes in the 1960's in which Plato and Socrates were taught without reference to the fact that they were contemplative mystics who believed in immortality and reincarnation. Everything that I learned in my formal undergraduate education about Christianity came through studying a little Thomas Aquinas in a philosophy course, and even there we focused more on the logical sequence of his arguments than on the fundamentals of the Christian doctrine that he espoused.

I recall that Dostoyevsky was presented as an existentialist, with hardly a nod given to the fervent Christian beliefs so clearly apparent in his writings. I even recall my professors referring to their Christian colleagues, somewhat disparagingly, as "Christers." I learned about mystical and spiritual interpretations of Shakespeare's sonnets and plays many years after taking college English courses.

We can see the significance of omitting teaching about religion and spirituality in the discipline of psychology and, in particular, in my own field of clinical psychology. I am a member of the Task Force on Religious Issues in Graduate Education and Training in Division 36 of the American Psychological Association, a panel chaired by Edward Shafranske of Pepperdine University. In this work, I have discovered that graduate programs generally do not require students to learn anything about the role of religion in people's lives.

Almost no courses are available to teach psychologists how to deal with the religious values or concerns expressed by their clients. Nor are such courses required or generally available at the undergraduate level for psychology majors. Allusions to religion and spirituality often are completely missing in textbooks on introductory psychology, personality theory, concepts of psychotherapy, and developmental psychology.

Recent attempts to add a multicultural perspective to clinical training almost completely ignore the role of religion and spirituality as core elements of many racial, ethnic, and national identities. Prayer is widely practiced, yet poorly understood and rarely studied by psychologists. When presented, religious ideas are usually found in case histories of patients manifesting severe psychopathology.

Yet spiritual and mystical experiences are not unusual in our culture. And research has shown that religion is an important factor in the lives of many Americans; some studies have suggested that a client's religious identification may affect the psychotherapeutic relationship, as well as the course and outcome of therapy. Some patterns of religious commitment have been found to be associated with high levels of mental health and ego strength. A small number of psychologists are beginning to actively challenge the field's inertia and indifference by researching and writing on topics related to religion and spirituality. Their efforts have not as yet, however, markedly affected the climate or curricula in most psychology departments.

Is it any wonder that religion for the typical psychotherapist is a mysterious and taboo topic? It should not be surprising that therapists are not equipped even to ask the appropriate questions regarding a person's religious or spiritual life—much less deal with psychological aspects of spiritual crises.

Or consider the field of political science. Our scholars and policy makers have been unable to predict or understand the major social and political movements that produced upheavals around the world during the last decade. That is at least partly because many significant events—the remarkable rise of Islamic fundamentalism, the victory of Afghanistan over the Soviet Union, the unanticipated velvet revolutions in Eastern Europe and in the Soviet Union, and the continuing conflicts in Cyprus, Israel, Lebanon, Northern Ireland, Pakistan, Sri Lanka, Tibet, and Yugoslavia—can hardly be appreciated without a deep understanding of the religious views of those involved. The tender wisdom of our contemporary political scientists cannot seem to comprehend the deep spirituality inherent in many of today's important social movements.

Far from being an anachronism, religious conviction has proved to be a more potent contemporary force than most, if not all, secular ideologies. Too often, however, people with strong religious sentiments are simply dismissed as "zealots" or "fanatics"—whether they be Jewish settlers on the West Bank, Iranian demonstrators, Russian Baptists, Shiite leaders, anti-abortion activists, or evangelical Christians.

Most sadly, the continuing neglect of spirituality and religion by colleges and universities also results in a kind of segregation of the life of the spirit from the life of the mind in American culture. This situation is far from the ideals of Thoreau, Emerson, or William James. Spirituality in our society too often represents a retreat from the world of intellectual discourse, and spiritual pursuits are often cloaked in a reflexive anti-intellectualism, which mirrors the view in academe of spirituality as an irrational cultural residue. Students with spiritual interests and concerns learn that the university will not validate or feed their interests. They learn either to suppress their spiritual life or to split their spiritual life apart from their formal education.

Much has been written about the loss of ethics, a sense of decency, moderation, and fair play in American society. I would submit that much of this loss is a result of the increasing ignorance, in circles of presumably educated people, of religious and spiritual world views. It is difficult to imagine, for example, how ethical issues can be intelligently approached and discussed or how wise ethical decisions can be reached without either knowledge or reference to those religious and spiritual principles that underlie our legal system and moral codes.

Our colleges and universities should reclaim one of their earliest purposes—to educate and inform students concerning the spiritual and religious underpinnings of thought and society. To the extent that such education is lacking, our colleges and universities are presenting a narrow and fragmented view of human experience.

Both core curricula and more advanced courses in the humanities and social sciences should be evaluated for their coverage of religious topics. Active leadership at the university, college, and departmental levels is needed to encourage and carry out needed additions and changes in course content. Campus organizations should develop forums and committees to examine the issue, exchange information, and develop specific proposals.

National debate and discussion about the best way to educate students concerning religion and spirituality are long overdue.

3

Every Moment Meditation: Teaching English as Spiritual Work

Karen Carlton
Humboldt State University
Chalon Emmons
University of California, Berkeley

Oh you who are anxious to learn what it is to enjoy the Word, prepare not your ear but your soul.
—St. Bernard of Clairvaux, "Sermons on the Canticles" (cited in LeClercq, 1978, p. 329)

So that he may bring the trainee to the ultimate of Truth
The master uses skillful means.
Trainees embrace the ultimate,
Masters contain the means.
Correctly blended,
This is good.
—Zen saying (in Jiyu-Kennett, 1990, p. 63)

While we were visiting a Cistercian monastery one summer, a friend of ours asked Myriam, one of the monks, to explain the difference between prayer and meditation. Our friend's question surprised both of us, and caused us to think about these spiritual practices in a new way. Although we are mother and daughter, we are followers of different religious paths, and each of us had her own definitions of the

17

two terms. Prayer, Myriam finally offered, is an address, a conversation with the eternal divinity outside oneself, whereas meditation is a looking inward, a communion with one's own divine nature. Both, she said, are necessary.

When we began to write this chapter, we thought again about prayer and meditation, and what these practices could reveal about our work in education. As teachers of English and as students of monastic Catholicism and Buddhism, we recognized the insight of Myriam's explanation. Intellectual and spiritual education is a product of both kinds of activities: outward relationship—a kind of prayer—between teacher and student, and inward reflection—meditation—by the student and the teacher. Thinking in this way about education has caused us to re-examine our classroom exercises and our interactions with students. We explore the results of this re-examination later in this chapter.

The monastery has provided us with a useful lens through which to view our professions in the academy. We have been drawn to sacred spaces of the monastery, spaces revealing a communal presence of mind and soul that recognizes and honors life even in what appears to be inanimate: a neat stack of firewood, a row of shoes, an arrangement of flowers on an altar. When we leave these holy spaces, we leave with a desire to live outside the monastery as we have lived in it—attentively, compassionately, aware that every being, task, or object can be a teacher. Our experiences in monasteries and our study of medieval European monasticism have shown us that we are never the only teachers in the classes we lead, and so we have investigated ways of incorporating prayer and meditation—and the various ways of being that these practices encourage—into the study of reading and writing.

The opening of the Gospel of John, "In the beginning was the Word," proclaims that the act of communication is at the center of human existence and divine consciousness. The movement of being to utterance, from the thought that dwells within to the word that emerges—the mystery of that process is the mystery of divinity taking form in humanity, of spirit finding life in the flesh. Language can be, as the Cistercians say, a signature of the soul. Because of this, we find spiritual relevance in our work in English classes, just as, we are sure, teachers of math, history, or art find central mysteries manifest in their subjects. Language can be a way to integrate body, mind, and spirit—aspects of humanity that tend to be divided into separate spheres: the body valued in the marketplace, the mind valued in the academy, and the spirit valued in the church or temple. Such divisions cut us off from important self-knowledge. When we can encourage students—and they can dare—to speak, read, and write from their bodies and spirits as well as from their minds, they often seem to capture a kind of energy and coherence. Words become a means of grace.

We begin here with a brief discussion of medieval Europe's monastery and scholastic schools, giving special attention to the reasons why the scholastic schools may have prevailed over the monastery schools in influencing the modern university and particularly literary studies. Because we believe the philosophy and practices of the monastery schools are worth remembering, and because some are worth implementing, we refer to this background material in subsequent sections, where we reflect on the classroom as community, on ways to approach and create texts, on students and our relationships with them, and on our roles as teachers.

To some extent, the opening of the literary canon, the recognition of multicultural literature, and the affirmation of reader-response literary theory suggest that there is readiness, in English studies, to help students widen and deepen their thought processes, to help them journey inward to the soul and the divine. And yet we must, at the same time, acknowledge the skepticism in academia that has kept words like *soul* and *divine* out of the vocabularies of many English teachers, despite the genesis of literature in the struggles of the human spirit. In many university environments, where the teachings (or popular corruptions of the teachings) of Darwin, Marx, and Freud are the backbone of general education, nothing seems easier to mock than the universal longing for spiritual, emotional connection and the desire to understand and express the deepest parts of the human heart. But we have found it impossible to keep the monastery and the university separate in our own lives; the quest of the soul and the quest of the intellect are not, we believe, antithetical. "Spiritual care," the Tibetan Buddhist teacher Sogyal Rinpoche (1992) insists, "is not a luxury for a few; it is *the* essential right of every human being, as essential as political liberty, medical assistance, and equality of opportunity. A real democratic ideal would include knowledgeable spiritual care for everyone as one of its most essential truths" (p. 209). And so we go against the grain, reaching far into the past (and into present day monastic life), as we aspire to make the teaching of English spiritual work.

The practices of prayer and meditation have helped shape this chapter as well as our teaching because our writing comes out of our conversations with each other and from our solitary contemplations. Our voices merge and separate in the following pages, reflecting both the new perspective on teaching the daughter brings, and the perspective of long experience brought by the mother. Because one of us (Chalon Emmons) has been working with students for five years, while the other (Karen Carlton) has been an educator more than thirty, we have different kinds of stories to tell, and different kinds of voices in which to tell them.

PREPARE NOT YOUR EAR BUT YOUR SOUL: HISTORICAL BACKGROUND

Karen Carlton

Although it is common knowledge that the Western academy has its beginnings in medieval monasticism, the evolution of higher education from these roots is not so clearly understood. Because of my interest in Eastern and Western forms of meditation and mysticism, I have had occasion to look at medieval monasticism, particularly 8th-through 12th-century English and French monasticism and its educational practices, only to discover the existence of two separate schools: those within monastery walls, the monastery schools, and those without, called the scholastic or clerical schools. These schools differed dramatically in their pedagogical methods, intellectual thought processes, and spiritual values, although both sought to promote the humanities and Catholic theology. Most interesting was my realization that it was the scholastic school, not the monastery school, that shaped the philosophy and practices of our present day western academy, despite the fact that monastery schools, up until about the 14th century, were thought to be superior. Why did the influence of scholastic schools prevail, I wondered, and what happened to the monastery schools that had such a powerful and positive influence on medieval and Renaissance cultures?

Monastery schools emerged first on the continent and in England around the eighth century. During the next hundred years they grew in size and number, fortified especially by Charlemagne's desire to restore Roman liturgy and literary culture, and to teach Latin to Anglo-Saxon monks so that church doctrine might be received, read, written, and preached in its purest form. In these monastery schools, students read Latin manuscripts of classical authors such as Pliny, Ovid, Lucan, Statius, Lucretius, and Virgil, and of orthodox church fathers such as St. Augustine and St. Gregory. They were taught to use, but at the same time to transcend, Latin grammar and classical reasoning—to give attention primarily to the life of the spirit and its search for understanding of the mysteries of life and death.

Patterned after ancient Coptic and Buddhist monasteries, these "interior" schools, as they were also called, stressed the presence of God in each person and in the world, as well as each person's presence before God. Students thus experienced the love of learning and the desire for God as being one and the same. In a liturgical setting, where chanting, reading, writing, painting, singing, meditating, and praying were the primary modes of knowledge and expression, they studied literature, philosophy, and theology. Monks and students alike approached all subjects through *gnosis*, a personal apprehension of spiritual truth that is the complement of faith and that reaches fruition in prayer and contemplation. They valued poetics over logic, mystery over clarity, wisdom and belief over analysis and doubt. Rather than abstract and theoretical language, concrete images dominated the writings of these students and monks:

> William of Saint Thierry: I fled paradise and in exchange for the place you gave me, I found a sewer and submerged myself there. I kept the seal of your face. (cited in DeGanck, 1991, p. 104)

St. Gregory: The bridegroom hides, when he is being sought so that, not finding him, the bride will search for him with renewed ardor; and the bride's search is prolonged so that the delay will increase her capacity for God. (cited in LeClercq, 1978, p. 108)

Peter the Venerable: He cannot take to the plow? Then let him take up the pen; it is much more useful. In the furrows he traces on the parchment, he will sow the seeds of the divine words. (cited in LeClercq, 1978, p. 154)

Henry of Pomposa: Admirable clemency of God towards His own! It renders their faith so fervent that, famished, it feeds without ever becoming full; thirsty, it drinks and grows thirstier still. (cited in LeClercq, 1978, p. 157)

In these passages and in their other writings, monks and students in the monastery schools cultivated a knowledge of self and a knowledge of God; they searched for deep personal truths and for the ways these truths embodied themselves in common states (marriage, hunger, and thirst) and in common objects (the seal, the pen, and the plow). Valuing simplicity over complexity, sincerity and humility over pride, they wrote in genres that showed the processes of their search—poetry, letters, dialogues, histories, stories. They attempted to look at themselves and the world from God's perspective, hoping thereby to achieve an understanding of all creation. In short, they cultivated a spiritual intelligence, based on the belief that love itself is knowledge; the more one loves, the more one knows.

The scholastic schools emerged sometime after the monastery schools, but the two were related and even complementary to each other. Whereas the monastery schools were open to children preparing for monastic or religious life, the scholastic schools were available for those children who would engage in the "active" (rather than the "contemplative") life. In the beginning, all students were male and were drawn from the noble class. Although the teaching in these scholastic schools was entrusted to the clergy, the goals, philosophy, and practices were very different from those of the monastery schools.

Scholastic schools followed the tradition of Aristotle, approaching philosophy and theology through the modes of speculation and skepticism. Doubt replaced belief; questioning texts was more important than experiencing them. Rather than accentuating the poetics of language and literature, teachers in the scholastic schools emphasized logic, analysis, and dialectics. There were verbal battles between teacher and student, and among students, always in the service of argumentation and objectivity. Rational knowledge took precedence over mystical knowledge; knowledge of the material world was valued over knowledge of the self and God; innovation prevailed over tradition.

The differences between the scholastic and monastery schools are neatly summarized by St. Bernard in his discussion of speculative knowledge (cultivated by the scholastic school) and knowledge through contact, the *affectus* (promoted by the monastery school):

> There [in the scholastic schools] we hear Wisdom teaching, here [in the monastery schools] we welcome it within us. There we are instructed, here touched; instruction makes learned men, contact [with the divine] makes wise men. . . . It is one thing to know many enriching truths, another to possess them. (cited in LeClercq, 1978, p. 266)

It can be argued, then, that the ultimate victory of the scholastic schools over the monastery schools was a victory of Aristotle over Plato, of the secular over the sacred (LeClercq, 1978). But this analysis still does not explain why the scholastic schools prevailed and why the monastery schools disappeared. Some scholars argue that there was a distinct decline in the influence of monastery schools and the quality of literary activity after the Norman Invasion in 1066, that the chaos of war, the clash of ideologies, and the cultivation of trade placed new emphasis on the values promoted by scholastic schools (Bynum, 1987; Cantor, 1993; Manchester, 1992). In response to the times, the purposes of education shifted. Rather than preserving traditional values and teaching men to live in harmony with the divine, to find the source of all meaning in a God that is both immanent and transcendent, education began to emphasize the material and intellectual world, particularly science, law, and philosophy. It focused on helping men gain financial and political power rather than spiritual strength.

No doubt these external forces of war, commerce, and science played a significant part in transforming education on the Continent and in England. But there was also an invasion of monastery schools and monastic life from within—by women. Beginning in the 11th century, scholars estimate, thousands of women entered monasteries (DeGanck, 1991; Flinders, 1993). Some characterize this movement as the problem of too many unmarried women; wars, crusades, disease, and the canonical celibacy of the quite numerous clergy resulted in an unusual surplus of women over men. But many women came to religious life because they wanted to avoid marriage and devote themselves to learning, reflection, and prayer.

In monastery schools and in the small hermitages close by, women learned to read and understand Latin, although only a few were taught to write. Excluded by church law from active ministry in the church, women were more likely than men to spend long hours in contemplative prayer, chanting, and singing. Perhaps because their energies were directed toward mystical knowledge and gnosis, many of these women had powerful revelations. When they were not able to record their revelations, monks served them as scribes, with the result that many texts describing these revelations or visions began to circulate among monks, church leaders, and even lay people. While Julian of Norwich and her "God as Mother" Showings are familiar to many readers, she was not the only woman to influence the Catholic Church with mystical writings.[1]

---

[1]The texts of mystical writings by women from both the Continent and England were widely circulated throughout the Middle Ages. Margery Kempe, an English contemporary of Julian of Norwich, wrote the first autobiography in the English language—an

It is my suspicion that the values, methods, and products of monastery schools—this environment that embraced women in a misogynist age—finally threatened the structures and dictates of the Catholic Church, which compelled submission to its authority. Mystical doctrine, as taught and lived in monastery schools, had no need for the ecclesiastical dispensation of grace. Without the mediation of church authority, monks and nuns entered into a direct relationship with God; they sought purity through their own study, faith, prayer, and meditation. Furthermore, several abbots of monastery schools, St. Bernard among them, presumed to judge church leaders, accusing bishops of "serving antichrist" and "betraying the Lord" (Cantor, 1993, p. 342). Ultimately, the church had no choice but to end its support of monastery schools and attempt an eradication of mysticism and gnosticism. This denouncement, which later took the form of witch hunts and book burnings, together with the growing emphasis on speculative thought, law, science, and math, resulted in the demise of monastery schools. By the 16th century, only scholastic schools remained as a model and foundation for the Western academy.

What if monastery schools had survived? If we were to teach according to monastery school methods and values, how would this change our goals and practice as teachers, our relationships to our students and to the texts we assign? Of course, I remain conscious of my actual role as a teacher in a late 20th-century classroom, almost a millennium after the triumph of scholasticism, and so I attempt to bridge the ideal and the real worlds of teaching. As my daughter and I examine the potentialities of the English classroom as a sacred place, of reading and writing as holy acts, we are repeatedly confronted by present and past teaching experiences, which remind us how truly difficult—and yet worthy—is the implementation of such a dream.

SACRED PLACE, SACRED TIME:
THE CLASSROOM

Chalon Emmons

During my first meditation retreat at a Zen Buddhist monastery, monks taught me to make *gassho* by pressing the palms of my hands together and bowing. This physical posture, the monks said, is a way to remind the Zen student to return his or her attention to the present, to recognize and express gratitude

account of her personal union with God. Prior to Julian of Norwich and Margery Kempe were Flemish, French, and German women whose mystical writings were influential for a period of several hundred years. Such writers include Hadewich and Beatrice of Nazareth, both from Belgium; Marguerite Porete and Heloise of France; Mechthild of Magdeburg and Hildegard of Bingen, both from Germany. See Wilson's (1984) *Medieval Women Writers* for more on these women and their work.

toward the Buddha Nature or the divine in each of its manifestations. For a week, I was bowing all the time. I would bow as I entered the dining hall or bathroom, as I passed a monk in the cloister, as I approached my meditation cushion. The meditation instructions I received were deceptively simple: to watch my thoughts arise and pass without holding on to them or pushing them away; to sit when I was sitting; to eat when I was eating; to sweep when I was sweeping. Making *gassho* so often was an extension of the formal meditation we did on our cushions because our goal was to carry the meditation hall with us to every place and in every activity.

When the retreat was over, I returned home and went back to school. Although I wanted to continue to live as attentively as I had in the monastery, I had difficulty making *gassho*—even inwardly—as I entered my classrooms. Lit by buzzing neon tubes, crowded with desks bolted to the floor, littered with copies of the school newspaper, the classroom was a hard place to recognize as a meditation hall. My students, too, seemed unmoved by any Buddha Nature or divinity lurking in the classroom; they would put their feet up on the desk and drink soda from Big Gulp cups until the bell rang to release them. The bell itself—unlike the bells ringing in the monastery to call students to meditation—became one more distraction because it invariably cut class short just as we were beginning a satisfying discussion or exercise.

But if I couldn't bring the meditation hall to the classroom, perhaps I could find out more about the classroom and the people who inhabited it. "Why are you here?" I asked my students. "Why are you taking this English class?" Some of them said what I hoped they would say, that they felt reading and writing helped them to know themselves and the world around them better. But a few students candidly told me they were sitting in my classroom so they could get a good job later on. A lawyer or bank manager has to be able to write and read; therefore, a future lawyer or bank manager should take my class to gain these skills.

Like many English teachers, I have found myself justifying my courses to students and myself with similar economic arguments and assumptions. I teach my students analytical skills by asking them to examine politicians' speeches and magazine advertisements. I emphasize the practical applications of analysis: you will be able to see through political rhetoric, so you can vote for the person most likely to create jobs or lower taxes. And, you will be unswayed by emotional sales pitches, so you can buy the cheapest and best products. Learning to write, I tell them, will give you your own rhetorical tools, so you can most effectively get what you want as a citizen, worker, and consumer.

These skills are important. But what troubles me about my students' and my reliance on economics to justify education is the effect of this reliance on the classroom environment. By stressing the importance of communication skills in the workplace, my students and I are in effect saying, *"This* place—this class-room—and *this* time—now—are not the place and time that really matter. We are preparing for a more important place and time . . . the future, somewhere else." This kind of thinking is common, and certainly not limited to students and teachers in required English classes. It is the thinking that followers of Zen Buddhism and other religions hope to move beyond, so that they can recognize here and now (wherever and whenever that might be) as important, as full of divinity. By bringing my attention back to the present moment, I hope to reclaim and preserve the environment of the classroom, an environment threatened just as the natural environment is: by laziness, by ignorance, by inattention.

The environment of the classroom is important, because it can nurture and sustain minds, souls, and selves. The poet Carolyn Forché suggests that our pressing duty as educators is to become "ecologists of the mind." Whole realms of consciousness, she warns, are in danger of destruction: The places within ourselves where we go to meditate, to write poetry, and to find God are becoming lost Edens for us—places from which we have exiled ourselves and that most of us have forgotten. When we read and write, my Buddhist teachers would say, we should just read and write. The classroom, the book, the paper—these are the meditation hall; these are manifestations of the sacred.

ENCOUNTERING THE TRANSCENDENT: APPROACHES TO TEXTS

Karen Carlton

Although the earliest literature was sacred and cosmological, and although much of modern literature can be seen as a secularization of ancient, holy texts, it seems that few English teachers attend to this connection or emphasize the spiritual dimensions of reading and writing. Perhaps many of us who teach English avoid issues of moral and spiritual education in response to the recent popularity of deconstruction, a mode of reading that emphasizes the separation of word and world, and that holds that nothing can be finally determined, including meaning itself. Indeed, deconstruction appears to repudiate the theological and metaphysical roots of literature because, as George Steiner (1989) writes:

> . . . the origin of the axiom of meaning and of the God-concept is a shared one. The semantic sign, where it is held to be meaningful, and divinity "have the same place and time of birth" (Derrida). . . . The issue is, quite simply, that of the postulate of the existence of God. "In the beginning was the Word." There was no such beginning, says deconstruction; only the play of sounds and markers amid the mutations of time. (pp. 119-20)

But there are other reasons why we, as English teachers, may hesitate to explore the transcendent dimensions of texts in the classroom. I worry, for example, that if I discuss spiritual matters in my class I may be identified with the growing (Christian, Jewish, Islamic, Hindu) fundamentalist movements, whose members are seen as seeking every opportunity to voice their beliefs and impose those beliefs on others. I wish to avoid implying that a certain group of texts are the touchstones of great literature. Most significant, perhaps, may be my susceptibility to the power of the prevailing philosophy (educational, political, economic) of materialist individualism that leaves me embarrassed to give witness to the mystery and numinosity of poetic language. I haven't the courage to face the ironic smile of the defensive student, the empty eyes of the indifferent student, or the constant appeals of the needy student.

Most people in school have lives that are complicated not only by the realities of work, play, and relationships, but by a cultural noise that makes deeply serious reflection difficult if not impossible. Except in a very few places, the drone of television, radio, video games, and machines captivates our senses and distracts our attention. The time and quiet and guidance required to contemplate spiritual questions are seldom available to any of us, least of all to students in crowded classrooms and dormitories.

And yet, I believe that most of us need to explore possibilities of meaning and truth that resist empirical proof. We need occasion and opportunity to explore what is deepest, most mysterious, and least expressible within ourselves. And what better way to explore these depths than through books, which Edna O'Brien (1994) calls "our soul's skeleton" (p. 20), and through writing, which St. Bernard termed "the signature of our soul" (cited in Gilson, 1940, p. 63)? "You must change your life," says Apollo to the observer in Rainier Maria Rilke's famous poem (1981, p. 147). All serious literature can challenge us in this way, can call us toward transformation. Our own thoughtful writing can confront us as well, posing the most private and profound of questions: "Who are you? What do you feel and think? Where are you going? What are the great possibilities in your life and how may you best fulfill them? How will you die?"

Clearly, reading and writing alone are not enough to enable students in their apprehension and integration of spiritual values. Texts must enter into them and they must enter texts; readers and writers must feel an encounter with transcendence in the experiencing or creation of literature. Put another way, students must empty themselves of preconceptions and preoccupations through engaged reflections on—as well as critical and objective analyses of—the works they encounter and compose.

The texts that are (and were) read in monasteries are carefully chosen, selected for their spiritual themes, for their brush with the divine, for their abilities to shift the boundaries of consciousness to something larger, something both familiar and deeply startling. Monks seek a practical end: to guide themselves to the sacred in life and toward union with the divine forever. In doing so, they make every effort "to find a good intention" in each text, as the Cistercians so gracefully put it.

We in our secular classrooms, of course, seem very far from this sort of religious "canon." Like many English teachers, I want to offer my students a range of reading experiences so that they have some sense of and empathy for the richness and complexity of world literatures, peoples, and ideas. Also, it is not enough merely to think of what students ought to read. I want to offer them literary choices that link their past experiences and present levels of emotional maturity to their potential for experiencing literature in the most vital way. A transforming experience of the student in response to a text is really what I aim for—a discovery by each reader of a life, a divinity in the text: in the language, the syntax, the ideas, in all their harmonies and contradictions. To help students find this life in the literary models we study is, at one and the same time, to develop their linguistic capabilities, their appreciation of literary subtlety, as well as their moral and spiritual sensibilities.

In helping students make this discovery in their reading, I have found that many traditional teaching methods, all inherited from monastery schools, work well. Most of these methods are time-consuming and require a commitment to the text by both student and teacher, a willingness to listen carefully and respond seriously to the challenges posed by a piece of writing. Therefore, the text must provide serious challenges; it must pose aesthetic, rhetorical, intellectual, and spiritual problems for the reader to explore, through which the reader can see the complexities and possibilities of life. Such stipulations about the texts we read—that they be multifaceted and challenging enough for students and teachers to be committed to reading them—can lead educators to draw up lists of texts that meet these criteria. And indeed, thoughtful people both inside and outside the academy vigorously debate the issue of which texts to teach, because what we read shapes the people we become, and the people we can imagine ourselves becoming.

Like many issues that pass from the realm of possibility to the realm of practice, my choice of texts to assign is a product of both chance and negotiation, my "canon" a fluid contract between myself and my students, as well as a result of my own evolving reflections. In the very question of which texts to read, I find manifest the many paradoxes of spiritual life: Each text, no matter how mundane or even offensive, does contain a spark of the divine; my belief in this divinity of texts is an act of faith; the canons of literature we read in English classes—whether traditional or nontraditional—result from readers agreeing and disagreeing on the worth of those canons, and from struggling to define what makes a text worthy.

As I select poems, novels, and essays, I try to be mindful of these concerns. I try also to be as careful in what I choose to do with the texts in my class as I am in choosing the texts themselves, and hope that the practices I have adopted from monastery schools will help illumine literature for my students and myself. Although unfashionable in some classrooms, activities such as reading texts aloud, memorizing and performing excerpts of texts, and chanting or singing poetry are ways not only of interpreting but of answering texts. Each performance of a piece of writing is a lived critique, an act of penetrative response that makes possible the deepest sense and understanding of the work.

When students memorize texts, they feel the words by body as well as understand them by mind; that is, they directly incorporate the rhythms of the text into their physical and emotional rhythms, not only deepening their grasp of the work but establishing an ongoing and ever-changing reciprocity between themselves and that which they know. Their internalization of texts serves to help them recognize and discover worlds within themselves as well as worlds without. That which they know by heart and perform is that which they can come to love; texts become aspects of their selves, rooms in their souls to which they can continually return for rejuvenation and restoration—for revision of their lives. Perhaps, too, the memorization of a text enlivens or humanizes it as no other kind of reading can, as the text becomes a part of the reader's life, a part of the reader's humanity.

I believe that art, dance, and creative dramatics can work for students in much the same way as reading aloud and memorizing texts. That is, these activities, used in response to the images, ideas, and feelings within a text, help students experience language in a primary, deep and unmediated way. Again, interpretation (whether it is through reading aloud, artistic representation, dramatic performance, dance, or mime) is understanding in action; it is the immediacy of translation. In short, all such interpretive and artistic activities help students discover and live the spiritual values expressed in literary works.

But there are other monastic methods, less well known and, I suspect, seldom practiced, that might be helpful in enabling students to encounter the transcendent in literature and composition. One is the practice of *glossing*. The gloss provides an explanation of each word of a text, a clarification of one word by another. To look for and find an equivalent for each word necessitates not only a superficial reading of a work, but a minute, attentive study of all the details—connotation, denotation, etymology, grammar, punctuation, syntax. The gloss, an immediate yet ever-unfolding commentary, can help the reader (who also becomes a writer of the text's various and possible meanings) appreciate an author's creative process. Through this kind of *grammatica*, through penetration of the literal, moral, allegorical, anagogical, and spiritual aspects of a passage, students may find a surprising wisdom, a presence, a spark of the divine (LeClercq, 1978, p. 150).

The oral commentary, yet another monastic method, gives students the benefits of the experience of glossing a text along with the advantage of working with another person. In pairs, with access to dictionaries and other reference books, students read and explain passages to each other, focusing on the grammatical forms of words as well as on their meanings. Two minds looking together at the interpenetrations between syntactic and rhetorical aspects of a text can produce insights of exceptional depth and authority. Related to the oral commentary, but private in its execution, is the *lectio divina* or "active" reading,[2] an ancient practice that allows students to "learn by mouth"

---

[2]*Lectio divina* is a prayerful reading aloud of a text (usually holy scriptures), that allows the reader to experience the passage as a "divine lecture." More important than the

(LeClercq, 1978, p. 21). A reader pronounces words out loud in order to retain them; the audible reading and the exercise of memory and reflection that follow are the three necessary phases of the same activity. Meditative or active reading involves learning a text with one's whole being: with the body, because the mouth pronounces it; with the memory that fixes it; with the intelligence that understands its meaning; and with the will that desires to put into practice its beauty and wisdom.

Literary imitation is yet another writing device used by monastery schools that helps students appreciate the strengths of a text and, at the same time, develop their own linguistic abilities. By becoming saturated, through meditative reading, with the language of the work, students are able to respond to art with art; that is, they are able to use the linguistic structures and generic forms of the text they are imitating to envision a new work. Their imitation of a literary piece may be the best means of expressing their own deep truths as well as demonstrating their appreciation and understanding of a given text.

Many of the techniques just discussed are used routinely by creative writing classes, in which teachers and students recognize a deeper place than everyday consciousness as a source of creativity. But it is symptomatic of our society's ambivalence toward artists (on the one hand, we glorify them and mystify their process, whereas on the other hand, we devalue their work and ridicule their subjectivity) that many teachers are afraid to incorporate such techniques into literature and composition classrooms. But Dorothy Sayers (1941), believing that the "creative mind is . . . the very grain of the spiritual universe" (p. 185), warns against confining humans to uncreative activities and an uncreative outlook. To do so, she writes, is to do "violence to the very structure of our being" (p. 185). Unlike those of the modern academy, monastery school values and methods seem to honor the spiritual structure of each student—the creative mind and searching soul as well as the worldly persona. These values and methods acknowledge that thoughtful reading of serious literature and writing on matters of the spirit are, finally, religious acts . . . acts that explore and dramatize the relations of human beings, not only to each other and the world, but to the existence of something beyond themselves. Such acts, although rooted in substance, bind us to that which transcends, allowing us to glimpse and experience for a moment the continuum between temporality and eternity, between matter and spirit. Put simply, to read and to write can be a means by which we experience that numinous Presence, that eternal Self, which some call God.

Liberal skepticism may keep us, and our students, from using the language of the monastery schools, or from embracing many of their religious propositions. But I suggest we not let our doubts keep us from experimenting

---

choice of text is the reader, and the benefit he or she derives from the prayerful, meditative reading of the work. To read in such a way is to "attach oneself closely to the sentence being recited and weigh all its words in order to sound the depths of their full meaning" (LeClercq, 1978, p. 90). In the monastery schools, the *lectio divina* was a form of prayer—prayer for the purpose of achieving wisdom and an experience of the divine.

with those practices in monastery schools that might bring us closer to an understanding of the poets and writers whose works we read and hope to imitate in our English classrooms. Many of these artists speak or write unapologetically about the powers of the divine in the creative process. Here, for example, is D. H. Lawrence on the subject: "I always feel as if I stood naked for the fire of Almighty God to go through me—and it's rather an awful feeling. One has to be so terribly religious to be an artist" (cited in Steiner, 1989, p. 228). Annie Dillard (1990) instructs aspiring writers to

> Write as if you were dying. At the same time, assume you write for an audience of terminal patients. That is, after all, the case. What would you begin writing if you knew you would die soon? What could you say to a dying person that would not enrage by its triviality? (p. 68)

Language, these writers assert, is a serious enterprise, a grave responsibility. I would like my students to experience this "awful feeling" of shaping and being shaped by words, this vital encounter with the transcendent, not only so that they may become better readers and writers, but so they may become artists as well.

TRAINEES EMBRACE THE ULTIMATE: THE STUDENTS

Chalon Emmons

Five years ago, when I first began to teach, I felt I was failing because my job required me to maintain relationships with forty people who were strangers to me. Had we met outside the university, I would have liked some of them as friends; others would have remained no more than acquaintances. Because I hoped for satisfying, successful relationships with all forty, I was bewildered by some students' hostility and found myself angry at them. It became easy for me to see a student as a writing problem (those comma splices! that lack of development!) or a discipline problem (that Walkman! those absences!) and to see my relation to the student as my relation to a problem. Often my authority in the classroom seemed to depend on my ability to master the problems—to point out and correct deficiencies in writing skills, to spot and punish unacceptable behavior. As a new teacher, I thought a lot about the sources of my "authority." My age (24), gender (female), and educational status (graduate student) did not confer authority on me; the authority seemed to be bureaucratic, weighted by the size of the university, by institutional position papers and departmental memos. I had authority insofar as I was a surrogate for the program, an individual manifestation of the collective teacher. Although this may be a problem primarily for graduate teaching assistants, I think it is a function of the hierarchical structure of the university, which cultivates a star system of famous (publishing) scholars and less famous (teaching) understudies, who are seen as filling in, substituting in their own classes. The result for all participants is a profoundly dislocating experience; the work occurring between two abstractions (a writing problem and an institutional representative) is work that itself has no current authority or value because it is merely training, merely practice for future, "real-world" transactions.

But more than my own authority, I thought about my students' authority. In my composition classes, I saw students struggling for identities as readers, thinkers, and writers in modes such as literary analysis, with which they were unfamiliar. How was I to recognize and honor the authority of these emerging voices? What were they coming here to learn, and what did I think I was coming here to teach them? It seems to me that there are two complementary approaches to these questions. One has to do with the tasks we assign in the English classroom, and the ways of thinking such tasks encourage in our students; the other has to do with our spiritual recognition of students, and the ways of thinking such recognition encourages in us.

As my mother and I have observed, literature and composition classes require that students use language to analyze, to conclude, to argue, to persuade. Following the traditions of the scholastic schools, English teachers often stress separation and doubt—the student writer's separation from and doubt of his or her subject (and therefore the possibility of analysis), and his or her separation from the reader (and therefore the possibility of persuasion). Such separations lead naturally to hierarchies that are very real in the classroom: A literary subject is above the beginning writer, who may be unable to perceive literary "merit," whereas a rhetorically skilled writer is above the gullible reader. The student writer thus comes to see his or her subject in much the same way that I sometimes see my students: as a problem to solve. To the extent that the writer solves the problem—pulls the "secrets" from a text, convinces the reader that these "secrets" are the keys to the text—the writing is successful.

And yet this is not why I write, nor why I want my students to write. In college, even when I was involved in the very activities that are the legacy of the scholastic schools, I learned about myself through reading and writing. Although I coaxed hidden nuances from literary texts and constructed arguments to convince readers, my unspoken purpose—and my unspoken achievement in the writing that satisfied me most—was to affirm something about life, to experience and to articulate something true about my own soul. I realize now that I was trying always to make my own writing sacred, just as I had discovered a sacred life in the language of others. Whatever other goals I might have adopted for my writing—originality of thought, order, persuasiveness—I adopted because they were the conventions, but I see now that they were secondary considerations. Now I realize that, although trying to be "original," I was in fact writing the same essay over and over again: whether writing about John Milton or Charlotte Brontë or William Shakespeare, I was always struggling to determine how language expresses the soul. In each essay I discovered that it simultaneously does and does not. That paradox struck me again and again as wonderful, as breathtaking.

My writing students, who may not be as single-minded as I was in college, often approach writing with fear—fear of making mistakes, fear of getting bad grades, fear of exposing themselves to strangers—but many of them also approach it with faith that the acts of reading and writing will make them better people. A number of my students tell me they believe that education will enrich not only their careers but their lives as well. They appear in my classroom willing to experience the mystery of language, a mystery that, as the poet Jorie Graham (1990) points out, permits "the soul-forging pleasures of thinking to prevail over the acquisition of information called knowing" (p. xx).

Too often, however, I find myself addressing student fears and not speaking to their faith. I talk about "writing strategies," "counterarguments," "rhetorical appeals"—dramatic terms that compare writing and reading to war or to blackmail. Although I stress the importance of the writing process, leading my students through draft after draft, in the end I assign the final product a grade that, for many students, reduces their efforts to "success" or "failure." Whether or not my students are successful (by their definition or mine) at adopting the language of mastery and therefore "winning" the rhetorical battle, their attempts to do so weaken their faith in the creative powers of reading and writing; these activities become tools—weapons or currency—rather than paths inward to self-knowledge and outward to community. If my students and I can rediscover these paths, we can make reading and writing into the necessary soul work of prayer, of meditation.

I have come to believe that we are seeing things backward when we treat voice as a luxury in writing. Indeed, in the graduate writing classes I take, my professors and fellow students talk about "voice" in reverent tones. "You can't acquire a voice—you can't learn it," one professor said. "You either have it or you don't." Another contrasted "voice" with "tone," defining tone as a verbal attitude which any writer can adopt and voice as a sign of spiritual maturity. Such mystification of voice amounts to a refusal by students and teachers to take on the work of cultivating it. How, after all, do we cultivate something we can barely define? But if we accept voice as something we "can't learn," as a sign of spiritual maturity—and I do accept these descriptions—we have a responsibility, I believe, to attempt the journey through language to voice, and to help our students, our fellow voyagers, on the way.

Such journeys might begin with writing projects that rely on a personal tone (if not a voice): the journal, the letter, the essay. Although some critics, who hope to combat what they see as a lowering of standards in U.S. education, argue that emphasizing personal experience and authority in writing encourages sloppy work, I believe that this kind of writing can be much more than a "virtually standardless exercise in 'self-expression' that 'empowers' students," as George Will (1994) describes the journal (p. 93). These projects are, in fact, opportunities for teachers to encourage students to listen closely, to move through "self-expression" to an awareness of a life beyond self, beyond language.

To guard against accusations raised by Will and the suggestion that striving for an awareness that transcends self or language is a hopelessly vague and romantic goal for writing classes, I am beginning to focus on the formal demands of genre. By reading *The Diary of Opal Whitely*, the correspondence of George Sand and Gustave Flaubert, the memoirs of Isak Dinesen, and the essays of Lewis Thomas, I can ask myself and my students, "What do the journal, the letter, and the essay do? How have these writers and others satisfied and redefined generic constraints? What do these genres ask of us as writers?" As a writer and a reader, I find that the journal, the letter, and the essay demand honesty and an examination of the writer's complex relationship to self—a relationship characterized by what Robert Atwan (1992) calls a "tension between self-effacement and self-importance" (p. 3).

Because the name *essay* suggests "an attempt," I see this genre as an approximate translation into language of the spiritual quest itself: formally demanding yet ever flexible, shifting with time and circumstance, reaffirming that the process is as important (is perhaps the same) as the goal. My students may not see or feel this connection. To them, perhaps, the formal constraints of the journal and essay are as tedious as the formal constraints of the research paper. But in my experience, this has not been so. My students have been frustrated by the demands of writing the personal essay, but not bored. Often, their frustration points to their discovery that "self-expression" is not "virtually standardless," that "empowerment" requires the hard work of facing themselves and making themselves intelligible to the world.

Yet, paradoxically, I must recognize and accept that my students' spiritual awareness or growth is in some ways not my concern. As my mother does, I think about my students' spiritual development; like her, I look for ways to foster that development in my classes. But the Buddhist monks at the Zen monastery I visit remind me that I can only work on myself, that I cannot and should not attempt to do the spiritual work of others. Whether my students perceive writing essays or anything else we do in class as sacred or meaningful is up to them. They will, perhaps, be moved by different things than I am, or at different times. Acknowledging that I cannot control my students' spiritual experience—that I cannot "teach" voice, cannot show beginning writers how to infuse their work with a wordless force their readers will recognize as unique—could lead me to throw up my hands. Instead—again, paradoxically—this recognition pushes me to teach in ways that recognize that spiritual experience is possible. The Buddhist monks warn me not to "sell the wine of delusion," not to do things that will cause others to act from greed, anger, or delusion (Jiyu-Kennett, 1987). Although I cannot ensure my students' spiritual development, I must at all times be aware of their spirits, and not hinder their potential for growth.

As I respond to student essays, it seems important to give up my own institutional authority—the voice of the collective teacher—and to claim a different authority of personal voice or soul so that I can hear and honor each student's own emerging voice. By acknowledging in my assignments that I expect writing students to attempt the frustrating but rewarding journey toward voice and self-knowledge, as well as to convey information and persuade readers, I hope to speak to students' faith in language, in me, and in themselves.

A shift in my understanding of classroom goals—from skills acquisition to cultivation of voice, gnosis, and self-realization—has required a shift in my understanding of students themselves. No longer can I allow myself to see students as problems that need to be solved. I must see them as the same, in a religious sense, as I am; I must have faith in them, and in their embodiment of the divine. In an annual Zen ceremony, senior priests representing Buddhas bow to laypeople gathered in the monastery, recognizing the Buddha Nature in them. Such recognition in the classroom is an act of mindfulness and meditation, an attempt similar to the monastery school students' endeavors to look at the world from God's perspective. I have come to see my duty as a teacher as the responsibility to make my relationship with each student sacred in this way, to make it as honest and respectful as I can.

I find this difficult at times: when a student misses class, turns in late or sloppy work, or yells at me about my grading standards. In such a case, I get angry or discouraged, and find myself fretting over the incident hours or days later. I try to think of ways to minimize or eliminate these situations—I could revise my absence policy, I think, or give everyone an A. But I realize immediately that my desire to control student behavior and emotion is as futile as my desire to regulate their spiritual growth; instead, I must learn to use my behavior and emotion as aids for my own spiritual development. Following the suggestion of my Zen Buddhist teachers, I try to sit with my emotion, neither clinging to it nor pushing it away, so that it arises and passes naturally. Although my impulse is to label my tiredness, despair, and agitation as negative (and my elation over a successful class as positive), the challenge I face is to accept all of these reactions with compassion. I hope to recognize—and help my students recognize—that the emotions we express in the classroom, rather than obstructing our learning, can teach us even more.

TOWARD THE LIGHT WITHOUT LIMITS: OUR ROLES AS TEACHERS

Chalon Emmons

I believe that attentiveness in the classroom to students' spirituality and to our own emotional challenges can lead us to acknowledge that we are doing spiritual work when we teach. At the end of the century, citizens of industrialized countries are thinking very seriously and very anxiously about the term *work*. People are working harder than they have in the recent past, or they are not working at all. Although many people find meaning in their families, their religions, and their avocations, our society primarily values its citizens' professional contributions; and so we tend to value ourselves according to our professional work. Although an academic profession includes a great deal of solitary toil—research, writing, preparation for class—and a great deal of interaction with peers—service on committees, participation in conferences—many of us measure our professional selves by our roles as *teachers*. Our ideas about our own "work" depend on the ways we construct our personae in the classroom.

Two reflective essays by women in the academy have explored the way teachers commonly think about their work, and have suggested new ways of thinking about the teacher's roles. These new ways of thinking, the essayists hope, may help make teaching a more human and humane endeavor. In "Pedagogy of the Distressed," Jane Tompkins (1990) analyzes what she calls the "performance model," which many academics unconsciously adopt. As a performer, the teacher focuses less on the students' needs and more on conveying to students her own intelligence, knowledge, and preparedness for class. Tompkins argues that such a model, based on "fear of being shown up for what you are" (p. 654), communicates that dread to students. The fear pervasive in performance-based classrooms results from the split personalities both students and teachers take on. Students feel divided because they must perform and display their required skills to the class, while suppressing what they consider to be their personal voices. Teachers, too, must foreground their institutional authority, and hide what Tompkins calls "the real backstage self." Tompkins urges teachers to bring their backstage selves onstage so that students too can begin to speak with their true voices. These backstage selves and true voices, she admits, are rowdy and at times embarrassing. They express feelings, hopes, and desires. They show students and teachers to be bodies and spirits as well as minds. Part of classroom work, then, is to recognize and tend to these bodies and spirits. Tompkins concludes her essay by describing her new sense of teaching as "a maternal or coaching activity," a model that, she claims, allows her to shift responsibility for the success of a course to her students, and allows her to attend to students' needs rather than her own.

Although Tompkins admits that she adopted this model in order to work less, Diana Hume George (1994) argues in "How Many of Us Can You Hold to Your Breast? Mothering in the Academy" that a maternal model often pressures women teachers to work more. Such a model requires the female professor to do emotional work in addition to intellectual, "professional" work. As we attempt to "humanize" the academy, George warns, we are duplicating in the university the phenomenon of the "double shift." Male teachers, she points out, have not stepped in to "mother" students as women have. George recommends that female professors, especially women writers who silence their own voices as they nurture the voices of students, learn not to integrate personal and professional selves—this they do too well—but to separate them. She views this kind of separation as the teacher's healthy move to claim her own privacy, individuality, and writing voice. George does not defend or reinstate the kind of performance-for-public-approval that Tompkins critiques. Instead, she encourages teachers who are also writers to give less of themselves to teaching so that they can give more of themselves to writing.

Each of these essays expresses the author's physical, mental, and emotional exhaustion; each author tries to define the teacher's self and to find a place for it, a place where that self—or soul—can rest and regain wholeness. Should the teacher "perform" more (and thus split herself in two) in order to nurture her private self, or should the teacher "mother" more (and thus bring public and private selves together) in order to nurture her students? Who is the teacher? this debate asks. What kind of work should she do?

As the title of our chapter suggests, my mother and I believe that the teacher's work is spiritual, and that it requires us to focus both more and less attention on the self. As teachers, we need to attend more to ourselves, or to our souls, because we, like our students, are growing spiritual beings; our teaching is an opportunity to open ourselves up to that growth. We need to attend less to ourselves, or to the roles we play, because, like all spiritual work, teaching is selfless. Although teaching does incorporate both performance and coaching, combining high ritual and an intimate trust between teacher and student, we cannot let ourselves be distracted by either aspect of the profession from the work in front of us. We must remember our own humanity by dealing compassionately with our students and ourselves. We must also do the physical, emotional, and intellectual work of teaching with the mind of meditation—that is, without letting our personal attachments get in the way.

TEACHING AS SPIRITUAL WORK: CONCLUSION

Karen Carlton and Chalon Emmons

Despite the resistance we face from colleagues and students, despite the resistance within ourselves (as we struggle to respond to endless rounds of student papers, to the often meaningless committee work of academic life, or to the weight of collective indifference—even hostility—to matters of the soul), we hope to bring passionate and loving attention to every classroom experience: to each reading, each writing, each discussion, each conference, each response to each paper, each grading, each private agony following a class or an exchange gone wrong. In order to enrich the university environment of minds, bodies, and spirits (our own and our students'), we look for ways to furnish our classrooms with objects which are spiritually nourishing—paintings on the walls, imaginatively selected books and music, chairs or desks arranged to foster conversation, plants and natural objects near the windows or walls. When we cannot shape the physical environment, we can try to make the class time more sacred by beginning sessions with a writing exercise or a formal reading, to help return our attention to the present moment.

Following the example of teachers in the monastery schools, we would strive to cultivate "God's perspective" in ourselves and our students—that is, a perspective that sees infinite value in each person, each moment, and that views the love of learning and the desire for something beyond ourselves as one and the same. This is the perspective that dissolves hierarchies, separations, and doubts, and that fosters compassion, justice, and faith; it is the perspective that honors being and feeling as well as thinking.

Specifically, we want our students to encounter the transcendent through direct, immediate and lived interpretations of texts and their genres. That is, we want to enable our students to *experience* literature, to have bodily knowledge of its beauty, power and transformative wisdom. Moreover, we want our students to see themselves and others as spiritual beings who have the capacity to find purpose and meaning in life through writing as well as reading. We want to speak to the faith rather than the fears of students by bearing witness to the value and uniqueness of their creative and interpretive endeavors.

We want to resist any role or situation which causes us to see our students as objects or problems. Indeed, we try to keep in mind that our students are also our teachers, people who contribute to our own spiritual growth. We want to enter into our classrooms with these conscious thoughts: "Here is a community of souls; we all have spiritual relationships with each other. What matters is not only the environment we create, the words we say, the books we read, the skills we teach and learn. What matters, too, are the thoughts that fill us, the reverence, gratitude, and wonder we bring to that which is before us. Our work as teachers and students is sacred and the classroom is our temple. Let us care for each soul, including our own, through the work we do here."

We believe that such a commitment to the spirit in education can transcend religious divisions and denominations, and can respect the faiths and doubts of all students and teachers. Although our reflections have been shaped by historical and contemporary monasteries, we recognize that universities and monasteries are unique institutions, which support human society in different ways. We aim not to promote a particular religious viewpoint. Indeed, we wish to honor the separation between church and state, which protects each person's freedom of conscience. And yet, symbolically, we hope to recognize the church, the meditation hall, the synagogue, the sacred circle everywhere and in every moment. By widening our vision to include the nonvisible, the nonmaterial, the spiritual, we hope to keep bodies, minds, and spirits in balance, and, as teachers following the admonition of the Zen saying, to "contain the means" that will allow our students to embrace their own ultimate truths.

REFERENCES

Atwan, Robert. "Introduction." *Ten on Ten: Major Essayists on Recurring Themes.* Ed. Robert Atwan. Boston: Bedford/St. Martin's, 1992. 1-6.

Bynum, Caroline Walker. *Holy Feast and Holy Fast.* Berkeley: University of California Press, 1987.

Cantor, Norman. *Civilization in the Middle Ages.* New York: Harper, 1993.

DeGanck, Roger. *Beatrice of Nazareth in Her Context.* Kalamazoo, MI: Cistercian Publications, 1991.

Dillard, Annie. *The Writing Life.* New York: Harper, 1990.

Flinders, Carol Lee. *Enduring Grace.* New York: Harper, 1993.

George, Diana Hume. "How Many of Us Can You Hold to Your Breast? Mothering in the Academy." *Listening to Silences: New Essays in Feminist Criticism.* Ed. Elaine Hedges and Shelley Fisher Fishkin. New York: Oxford University Press, 1994. 225-44.

Gilson, Etienne. *The Mystical Theology of Saint Bernard.* Trans. A.H.C. Downes. London: Sheed, 1940.

Graham, Jorie. "Introduction." *The Best American Poetry 1990.* Ed. Jorie Graham. New York: Macmillan, 1990. xv-xxi.

Jiyu-Kennett, P.T.N.H. ed. *Zen is Eternal Life.* 3rd ed. Mt. Shasta, CA: Shasta Abbey, 1987.

_____ . *The Liturgy of the Order of Buddhist Contemplatives for the Laity.* 2nd ed. Mt. Shasta, CA: Shasta Abbey, 1990.

LeClercq, Jean. *The Love of Learning and the Desire for God.* Trans. Catharine Misrahi. London: Billings, 1978.

Manchester, William. *A World Lit Only By Fire.* Boston: Little Brown, 1992.

O'Brien, Edna. "It's A Bad Time Out There For Emotion." *New York Times Book Review* 14 Feb. 1994: 1+.

Rilke, Rainer Maria. *Selected Poems of Rainer Maria Rilke.* Ed. Robert Bly. New York: Harper, 1981.

Rinpoche, Sogyal. *The Tibetan Book of Living and Dying.* San Francisco: Harper, 1992.

Sayers, Dorothy. *The Mind of the Maker.* San Francisco: Harper, 1941.

Steiner, George. *Real Presences.* Chicago: University of Chicago Press, 1989.

Tompkins, Jane. "*Pedagogy of the Distressed.*" College English 52.6 (1990): 653-60.

Will, George F. "Radical English." *Reading and Writing Short Arguments.* Ed. William Vesterman. Washington, DC: Washington Post Writer's Group, 1994. 91-93.

Wilson, Katharina M., ed. *Medieval Women Writers.* Athens: University of Georgia Press, 1984.

4

Teaching—and Living— in the Meantime

Virginia A. Chappell
Marquette University

Almighty God, give us grace to cast away the works of darkness, and put on the armor of light, now in the time of this mortal life in which your Son Jesus Christ came to visit us in great humility; that in the last day, when he shall come again in his glorious majesty to judge both the living and the dead, we may rise to the life immortal. . . .
—Collect for the First Sunday of Advent, *The Book of Common Prayer* (1979)

This prayer for grace, courage, and light with which the Episcopal Church begins a new church year and the observance of Advent usually finds me eager to don the armor of its central image. As afternoons get increasingly gloomy, my final four weeks before Christmas get increasingly hectic. The darkness that besets me grows from work to be done or left undone. Professional obligations contend with and usually overshadow personal delectations. Hunkered down as I am, at least psychically, I come to the flowerless Advent altar eager for refuge, ready for hope.

I imagine the armor of light (Romans 13.12) wrapping a protective glow of calm around me as I bob and weave through the pressures of seasonal gaiety, as I make the sometimes pleasant, sometimes painful, choices that abound in the month before this precious holy day that every year seems more secularized. But as I savor the prayer, I run smack into a piece of doctrine that bewilders me: the last day. Jesus as son of God I can imagine, I can believe. Life immortal I can believe in, although I have never felt successful at imagining it. But the promise of a second coming, I find, well, rococo. It seems an elaborate adjunct to the basic Christian story of salvation through incarnation and resurrection. Intellectually, I just really don't know what to make of it.

On the first Sunday of Advent several years ago, the preacher at the church I belong to, St. Mark's Episcopal Church in Milwaukee, Wisconsin, put the paradox of this dual anticipation of Christmas and the Second Coming at the center of his sermon. Christians profess and live the belief that God has shown the world "an all-sufficient saving love, which needs no reinforcement, no final act, to resolve all things," Father Julian Hills reminded us.[1] Yet Christianity preserves and professes a biblical promise that Christ will come again. "In a sense," he said, "we are living in the meantime, between Calvary and some unknown final end." This meantime—unnervingly provisional and tentative in its very naming—was not the refuge or comfort I might have hoped for. Yet it is, I am coming to believe, what the armor of light equips me to confront. In the meantime, between the promise and the fulfillment, faith helps me face the uncertainties of this mortal life, including the paradoxes of intellect and belief that I find in my communities of work and worship.

Father Hills had begun his sermon by describing the hundreds of beggars, panhandlers, and hustlers he encountered in San Francisco during a religious studies convention the previous weekend. The image of the poor outside the academics' luxurious meeting rooms served him as a type for individual suffering. "Life in this meantime is not easy," he said. "Whatever the depth of our sharing in the lives of others, from time to time we are reminded—as I was, by all those begging people—that we are alone, single, individual." The suffering comes because "our God-given yearning for life and love collides with the jaded expectation and sad history of much of the world we live in." I listened from a far corner of the sanctuary, alone in my acolyte's garb. These robes were once denied me, a girl; now, recapturing some of that girl's enthusiasm, I relish playing a small costumed liturgical role, particularly on special Sundays such as this one. But I had been thinking about hope and light as I anticipated the service, not hunger and loss. It was difficult to sit still on the backless acolyte bench.

The world, Father Hills was saying, summons us "to participate in an economy of self-interest, self-improvement, and self-promotion." A tempting call. "But Advent reminds us that the Christian church stands in defiant opposition to this paradigm." It proclaims a gospel that speaks not only of God's love for the world but also of "our real, tangible, and necessary responsibilities for each other. . . . The world is again waiting to see just what we're made of." I was sitting up straighter. These responsibilities were not a matter of giving to

---

[1]The Rev. Dr. Julian V. Hills, associate professor of theology at Marquette University, serves as assistant priest at St. Mark's Episcopal Church in Milwaukee. With his permission, I quote throughout this essay from an electronic copy of his sermons from Advent 1992. Father Hills' observations about our congregation's life and work in the world have helped crystallize my thinking about my work and faith, and I am grateful for the light cast by his eloquence and conviction.

the point of exhaustion and hoping that someone else would then step in. No, these responsibilities are the careful choices we each must make in the ordinary course of our lives. I was buoyed by Father Hills' own proclamation: "I believe that . . . everything that we say or do has an impact on the life of the world. Every choice, every decision, has a role to play in the great web of interconnections that unite person to person and community to community." As the sermon drew to a close, I recognized, not for the first time, that putting on the armor of light means more than becoming calm enough to withstand the tensions of diminishing daylight and holiday deadlines. It means, Father Hills declared, that "we stand for something, something full of hope, and promise, and life."

In a commonly used prayer near the end of the Eucharist, Episcopalians corporately ask God to "send us out to do the work that you have given us to do." I teach rhetoric and composition, so when I consider the work I have been given to do, I think first of my writing classes. And I recall that the authors of *Habits of the Heart* portray the problem of individualism's dominance over community-based traditions in terms of Americans' need "to find a moral language that will transcend . . . radical individualism" (Bellah, Madsen, Sullivan, Swidler, and Tipton, 1985, p. 21).[2] They observe that one of their four representative Americans, Brian Palmer, "lacks a language to explain what seem to be the real commitments that define his life, and to that extent the commitments themselves are precarious" (p. 8). My work, it seems to me, is to enliven in students the rhetorical and linguistic ability with which they can articulate their commitments and write about the somethings for which they stand. My hope is that this process will develop their facility with the "second languages" that form the basis of what *Habits of the Heart* describes as the civic republican tradition. In this tradition, "public life is built upon the second languages and practices of commitment that shape character . . . . [These] form those habits of the heart that are the matrix of a moral ecology, the connecting tissue of a body politic" (p. 251). The temptations to disengage from the larger society, especially from politics, are many and persistent, Robert Bellah and his colleagues note a decade later, expressing grave concern over what they term a deepening "crisis of civic membership" (Bellah, Madsen, Sullivan, Swidler, and Tipton, 1996, p. xi). The work to which I am committed asks me to nudge my students back toward engagement, to broaden their thinking about the communities to which they are responsible. Like Bellah and his colleagues, I would like them to conceive of a community that goes beyond neighbors and friends but is instead "a cultural theme that calls us to wider and wider circles of loyalty" (Bellah et al., 1996, p. xxx). I want my stu-

---

[2]This frequently cited 1985 book was a bestseller, widely read beyond academia. For a critique of its perspective as too narrow—too White and too middle class—see Harding's (1987) essay and the responses from Bellah and others (Communications, 1987). The 1996 paperback edition includes a new introduction that addresses problems of growing economic disparity and deep racial divisions—consequences, the authors argue, of radical individualism.

dents to become sensitive to a given community's culture, to recognize diversity within that community, and, indeed, to write about ideas and principles that will give their communities hope, promise, and life.

Father Hills' description of the San Francisco beggars reminded me of my work at Marquette with students' essays about their encounters with "the homeless" in Milwaukee. In my upper division writing classes, where I leave paper topics largely up to each student, I often find myself reading personal narratives about helping street people, or not helping them. These essays are written by bright, caring students who have been taught in school, family, and religious formation classes about the value of both charity and hard work. My discussions with them about these papers go deeper than advice about matters of style and organization. They involve helping students articulate their responses to a city, and world, that contain more pain and contradictions than they had thought. Until now, their safe, relatively affluent schools and neighborhoods have sheltered most of them from the handout-requesting, eye-to-eye, guilt-inducing encounters with poverty that have become common in the downtowns of cities the size of Milwaukee. The shock of such contrasts and the emphasis on community service at Marquette lead many students to volunteer in tutoring or food programs that serve area residents directly. The experience energizes these students' writing about social problems.

Yet, as I read or listen to essays on issues such as homelessness, I typically want more depth, more detail, more examination of the larger context of the students' encounters. I want essays in which students scrutinize themselves and their connection to their subject more painstakingly than might the San Francisco tourists that Father Hills described, "handing out a dollar here and a quarter there." Early drafts tend to paint poverty and mental illness with broad brush strokes. Some bleed with sympathy for their subjects' plight; some bristle with indignation over a panhandler's audacity or drunkenness. It is not difficult to find fault with these papers, especially when one has read many of them. I owe it to the academy, and the student, to point out problems of clichés or easy moralizing when I see them. But I also owe every paper respect and patience. I remind myself that the lenses of privilege and naiveté through which my students view their subjects are also lenses of concern and discovery. These writers are searching for an adequate response to situations difficult for trained professionals to understand, let alone young college students. A writing teacher's responsibility is not merely to burnish student texts, but to provide students with strategies for developing the meaning and effectiveness of those texts. Ultimately, those strategies depend on writers' understandings of both themselves and their roles in the communities for which they write.

For the students behind these essays about hunger and handouts, writing about poverty on such immediate terms is usually a new effort, and it can be an overwhelming one. When a subject is new or painful, "what I really mean" is not easy to articulate. Sentimentality and self-righteousness can mask despair, not just in the people the students meet, but in their own response. Neither a brisk teacherly call for sophistication nor an indulgent gush of emotion will serve anyone well. My comments in conferences or workshops and my notes in the margins of the students' texts must probe tenderly. I listen carefully and try to say back to students what their texts seem to be saying. I point to places where I and perhaps other readers resist the writer's assertions or need more substance to be persuaded. It is not a question of disagreement, I explain; it's that I am looking for greater depth. My intent is to show students how to do the same kind of critical reading. I encourage them to articulate their own resistance to texts, and to recognize when a piece, even a published piece, would improve with additional supporting evidence or a sharper articulation of its concerns. By reading and listening critically, to themselves and to others, they can begin to learn how to wrestle with contradiction and complexity.

As the saying goes, I ask to be shown, not told. Then I ask for more. Why is the man to whom the writer handed a sandwich, "not just a bum any-more"? A description of a fraternity man with an expensive haircut and over-coat seems to condemn him—is that fair? Are we supposed to laugh at the way the drunk fell down? Why? Does that woman in the plaid shawl asking for money in front of the church every night have other options? How seriously are we to take the disheveled bus rider's grandiose story of money made and lost on the stock market? Is it a story about economic hard times, or might it have been fabricated by illness? How does a reader's awareness of that possibility change the meaning the writer wants to construct?

The purpose of such discussion is to uncover how writing can help us explore together how we should, or can, or want to respond to ambiguity, uncer-tainty, and need. We begin to look at what might be the differences among a personal response, a community response, a governmental response. All this is meant to help students write better papers, of course. But I also want students to learn to use writing as a means of discovering and articulating constructive responses to the collisions they perceive between what Father Hills described as a childhood "Eden of wonder" and "a hard world of insecurity and mortality."

My approach seeks to take pedagogical advantage of what Stephen Fishman and Lucille Parkinson McCarthy (1996) point out as John Dewey's con-fidence in the value of perplexity, of a "*forked-road* situation," to stimulate think-ing (p. 345). The members of a creative nonfiction workshop, for example, loved one writer's clever personifications of her money clamoring to be given away while she told drunks who accosted her that she had none. Then, in the essay's final scene she handed a fair chunk of cash out her car window to a neatly dressed man holding a "Will Work for Food" sign at a busy intersection in the suburbs. Her story was moving—funny at some points, painful at others. I confessed, how-ever, that I was disturbed by the implication that it is easy to know when a hand-out will be well spent and when it will not. What did she intend for us to conclude about when to give money to someone? Discussion lapsed into anecdotes of oth-ers' quandaries about similar encounters. The issue was unresolved when the ses-sion was over, but the spotlight had shifted. Later, the student brought us a revised version that was more about her responses to panhandlers and less about their deservedness. We all agreed that it was better—more interesting, more compelling. It had set moralizing aside and become an essay that reflected on decision making instead of one that dressed clichés about guilt in clever detail.

I mean for my response to student writing to embody a pedagogical stance of active receptivity. By yoking these potentially paradoxical terms, I also mean to suggest the juxtaposition of intellectual and spiritual concerns. Active receptivity takes us beyond the dialogical or multilogical "critical thinking" of education theorists such as Richard Paul (1990). It suggests the importance of considering and accepting the writer behind even poorly reasoned or politically discomfiting texts. Active receptivity describes not a curriculum nor criteria for assessment, but a way for an individual pedagogue to interact with students. Careful reading and listening constitute active and difficult work. So, too, does the careful scrutiny of writing that might initially seem easy to dismiss as half-baked ideas or sweeping generalizations. These are often the points where a writing teacher's most serious work begins—not the work of correction, but the work of exploring and guiding. If one is concerned with a student's personal development, not just improvement of a particular text, one must remain open, receptive, to what the student has thought about so far. An actively receptive stance has allowed me to recognize that more than a few statements smacking of intolerance were bred of privilege and naiveté, not ill will.[3] This stance helps me keep an eye and ear out for the germ of an idea that can be cultivated into a discovery for both writer and reader. I have learned to listen for questions and responses—my own and the student's—that will prompt that cultivation. The work to which I feel myself called, in other words, is the teaching of writing not as performance but as a way of confronting and understanding a complex world. I would like to help make that complexity a little less treacherous for all of us.

A skeptic might observe that the sense of purpose I outline for myself—to facilitate students' articulation of their commitments in the face of daunting complexity—sounds just fine, but the abstractness of its terms makes its feasibility questionable. Fair enough. Abstractions need substance; assumptions need scrutiny. Commitment becomes more difficult when simplicity and truisms no longer suffice. Asking a student for a clearer text most likely means asking for clearer thinking, thinking that pushes toward commitment: *Here's what I really think.* Asking students for good, and then still better, writing inevitably means asking them to examine the values they have brought to college, values that will become enriched or diluted as they encounter new knowledge, new world views, in and out of class. *Here's what I think we all need to consider.* Asking students to articulate how someone else might view a subject means asking them, in turn, to take up active receptivity. *I recognize that people of good will might disagree here because. . . .* Challenging students to articulate new ideas can sometimes mean asking them to write provisionally, for the meantime. *Here's where my certainty turns into questioning.*

---

[3]Psychologist Fletcher Blanchard's (1992) research on what he called "interracial incompetence" examines the dynamics of this kind of naiveté.

Finding ways to help writers respond effectively to such challenges involves struggling alongside them with the contradictions and suffering they encounter. Deep talk with a writer about his or her work is like a walk along the ridgeline of Martin Buber's (1955) "between": "On the far side of the subjective, on this side of the objective, on the narrow ridge, where *I and Thou* meet, there is the realm of 'between'" (p. 204).[4] The walk can be precarious, the connectedness enormously rewarding. Active receptivity describes the effort to realize this "between," which, in Buber's words, "is rooted in one being turning to another as another, as this particular other being, in order to communicate with it in a sphere which is common to them but which reaches out beyond the special sphere of each" (p. 203). Buber says that "between" does not receive specific attention because it is "ever and again re-constituted in accordance with [people's] meetings with one another" and so is usually experienced as the soul or the world, the subject or the object (p. 203). Nevertheless, he designates it "a primal category of human reality" (p. 203). As such, it is for him the crucial beginning point for the establishment of genuine community, leading us beyond the alternatives of both individualism and collectivism (p. 204). It is for me a crucial beginning point for a pedagogy that helps build community.

It may be superfluous to note that the person-to-person, I-thou encounter of the "between" is not achievable with every student. But, in the language of Father Hills' sermon, one something for which I stand as a teacher is working to make the "between" accessible. Here in the mutuality of relation that Buber described, we can cultivate the seeds of the "hope, and promise, and life" that fill Advent's prayers and music. Through our connections with each other we build not just mutual understanding, but the hope and promise of a just and peaceful society. To enhance the possibility of students connecting with each other in the terms Buber described, I structure my syllabi to foster community. My classes begin with extended introductions on the first day and provide numerous in-class opportunities for person-to-person responses and collaboration. In a given class these might include group-prepared oral presentations, an e-mail forum on the campus mainframe computer, or writing groups in which classmates respond carefully to each other's drafts. The most public of these collaborations is the publication of a class anthology at the end of my advanced composition classes. Artifacts of community that students can show others, these little magazines become one way classmates remember each other. When I run into former students, we often enjoy reminding ourselves of others from the class in terms of, "Her magazine piece was the one about getting to know her sister's paraplegic fiancé," or, "Didn't he win a prize for that essay on the National Endowment for the Arts?"

These encounters make me feel good, but frankly, they're not enough. As Michael Buckley, S.J. (1992) observed in a lecture that examined Jesuit ideals

[4]Buber's (1955) notion of the "between" is central to Professor Andrew Tallon's Philosophy of Community course at Marquette. I thank Dr. Tallon for his generous guidance for my reading and thinking about community.

for humanistic education, "Deep care without a concomitant knowledge leads only into enthusiasms" (p. 103). The "real, tangible, and necessary responsibilities for each other" of Father Hills' sermon go far beyond warm memories of affective sharing. My intention is not that the community atmosphere of my classes serve as an end in itself; rather, I mean for the experiences of shared talk, affect, and work to prepare students for participating in the larger civic community. Philosopher Robert Paul Wolff (1968) describes three kinds of community: affective community, which is the reciprocal consciousness of shared culture; productive community, the sharing of common work; and rational community, the "collective deliberation upon social goals and collective determination of social choices" (pp. 191-92).[5] A classroom can become a community of the first two kinds, but it looks like the third only in very limited ways, such as shared decision making about due dates or, perhaps, evaluation procedures. Classrooms are where students prepare for the collective decision making about social choices in the rational community that Wolff describes. Personal essays give student writers important experience with reflective thinking and with language that articulates commitments. But the next step, and I take it to be crucial to their education, is to consider how those commitments might be lived in relation to a public good, the moral ecology of *Habits of the Heart*. This relationship to a public good goes beyond an individual's commitment to a given service program. As important as such commitments are, I want my students to extend their thinking further and examine the discourses that eventually formulate public policy.

In the past few years, I have increasingly stressed writing that examines public issues at a variety of levels, from the campus neighborhood to Congress. Writing classrooms, I am convinced, should foster in students a facility with language as a means of public dialogue, as a means of negotiating civic policy. Because this dialogue will inevitably include people whose assumptions differ dramatically, a key aspect of educating students to participate in it is expanding their perceptions of community. Who is included? Who is served? Whose voices have ready access to the public conversation? Whose don't? Why not? So what?

As theorists and critics such as Bellah and Fowler (1991) have pointed out, much of the contemporary search for community is flavored heavily with nostalgia for, as *Habits of the Heart* describes it, "a consensual community of autonomous, but essentially similar, individuals" (p. 206). Certainly, it is questionable whether this homogeneity ever existed in any comprehensive view of U.S. society, but I am reminded every semester that to many of my students it

---

[5]Wolff (1968) said his third form of community used to be called *participatory democracy*, a term that I realize can be understood as quite different from the civic republican tradition I draw from Bellah et al. As political scientist Robert Booth Fowler's (1991) discussion in The *Dance with Community* demonstrates, *community* is a rich and contested term and likely to remain so. My purpose here is simply to call on Wolff's helpful distinction of the political from the other two forms of community, not to privilege one notion of civic community over another.

appears to exist in the comfortable neighborhoods and schools from which they have come to college. As Bellah and his colleagues (1985) comment, "For all the lip service given to respect for cultural differences, Americans seem to lack the resources to think about the relationship between groups that are culturally, socially, or economically quite different" (p. 206). Indeed, the problem is underscored by the fact that this statement could serve as commentary on the limitations of the book in which it is contained. *Habits of the Heart,* for all its apologetic acknowledgments of its chosen White, middle-class orientation, and despite its updated introduction, itself provides only minimal resources for thinking about community in terms that consistently include racial and cultural diversity.

Education for active citizenship must, it seems to me, provide those resources. Reading and thinking about various kinds of differences and group relations serve as the ideal ground for writing that prepares one for dialogue with, and in the interests of, the full U.S. public. And so my assignments often ask students to stretch their imaginations beyond the familiar. Composition students read autobiographical material from people of color, do research so that they can explain what lies "at the heart of the matter" in a public controversy, and write at least one paper that addresses a "problem of community importance." Defining the community and the importance is part of the task. Teaching assistants and writing center tutors examine the social status of standard and nonstandard dialects and the class biases that make grammatical correctness so important. "Ours is a world . . . fissured by nationality, ethnicity, race, and gender," Henry Louis Gates (1992) observes.

> [T]he only way to transcend those divisions—to forge, for once, a civic culture that respects both differences and commonalties—is through education that seeks to comprehend the diversity of human culture. . . . [T]here is no tolerance without respect—and no respect without knowledge. (p. 37)

Whether the scene is a first-year class discussing Gloria Naylor's (1992) "Mommy, What Does 'Nigger' Mean?" or a group of graduate teaching assistants considering when and how to "correct" errors in student writing, discussion of difficult public issues is complex and can be uncomfortable. Yet it is essential. Without learning something of what it is like to live inside other people's skins, how can we expect to engage with them on Buber's narrow ridge?[6]

Now my skeptic might observe that although it is less abstract than my earlier statement, this further complication of my sense of purpose—to encourage student writing about encounters with difference as well as complexity—sounds daunting, and likely to incur resistance. Again, fair enough. It is; it does. And it gets more complicated than that, for frequently I have found more complexity than I wanted, as have many graduate teaching assistants who turn to me

---

[6]Amy Ling (1987) observes that she has always believed that what reading literature is all about is "getting inside other people's skins and experiencing their lives" (p. 153).

for guidance about responding to papers whose politics dismay them. When a text is not about compassion for the needy but about the public's response to homosexuality or the fairness of affirmative action, facilitative response can be difficult. Deeply felt but not always carefully examined positions are at stake. Student papers that carry implicit insults, often unintentionally, are difficult to respond to diplomatically; a critical response may be difficult for a student to hear. A teacher's insistence on factual detail from clearly cited sources might seem politically suspect. Nevertheless, young writers must recognize their obligation to provide substantive support and acknowledge potential resistance. They must learn to consider an issue or situation from multiple perspectives, including perspectives that may threaten their beliefs, and they must reflect on their judgments and avoid easy generalizations about guilt and blame.

In such situations, active receptivity turns my own certainty into questions, a stance I encourage the teaching assistants to take as well. The complexity and discomfort, including students' sometimes discordant responses to one another, make active receptivity a necessity for an instructor who wants not merely to lead lively discussions but to model inquiry. A teacher earns credibility by listening, and having earned the credibility, can ask others to listen. We need to understand many sides of an argument if we are to prevent impasse and outrage. To foster good writing we must point out strengths of arguments we oppose, weaknesses of positions we endorse. To gain our students' trust we must remain even-handed, and we must recognize that opposition is threatening, to us as well as to the students from whom we are asking for deeper reflection. My teaching becomes provisional, for the meantime, more concerned with the processes of discussion than the final decision.

In the encounter with difference lies the possibility of finding a "between" of new richness. I want the private to connect with the public; I want students to see that it can, that it does, perhaps in places they had not considered previously. I want them to set about discovering how their own private commitments might best connect with public ones. Through such connections we can imagine and build toward the public good. Doing so, I believe, is the work I am sent out from the Eucharist to do.

My approach to the teaching of writing finds validation in Marquette's Jesuit tradition, which dedicates the university to "pursuing truth, discovering and transmitting knowledge, promoting a life of faith, and developing leadership expressed in service to others" ("Marquette," 1993, p. 14). For the Jesuits, it is particularly important that this service be "rooted not simply in charity but in justice," as the current president, the Rev. Robert A. Wild, S.J., emphasized in his 1996 inaugural address, in which he declared that an essential part of the university's task is "to empower people to take leadership" in service to "the 'little ones' of the Gospel, those who are somehow disadvantaged or treated as outcasts in our society." This emphasis on leadership and justice, combined with the high value Jesuit education has always placed on clarity of expression (see Burghardt), makes preparing students for involvement in public discourse a central endeavor. My teaching focuses on equipping students to engage in this discourse, beginning with the effort, as I have said, to help them articulate their commitments. My personal values coincide with my institution's values in a hope that those commitments will be felt in some form of call to service (a concept Robert Coles, 1993, examines in detail). However, it is decidedly not my job to prescribe the particularity of those commitments. As Buckley puts it, the university "is not a place for ideologies or indoctrination however good these are judged to be. Turn the universities into propaganda institutions and you will destroy them as universities" (p. 82). Summing up an argument for the importance of ethically grounded social science classes, Buckley says students should not be inculcated with one kind of politics or one set of solutions, but instead, be

> introduced into some appreciation of the human condition of the vast majority of human beings and equipped with some of the tools that will enable them to discuss these questions and move to their resolution with a disciplined intellect as well as an educated sensibility. (p. 104)

To say that my teaching is for the meantime is in part to say that I use my knowledge, skills, and experience now to enhance the ability of my students to help their future communities move toward resolution of the questions and issues they will face. Individual students will make their own decisions about how to use their education, how to fulfill their personal promise, and in what measure they will do so through leadership and service. When it is time for me to work directly for what I conceive of as the public good, by advocating certain policies or supporting certain causes, I must do it outside the classroom, apart from my life as a faculty member. My work in the classroom is to foster the development of student voices, not to espouse specific political positions.

The part of my work in the world where I do make choices and take stands regarding politics and social policy has come to be centered at St. Mark's. Here I worship, listen, and talk in a setting that fits Wolff's (1968) definition of a rational community, "that reciprocity of consciousness which is achieved and sustained by equals who discourse together publicly for the specific purpose of social decision and action" (p. 192). Of course, parish and outreach work, too, are inevitably provisional. We do the best we can, in the meantime, with the time and resources that we have. But we do it together. My individual efforts for an outreach project or on a committee, in a study group or a carpool, are complemented and supplemented by the efforts of others. Together, sometimes almost invisibly, we support one another and one another's work. Furthermore, we are committed as a parish to projects that alleviate suffering in the larger community, offering a substantial portion of our budget, time, and talent to combatting hunger and its root causes. We are a Bread for the World congregation, a member of the nationwide Christian lobbying effort that, in the language of its masthead, "seeks justice for the world's hungry people." As Father Hills' sermon suggested, trying to consider, much less confront, the world's anguish alone can make one can feel quite vulnerable to despair. "Each one of us," he said, "could stand on those streets, and little by little, quarter by quarter, give away all that we have, and almost nothing would change." But the parish community gives me confidence that my offerings of energy and finances do not dribble away to emptiness. Indeed, the web of inter-connections that Christianity proclaims means, as Father Hills put it, that "when you decide to support some new initiative to provide employment or shelter for those who lack them, you have decided not only in favor of a good deed, but also in favor of a future that is structurally, essentially, more responsive than the pre-sent to the needs of God's people."

During Advent that year, as I ran up against the limits of my time and energy at both school and church, these matters of work and community were troubling me deeply. Where could I count on doing work that would be effica-cious? How could I see results? What would satisfy me? I was writing an essay for publication about the use of multicultural materials in monocultural writing classrooms. Neither in print nor in the classroom did I want to be discounted as too liberal, or as someone toeing a "politically correct" line. Yet I felt that mak-ing cultural pluralism more visible to my relatively sheltered and comfortable students was crucial. To support my argument for a pedagogy that legitimates difference yet takes care not to prescribe commitments, the essay described how students moved away from their resistance to talking about race as we worked with materials about the internment of Japanese Americans during World War II, which I had assigned for research work in a first-year composition class. "They don't want to feel guilty," one of my colleagues had told me. Scales had fallen from my eyes. I hadn't seen that students might see guilt on the agenda. I didn't want them to feel guilty. I wanted them to stretch their imaginations, and through that stretching I wanted them to develop some appreciation for the experiences of people who are racially different from them. I hoped, of course, that a "contraposition of different interests, different perspectives," as Gates (1992) puts it (p. 36), would motivate students to take responsibility not for the past but for the future.

Listening to sermons about putting faith to work in the world, I came to see—and accept—that in this meantime I could stop there, hoping for new motives, clearer commitments, new responsibilities. I could accept the fact that I was not likely to know about the ultimate gleanings of the imaginations I sought to enrich.

On the second Sunday of Advent, the Gospel reading told of John the Baptist's preaching in the wilderness (Matthew 3.1-12). Father Hills asked us to consider what we would have made of John's proclamation that a new era lay just ahead. It is naive, he said, to project on the Jews who went to listen to John a yearning for a new religion. "The fact is that then as now the greatest sense of need was not strictly religious, but social and political—local." He warned us against seeing "our primary calling at St. Mark's as the formation of a cozy community for the quiet enactment of our social destiny." God, Father Hills insisted, "has called us to more than this." Describing the promise of Christ's Incarnation in terms of a call to service, a call to alleviate suffering, he said, "In Christ, God has given me hands to work with, eyes to see, and a heart to feel with, and a mind to decide where the weight of my energy will further the loving purpose of God."

It was a great comfort to see my decisions about where to place the weight of my energy as God-given. This community, focused on liturgy and values, but creating itself weekly in shared work and decision-making about social actions, helps me make choices that, in Father Hills' words, "are not lost in the ether but become part of the new fabric of the world." My church community gives me strength and courage to go out and do the work God has given me to do—work with students, colleagues, papers, ideas. The community and the communion of the liturgy give me comfort each Sunday when I return from that work for renewal. Comfort, but not coziness, because renewal can be, perhaps ought to be, challenging.

On the fourth Sunday of Advent, responding to the Gospel story of Joseph's decision not to abandon the mysteriously pregnant Mary (Matthew 1.18-25), Father Hills said,

> For us, as for Joseph, the question is no longer, Shall I try to be a good person?—Of course we'll try, one by one, to be good, and true, and just. Instead the question is: How near to the divine mystery of incarnation, how near to the visible presence of God's work in the world, how near dare I tread, and what shape in my life . . . will this nearness take?

It is a question that bears asking more often than at Christmas, I realized, just as Paul hoped the Romans to whom he wrote would wear the armor of light throughout the year.

The concept of the Second Coming remaining a lacuna for me, I do my work in a Christian meantime, "between Calvary and some unknown final end," as if I knew for sure, grateful for what I have received, trusting the promise of more to come. That armor gives me courage to keep going in the face of uncertainty, to tread a little nearer. "It is, of course, a great gift to have a good heart, a caring mind, and all the best intentions," Father Hills said at the end of his final Advent sermon. "But these were never enough. From each of us it will take decision, commitment, and action, to show one another, to demonstrate to the world about us, that all the hopes of Advent really can give way to the joys of Christmas."

I teach at a university committed to engagement with contemporary urban problems and justice as well as to the intellectual and moral development of its students. The process of this development includes expanding students' often limited notions of community and developing their individual sense of responsibility within community—without imposing a political agenda upon them. My religious tradition and my parish community's commitment to serving the poor and working for justice provide me with opportunities for taking stands on public issues. Without certainty, but with conviction, my faith gives me the energy and courage to do my work in the academy. There I present educational opportunities designed in content to broaden horizons and in process to model ways for using written discourse to continue that broadening beyond the academy. Within the paradoxes of faith and uncertainty lies my belief, which makes possible my life in the academy.

REFERENCES

Bellah, Robert N., Richard Madsen, William M. Sullivan, Ann Swidler, and Steven M. Tipton. *Habits of the Heart: Individualism and Commitment in American Life.* Berkeley: University of California Press, 1985.

_____ ."The House Divided." Introduction to the Updated Edition. *Habits of the Heart: Individualism and Commitment in American Life.* Updated ed. Berkeley: University of California Press, 1996. vii-xxxix.

Blanchard, Fletcher A. "Combatting Intentional Bigotry and Inadvertently Racist Acts." *Chronicle of Higher Education 13* (May 1992): B1-2.

The Book of Common Prayer. N.p.: Seabury, 1979.

Buber, Martin. *Between Man and Man.* Trans. Ronald Gregor Smith. Boston: Beacon, 1955.

Buckley, Michael J., S.J. "Christian Humanism and Human Misery: A Challenge to the Jesuit University." *Faith, Discovery, Service: Perspectives on Jesuit Education.* Ed. Francis M. Lazarus. Milwaukee: Marquette University Press, 1992. 77-105.

Burghardt, Walter J., S.J. "Jesuit Education and the Faith That Does Justice." *Faith, Discovery, Service: Perspectives on Jesuit Education.* Ed. Francis M. Lazarus. Milwaukee: Marquette University Press, 1992. 1-22.

Coles, Robert. *The Call of Service.* Boston: Houghton, 1993.

Communications. "Responses to Harding's Darkly Radiant Dream." *Cross Currents, 37* (Spring 1987): 467-75.

Fishman, Stephen M., and Lucille Parkinson McCarthy. "Teaching for Student Change: A Deweyan Alternative to Radical Pedagogy." *College Composition and Communication 47* (October 1996): 342-66.

Fowler, Robert Booth. *The Dance with Community: The Contemporary Debate in American Political Thought.* Lawrence: University Press of Kansas, 1991.

Gates, Henry Louis Jr. "Pluralism and Its Discontents." *Profes*sion (1992): 35-38.

Harding, Vincent. "Toward a Darkly Radiant Vision of America's Truth." *Cross Currents 37* (Winter 1987-1988): 1-16.

Ling, Amy. "I'm Here: An Asian American Woman's Response." *New Literary History, 19* (Autumn 1987): 151-60.

Marquette University Self-Study Report for North Central Association, 1993. Milwaukee, WI, 1993.

Naylor, Gloria. "Mommy, What Does 'Nigger' Mean?" In *The Norton Reader: An Anthology of Expository Prose.* 8th ed. New York: Norton, 1992. 378-81.

Paul, Richard W. *Critical Thinking: What Every Person Needs to Survive in a Rapidly Changing World*. Rohnert Park, CA: Center for Critical Thinking and Moral Critique, 1990.

Wild, Robert A., S.J. *President's Inaugural Address*. Marquette University, Milwaukee, 1996.

Wolff, Robert Paul. *The Poverty of Liberalism*. Boston: Beacon, 1968.

5

Listening, Learning, and the Language of Faith

Jeannette M. Lindholm
Boston University

During my second year of teaching at a small state university, I asked my Introduction to College Writing students to write an informal response to a reading I had assigned during the first week of the semester. As I read through those responses, one essay in particular stood out for me. Its writer had prefaced his remarks with the comment, "I may be just [a] thick headed Christian. . . ." I winced when I read that phrase, not because I feared he was "one of those fundamentalists" I had heard teachers complain about, but because of the defensiveness in his remark and the stigma he attached to his religious tradition. He seemed to be seeing himself—or assuming I would see him—in the stereotype of the Christian buffoon, an object of ridicule, certainly not someone who would be taken seriously at a state university.

Although I was saddened by his comment, I could also appreciate the risk he took by identifying himself as a Christian. Although members of the academy have become increasingly sensitive to the ways race, class, and gender influence people's assumptions about knowledge or truth, many academics have either ignored or even openly denounced their students' religious backgrounds, thereby disconnecting formal education from many of the traditions that give meaning to human existence. Such attitudes may hinder students' academic or intellectual progress and discourage students from leading fully integrated lives by giving them the message that many of their life experiences, commitments, beliefs, and values have no relationship to the questions pursued in their academic disciplines. Moreover, these attitudes can ultimately inhibit a teacher's effectiveness. If part of our task as educators is to help students learn to examine ideas, perspectives, and situations critically, it seems only reasonable to encourage them to reflect on the range of influences that have shaped their outlooks. For many of our students, these include religious beliefs or spiritual experiences. Thoughtful, respectful attempts to understand those influences are well within the boundaries of the academic enterprise, even though as George Marsden (1992) notes, such attempts might require "some consciousness raising" in order to gain acceptance in many institutions of higher education (p. 40). Yet despite the challenges inherent in that task, efforts to make room for religiously informed perspectives are worthwhile, especially if teachers hope to create the possibility of meaningful educational experiences for their students and resist what bell hooks (1994) has observed as "a grave sense of dis-ease among professors . . . when students want us to see them as whole human beings with complex lives and experiences rather than simply as seekers after compartmentalized bits of knowledge" (p. 15).

In any institutional setting, it is important for teachers to model relationships and establish structures that allow students to determine and implement goals for their own learning. This includes giving students opportunities to make connections between their personal commitments and the new information they encounter in the college or university setting. The ways in which teachers structure their courses and relate to their students, however, are influenced in part by the nature of the academic institution itself. And in this chapter I refer to my teaching experiences at a large research university, a small state university, and an evangelical liberal arts college.

My convictions about the importance of facilitating connections between students' personal commitments and their formal schooling have been influenced by my own experiences as a student and the teachers who nurtured my development. They have also been informed by the work of educators such as Paul Freire (1970, 1978), Parker Palmer (1983), Mary Rose O'Reilley (1984, 1990, 1993), Henri Nouwen (1978), Ira Shor (1987), and writers in feminist collections such as *Gendered Subjects* (Culley and Portuges, 1985) and *Learning Our Way* (Bunch and Pollack, 1983) who advocate student-centered classrooms. These educators are committed to creating a learning environment in which students and teachers alike recognize the importance of honest, respectful dialogue, of the commitment to listen deeply to one another, and of the willingness to be transformed through the shared experience of learning.

Often, student-centered classrooms are characterized by frequent class or small group discussions, students' input regarding course topics and assignments, shared authority in the classroom, and alternative grading systems. Although these classroom structures are important for students' learning, perhaps more importantly, within them teachers can embody behaviors and attitudes that increase the possibility of relationships based on trust and commitment rather than competition or indifference. This possibility increases tremendously when teachers' work with students is motivated by love.

IMPORTANCE OF LOVE IN LEARNING

It can be difficult to speak or write about the relations between love and learn-ing, in part because the word *love* is used in so many different ways. Here I mean the kind of love that compels us as teachers to care deeply about the well-being of our students, to know them as human beings and not as objects for our manipulation or control. But more than this, love needs to be the motivating force at the center of any learning situation, particularly if an educator believes that the making of knowledge is a relational activity. That is, we cannot separate ourselves from one another or the world we attempt to understand; we are all profoundly affected by our relationships with one another.

Too often, as Palmer (1983) argues in *To Know As We Are Known: A Spirituality of Education*, scholars and teachers have been guilty of objectifying their subjects of study, distancing themselves from those subjects to the ultimate detriment of both the knower and the known. In this book, Palmer asserts that researchers/scholars tend to be motivated by mere curiosity or the desire to con-trol, motivations that can have devastating consequences. To illustrate this point, Palmer cites the creation of the atom bomb as a primary example of these motivations gone awry and taken to their terrifying extreme. In contrast, love as the primary motivation for our teaching and learning creates possibilities for understanding and wholeness rather than harm. As Palmer (1983) asserts:

> The goal of a knowledge arising from love is the reunification of broken selves and broken worlds. A knowledge born of compassion aims not at exploiting and manipulating creation but at reconciling the world to itself. The mind motivated by compassion reaches out to know as the heart reach-es out to love. Here the act of knowing *is* an act of love, the act of entering and embracing the reality of the other, of allowing the other to enter and embrace our own. (p. 8)

Palmer views love as crucial in any academic endeavor—in research and in teaching. Our lives are intricately connected to others, and we need a pedagogy that both acknowledges and nurtures the relational nature of our lives.

Love is important in the work of other educators, as well. Freire (1978), for example, in his efforts for literacy and work with the oppressed, viewed dialogue as necessary in the educational process. In order for that dia-logue to be liberating, love must always be present. He explains:

> Love is at the same time the foundation of dialogue and and dialogue itself. . . . No matter where the oppressed are found, the act of love is commitment to their cause—the cause of liberation. And this commitment, because it is loving, is dialogical. As an act of bravery, love cannot be sentimental; as an act of freedom, it must not serve as a pretext for manipulation. It must gen-erate other acts of freedom; otherwise it is not love. (pp. 77-78)

The love both Palmer and Freire embrace is neither sentimental nor possessive. It is the critical component of any educational process that aspires to the well-being of all.

Love or charity also figures prominently in Mark Schwehn's (1993) *Exiles from Eden: Religion and the Academic Vocation in America.* Like Palmer, Schwehn opts for a more "communitarian" vision of academic life, one that both nurtures shared quests for truth that are "linked inextricably to care taken with the lives and thoughts of others" (p. 44). For Schwehn, the presence of charity in a community fosters careful listening to others, including the thoughtful reading of texts. If we are charitable to others, we give them the benefit of the doubt; we struggle to understand their perspectives. Such an approach is critical in any attempt to find truth. The presence of charity does not eliminate the possibility of challenge or critique, but ensures that such critiques will be respectful and facilitate dialogue. Schwehn also viewed love as manifesting itself in both friendship and thoughtfulness, which, as he indicates in his paraphrase of Leon Kass, includes "the notion of being filled with reflections about important matters of human concern and the notion of being considerate of others" (p. 58). Finally, Schwehn believes friendship is important for the health of academic communities and relies heavily on Aristotle's assumption that the greatest friendships are those between virtuous individuals who wrestle with ideas and share the life of the mind. For Aristotle and Schwehn alike, friendships do not detract from teaching and scholarship, but rather enrich them (pp. 62–63).

Palmer, Freire, and Schwehn all reject both the possibility and desirability of objectifying knowledge, of separating the knower from the known. They recognize that love needs to be at the center of any educational endeavor, for the presence of love brings us closer to understanding the questions or answers we pursue and liberates learners themselves.

IMPORTANCE OF LISTENING

It is not enough simply to speak or write of love, however. Love must manifest itself in concrete ways. One of the most important ways love appears in educational settings is in the act of respectful, attentive listening. But listening is not always an easy task. Often, in classroom discussions, for example, I find myself too quick to jump in with a comment, or in individual conferences with students, too quick to give what I consider to be helpful advice. I have found that I must consciously remind myself to be silent and let my students speak, for I am convinced that something significant happens when teachers become comfortable with silence, when they give students opportunities to stumble through ideas, if need be, without interruption.

I recall, for example, a discussion we had in my Advanced Composition course at Gordon College, a small evangelical liberal arts institution. I had just assigned an essay in which I asked students to write about a place that was either fascinating or meaningful to them. In class I modeled a process they could use to help them carefully select the details they would like to include in their essays. To get us started, I chose a place they all knew well, Gordon College itself, and asked them to brainstorm a list of impressions they might include if someone asked them to portray the college in their essays. As the discussion progressed, a number of students shared details and stories that revealed Gordon as a caring community.

But as I was listening to their remarks, I remembered an earlier discussion we had in that same course. One afternoon I had asked my students if they ever felt silenced at Gordon, and many nodded or said, "Yes." When I asked them to elaborate, they told me about the pressures they felt to be good witnesses for God. Some feared that if they were completely honest about the doubts and struggles they faced in their lives, they might negatively affect someone else's spiritual life. They didn't want that to happen. Others feared that their friends would become overly concerned and feel the need to pray for them, while they, on the other hand, simply wanted to be heard and accepted.

So when some of my students spoke of Gordon as a caring community in our discussion about place, I pressed them further by reminding them of that earlier conversation and asked them if everyone would consider Gordon a community. Almost immediately, "Susan," one of the most insightful students in the group, shook her head to the contrary, but in the flurry of words that followed, she was unable—or unwilling—to speak.

Soon afterward she stopped by my office to talk about another matter. I mentioned that I noticed her nonverbal response to my question in class and that I was genuinely interested in her reaction. My comment sparked a 30-minute conversation. Listening to Susan, I learned about the alienation some of our students feel and the need for more accepting, authentic relationships at this college that strives to be a community. It was important for me as a teacher to hear what she had to say, and she told me that she appreciated being heard.

Listening can take many forms. It is not limited to hearing students out in classroom discussions or in the informal conversations we may have with them. We can also listen to students in their writing, echoing in our written comments what we think we hear in their work or asking them questions to prompt further reflection.

When teachers model listening, they give students the message that students' concerns matter, and such careful, attentive listening can initiate not only occasions for growth, but even healing in a person's life. If education is in part about seeking the truth in our lives, as Palmer and Schwehn both suggest it is, listening motivated by love can be a powerful force. In my own formal education at a Lutheran liberal arts college and a large research university, I was fortunate to have two teachers who listened carefully to me, a college mentor who heard me through my fumbling attempts to find a mature faith, and a graduate advisor who supported my desire to integrate my theological perspectives with my teaching and scholarship.

I am convinced that listening is essential if we teachers hope to establish learning experiences where "obedience to truth is practiced" as Palmer urges (p. 88), especially if we create opportunities for students to explore religious beliefs and spiritual experiences. We must listen attentively to students ourselves and encourage them to listen to one another. Together students and teachers alike must "[hear] one another to speech" (Morton, 1985, p. 55) and respond to one another with care and respect.

CHALLENGE OF COMMUNICATING BELIEF AND SPIRITUAL EXPERIENCE

Despite teachers' and students' best efforts to establish a supportive classroom community and healthy relationships with one another, challenges still remain when teachers encourage students to make connections between their lives of faith and their work in the academy. For a variety of reasons, it can be difficult for students to communicate their religious beliefs and spiritual experiences.

At one level, difficulties in communication emerge if students believe the language they use to convey belief or experience is stigmatized by individuals who do not share their assumptions. I think, for example, of a former student from my course, The Teaching of Writing, at a state university. She expressed concern about the possibility of sounding like a "Jesus freak" when reflecting on the ways her Catholic faith informed her commitment to teaching. At that same university, a student from The Personal Essay writing course expressed similar concerns to me after writing an essay alluding to his struggles over whether or not he should study for the ordained ministry. He feared the negative reaction of his peers, who, as it turned out, were actually very respectful of his beliefs. For these two students, writing about their beliefs was important enough for them to risk possible misunderstandings or negative reactions. But I suspect fears of potential rejection prevent other students from discussing their faith, particularly when such discussions have been openly discouraged or deemed inappropriate in much of their formal schooling.

Attempts to articulate human understandings of the divine are problematic in other ways, as well, for individuals are struggling to name or describe realities that they can never fully capture in language. Early in *Metaphorical Theology: Models of God in Religious Language*, Christian theologian McFague (1982) refers to "the great tradition of deeply religious people, and especially the mystics of all religious traditions, who feel conviction at the level of experience, at the level of worship, but great uncertainty at the level of words adequate to express the reality of God" (p. 1). Perceiving a tenuous relationship between language (including the language of Scripture) and the transcendent, Sallie McFague warned against approaches to religious language that make it idolatrous or irrelevant. Religious language becomes idolatrous, she explained, when people imagine a direct relationship between the language itself and the God it attempts to describe. It becomes irrelevant when the language is no longer meaningful to individuals whose range of life experiences do not resonate with the realities that language seems to construct or articulate. Ultimately, she claims, human relationships with God cannot be named and "all our language about God is but metaphors of experiences of relating to God" (p. 194).

Sensing the inadequacies of their words, students at any college or university may have difficulty finding language to articulate their experiences, whereas others may feel overly confident about the efficacy of religious language and slip into the traps of irrelevancy or idolatry that McFague identified. Take, for example, the conversion narratives that occasionally appear when composition instructors ask students to write about significant experiences in their lives, especially if those instructors request students to reflect on experiences that radically changed their way of thinking. Students from Christian fundamentalist or evangelical backgrounds in particular may often view their lives in a narrative structure paralleling the Fall/Redemption narrative of the history of the Christian Church.

From many of these students' perspectives, human beings fell from grace when Adam and Eve sinned by disobeying God. This original sin created a barrier between human beings and God until a restored relationship was possible through Christ's death and resurrection. Although Christ's coming made salvation from sin and eternal life possible, salvation does not become a reality unless people "accept Jesus Christ as their personal Savior." Often that acceptance involves a conversion experience which is later conveyed in a formulaic pattern. The narrative often includes a discussion of how empty, even debauched, a student's life was before he or she "accepted Christ." The narrative typically climaxes at the point of the student's conversion and then concludes with a romanticized account of life after the conversion. These narratives, whose structures closely resemble conversion narratives from 19th century America (Brereton, 1991, p. 6), often function metaphorically in ways similar to McFague's understanding of religious metaphor. Although the narratives may reveal particular characteristics of a student's religious experience, they may also obscure other characteristics of that experience, and students risk the danger of their narratives becoming irrelevant to their readers.

Similar narratives may appear with slight variation if students have grown up in fundamentalist or evangelical homes. These students may not have had radical conversion experiences but may have had times of experiencing backsliding in their lives, times when they no longer felt close to God. These students' narratives will typically discuss that period of backsliding and then climax with their re-dedicating their lives to Christ. I remember, for example, an essay I received while teaching at the large research university I attended as a graduate student. A student in my introductory composition course described a period of rebellion, then a time of tremendous struggle when he agonized over the apparent conflict between his own desires for his life and what he perceived to be the will of God. The essay concluded with the relief he experienced when he gave up his own wishes except for the wish to be God's "servant."

This latter paper illustrates not only a variation of the traditional conversion narrative but also some Christian students' tendency to resolve conflict neatly at the end of an essay with a reference to God's positive role in their lives. Fundamentalist and evangelical students come from traditions that regard narratives as extremely powerful. Stories—particularly the stories of Christ's death and resurrection or stories about God's work in individual lives—can bring others to the truth. For that reason, some of our students in any academic setting may feel compelled to tell their stories of faith. In addition, as my Advanced Composition students at Gordon College pointed out to me, they may resist writing about conflict or pain without resolving that conflict by referring to God's love and grace. They feel responsible for offering readers hope.

Narratives grounded in some of our students' religious traditions can be especially meaningful to those students, but for readers unfamiliar with such traditions, the narratives may seem confusing, irrelevant, or even offensive. Unfortunately, this can be true of much of the language used to describe religious faith or spiritual experience, for that language frequently derives from the sacred texts, doctrinal statements, hymns, dominant narratives, and metaphors embraced by an individual's worshipping community, which, in many instances, could be also viewed legitimately as one of the various discourse communities an individual may belong to. Within such communities, as Lester Faigley (1985) explains:

> people acquire specialized kinds of discourse competence that enable them to participate in specialized groups. Members know what is worth communicating, how it can be communicated, what other members of the community are likely to know and believe to be true about certain subjects, how other members can be persuaded, and so on. (p. 238)

Clearly, Faigley's definition could apply to members of various religious groups whose use of language marks them as members of those groups. For example, in addition to writing the conversion narratives I describe, students belonging to Christian fundamentalist or evangelical congregations may be more likely to use Scripture to support arguments in their essays, particularly if the Bible is the primary authority in their lives. Many of them may have memorized Bible verses as children so they could remember and draw inspiration from those verses in times of need. Fundamentalist students, in particular, very often grow up believing the Bible is a holy document containing facts and truths they could pull out and apply, even out of context. Many grew up hearing preachers do that very thing. It was accepted in their religious discourse community, so we should not be surprised that such a practice, often called proof-texting, sometimes appears in the essays they write.

I recall, for example, an essay I received while teaching Introduction to College Writing at a small state university. One of my students cited verses from the Bible to support her case against public rights for gays and lesbians. And at about the same time, one of our composition teachers expressed concern over a rough draft a student had written about the concept of grace. The teacher had asked students to write about a concept they were interested in exploring, and this student cited the words of the Apostle Paul as her primary means of support for her arguments.

Whereas proof-texting may be appropriate in some settings, it is not acceptable in writing situations where the audiences might not regard the Bible as authoritative—or if members of those audiences have different understandings of the proper ways Scripture should be interpreted and applied. Rather than being a cause for concern, however, the presence of proof-texting can provide rich opportunities for teachers to point out different understandings of textual authority and prompt students to think more deeply about their audiences' assumptions and needs.

It can be effective, for example, when students are writing research papers to hold class discussions on questions such as: What counts as convincing evidence? How do we determine whether or not a source is credible? How do various groups differ in terms of the kinds of authorities they will be likely to accept? Mentioning biblical proof-texting in the context of a broader discussion about sources not only helps all students to consider different understandings of authority, but also prevents teachers from singling out students who may already feel marginalized in the classroom.

Additional challenges related to students' use of the language of faith may appear when we consider the presence of intertextuality in discourse communities. According to James Porter (1986):

> We can distinguish between two kinds of intertextuality: iterability and presupposition. Iterability refers to the "repeatability" of certain textual fragments, to citation in its broadest sense to include not only explicit allusions, references, and quotations within a discourse, but also unannounced sources and influences, cliches, phrases in the air, and traditions. . . . Presupposition refers to assumptions a text makes about its referent, its readers, and its context—to portions of the text which are read, but which are not explicitly "there." (p. 35)

Although the religious narratives and practice of proof-texting I discuss earlier illustrate the kinds of intertextuality Porter described, I focus specifically on an example taken from a research paper I obtained while conducting dissertation research at an evangelical college in the midwest. The student wrote the paper for one of the college's required religion classes and could assume a Christian audience:

> Worshiping God is not just a once-a-day activity, but it should be a contin-
> ued, daily walk with God. The Bible calls us to bring glory to the name of
> the Father and our lives should be constantly doing this. As Christians our
> bodies are the temple of God and our hearts should be his throne. As we
> offer ourselves up to Him as living sacrifices daily, we will become more
> Christ-like until we see Him face to face and discover true worship around
> his heavenly throne. (Lindholm, 1992)

This example is especially rich because of its biblical metaphors and allusions
to specific passages in Scripture, but I will touch on just a few instances of
intertextuality apparent in the text. The phrase "daily walk with God," for
instance, or slight variations thereof, is quite commonly found in evangelical
circles (Hunter, 1983, p. 65) and has connections to a number of references.
Students at the college I studied are familiar with the popular admonition to
"walk the talk," which suggests it is not enough simply to profess Christianity
with words alone, but that a person must also follow through with correspond-
ing Christ-like actions. If we turned to Scripture, we would also find examples
of the "walk" metaphor in verses such as Psalms 23.4, II Corinthians 5.6-7,
Galations 5.25, and Ephesians 5.1-2 (Revised Standard Version). In addition,
these evangelical students would likely be familiar with the hymns "O Master
Let Me Walk with Thee" and "Just a Closer Walk with Thee," as well as others
relying on journey or pilgrimage metaphors to describe the spiritual life.

By mentioning the various instances of iterability in the student text,
however, I do not mean to suggest that the student was fully aware of the inter-
textual nature of his passage. He may have been to some degree, but as a member of an evangelical subculture, he was exposed to certain accepted ways of
speaking about religious faith and may not have traced many sources of his
expression.

In addition to the iterability I mentioned earlier (specifically, the ties to
hymns and passages from the Bible), the text contains a number of presupposi-
tions. Take, for example, the student's decision to invoke claims the Bible
makes about how Christians should lead their lives. In doing so the student
assumes readers will accept biblical authority and feels no need to justify the
legitimacy of that authority. It is the same assumption that underlies the convention of proof-texting, as well.

In any classroom setting, students, as well as teachers, might be unfamiliar with some of the discourse used to express religious belief or spiritual
experience. Students themselves using language to discuss their faith may be
oblivious to all of the sources and assumptions embedded in the language they
use. The matter is further complicated when we consider Joseph Harris' (1989)
claim that "the borders of most discourses are hazily marked and often trav-
elled, and that the communities they define are thus often indistinct and overlap-
ping" (p. 17). Nevertheless, the language students use does filter their perceptions of reality. So although teachers can create common ground in a course by

introducing students to the particular vocabularies, questions, and kinds of evidence embraced by an academic field or discipline, that ground may easily slip away when students attempt to explore their religious beliefs or spiritual experiences in relationship to their course material.

If communication and understanding are the goals, then difficult as the task may be, members of the class should be encouraged to express their perspectives in ways that will be more accessible to their listeners or readers. It is important for teachers to talk with students about the language in passages similar to the one I included on worship. Often these discussions can be most helpful if they take place in individual conferences. In that context a teacher can say something like the following: "I can tell your faith is important to you, and I'm interested in hearing more about this. But I'm not sure I'm understanding you here. Can you tell me what it means to 'bring glory to the name of the Father'? Or what it means for your heart to be 'his throne'?" A teacher can then encourage the student to express her or his beliefs in language that is more comprehensible to a broader audience. The teacher can also remind the student that it would be helpful for a Christian audience too, in this case, to get a more complete sense of what the student hoped to communicate. By taking this approach, teachers can affirm the importance of students' beliefs, but at the same time help them realize that the language of their religious communities isn't immediately comprehensible to individuals outside their own group. In these conversations, teachers can also suggest that it's important for students personally to explore the implications of their language. The words they use help them construct their understanding of God and are, therefore, worth examining.

In addition, teachers can feature various word choices in class discussion and explore the origins of particular discourse conventions. In the past, for example, I have asked students to bring in samples of writing from their churches, workplaces, or even dorms. We talked about the differences they noticed in format, vocabulary, assumptions about authority, the kinds of evidence writers included to support their points, and so on. Such discussions highlight the contextual nature of communication and help students realize even more fully that their audience needs to figure heavily in the choices students make with their language.

Although attempts to alter expression can prove to be difficult for students, particularly given the inherent challenges of discussing the spiritual life in general, they can be very beneficial. Members of a class may gain a greater understanding of one another when individuals have the opportunity to talk about the consequences of their word choices, as well as the assumptions behind the language they typically use to describe religious belief or experience. Exploring those consequences and assumptions may be particularly helpful to students who are well acquainted with the common phrases and conventions of discourse belonging to their faith communities but have not thoroughly examined them. The phrase, "walk the talk," I mentioned earlier, does imply after all that it can be relatively easy at times to "talk the talk." But that "talk" might not be particularly effective or beneficial.

IMPLICATIONS OF OUR EFFORTS

As I illustrated here, challenges do manifest themselves when teachers attempt to create opportunities for students to explore religious beliefs or spiritual experiences. And we must always keep in mind that students are vulnerable when they attempt to make connections between their personal lives and their work in the classroom. Because of the deeply personal nature of religious belief or spiritual experience, students are truly putting themselves on the line when they choose to reveal their commitments. We must remember the personal risks our students take and not discount those risks, doing everything within our power to offer students a safe hearing of their perspectives.

Yet despite the challenges, if, as McFague (1982) claims, our "knowledge is profoundly relational and, hence, interdependent, relative, situational, and limited" (p. 194), we have solid grounds for creating opportunities for students to explore their religious beliefs or spiritual experiences, even outside of the composition classroom where teachers are, perhaps, most intimately involved with students' ideas, feelings, and concerns. Creating such opportunities offers students the possibility of not only a more integrated, meaningful education, but also a more intellectually honest one.

REFERENCES

Brereton, Virginia Lieson. *From Sin to Salvation: Stories of Women's Conversions, 1800 to the Present.* Bloomington: Indiana University Press, 1991.

Bunch, Charlotte, and Sandra Pollack, eds. *Learning Our Way: Essays in Feminist Education.* Trumansburg, NY: Crossing, 1983.

Culley, Margo, and Catherine Portuges, eds. *Gendered Subjects: The Dynamics of Feminist Teaching.* Boston: Routledge and Kegan Paul, 1985.

Faigley, Lester. "Nonacademic Writing: The Social Perspective." *Writing in Nonacademic Settings.* Ed. Lee Odell and Dixie Goswami. New York: Guilford, 1985. 231-48.

Freire, Paulo. *Pedagogy of the Oppressed.* Trans. Myra B. Ramos. New York: Continuum, 1970.

_____. *Pedagogy in Process: The Letters to Guinea-Bissau.* Trans. Carman St. John Hunter. New York: Continuum, 1978.

Harris, Joseph. "The Idea of Community in the Study of Writing. *College Composition and Communication, 40.*1 (February 1989): 11-22.

hooks, bell. *Teaching to Transgress: Education as the Practice of Freedom.* New York: Routledge, 1994.

Hunter, James Davison. *American Evangelicalism: Conservative Religion and the Quandary of Modernity.* New Brunswick, NJ: Rutgers University Press, 1983.

Lindholm, Jeannette M. *Bearing Witness to the Word: Language, Faith, and Learning in an Evangelical College Community.* Unpublished doctoral dissertation. University of Minnesota, 1992.

Marsden, George M. "The Soul of the American University: A Historical Overview." *The Secularization of the Academy.* Ed. George M. Marsden and Bradley J. Longfield. New York: Oxford University Press, 1992. 9-45.

McFague, Sallie. *Metaphorical Theology: Models of God in Religious Language.* Philadelphia: Fortress, 1982.

Morton, Nelle. *The Journey Is Home.* Boston: Beacon, 1985.

Nouwen, Henri. *Creative Ministry.* New York: Image-Doubleday, 1978.

O'Reilley, Mary Rose. "The Peaceable Classroom." *College English, 46.*2 (February 1984): 103-12.

_____ ."Silence and Slow Time: Pedagogies from Inner Spaces." *Pre/Text, 11.*1-2 (Spring/Summer 1990): 134-43.

_____ . *The Peaceable Classroom.* Portsmouth, NH: Boynton/Cook, 1993.

Palmer, Parker. *To Know As We Are Known: A Spirituality of Education.* San Francisco: Harper, 1983.

Porter, James E. "Intertextuality and the Discourse Community."*Rhetoric Review 5.*1 (Fall 1986): 34-47.

Schwehn, Mark R. *Exiles from Eden: Religion and the Academic Vocation in America.* New York: Oxford University Press, 1993.

Shor, Ira. *Critical Teaching and Everyday Life.* Chicago: University of Chicago Press, 1987.

6

Goddess Spirituality and Academic Knowledge-Making*

Hildy Miller
University of Minnesota

I was reading about rationalism
the kind of thing we do up north
in early winter, where the sun
leaves work for the day at 4:15
Maybe the world is intelligible
to the rational mind:
and maybe we light the lamps at dusk
for nothing. . . .
Then I heard wings overhead. . . .
—Jane Kenyon (cited in Sewell, 1991, p. 240)

In this poem Kenyon captures a moment in which she suddenly apprehends mysterious creatures in flight—ironically—just after she has assured herself that reality must be both rationally constructed and rationally discernable. The imagery of dusk, when the sun no longer illuminates the world so clearly, suggests those moments when one privately questions accepted explanations or considers the information and experiences that contradict most culturally sanctioned kinds of knowledge. Like Kenyon, many of us find ourselves questioning the limitations of rationalist views of knowledge sanctioned by the academy—a

---

*A version of this chapter appears in the *Journal of the Association for Expanded Perspectives on Learning, 4* (1998-1999).

perspective most feminists would characterize as masculinist. We sense that some sort of counterbalance to it is needed. Yet, Beth Daniell (1994) points out, "As scholars and teachers in America, we have been carefully trained not only to separate religion from civic life but also to dismiss the spiritual" (p. 239). Indeed, academic knowledge-making typically delimits its domain by assigning "nonrational" kinds of learning to nonacademic contexts. Thus, spiritual belief is relegated to the province of churches, temples, and mosques. It is excluded because it is seen not simply as another way of knowing, but instead as a way of not-knowing, and so as altogether opposed to the kind of reason that we as academics should espouse. The mysteries of dusk must remain removed from the bright light of reason. To be sure, there are obvious dangers in attempting to admit spirituality to the academy if it serves to restrict or exclude any points of view. But by operating only within a rationalist tradition, we also limit what counts as knowledge, how we can go about making meaning, and who qualifies as legitimate meaning-makers. As a result, many of us are left, like Kenyon, feeling intellectually fragmented when kept within such narrow straits.

Certainly, for intellectual growth to occur, we must be free to draw on a full range of knowledge, including that of spiritual belief, no longer completely divorced from the enterprise of academic research and teaching. In particular, I propose that spiritual belief can be an alternative way of making meaning that can enhance as well as challenge our traditional notion of academic knowledge-making. And I illustrate this point by showing how I am integrating spiritual ways of knowing into the reading and writing that students do in my literature and composition classes from the perspective of goddess-centered spirituality.

My own connection to this tradition grew out of my longstanding interest in feminism. Early on, in the 1970s, I participated in consciousness-raising groups in which circles of women gathered privately to try to interpret personal experience through the social lens of gender for the first time. As I would discover later, such circles worked well not only for social issues but for spiritual ones. Out of these shared experiences, women generated a coherent and increasingly complex feminist theory that transformed masculinist approaches and assumptions in many sociopolitical areas. Always, I read and watched these transformations with interest. By the late 1970s, the women's movement had begun to change spirituality too, as the movement to reclaim lost feminine spiritual traditions began. It was during this time that a group of women gathered in Boston for a first spirituality conference (Christ, 1987). My own exposure to this development began when I read a book by Merlin Stone (1976) called *When God Was a Woman*—a watershed study, the first to document ancient and widespread matrifocal spiritual traditions. It was, in fact, also the first time I had ever felt the negative impact of the way in which our culture typically anthropomorphizes a supreme being as masculine—and I was thunderstruck. As I read about ancient goddesses, I found myself first struggling to even imagine a god-figure with feminine qualities, then after only partly envisioning this phenomenon, feeling overwhelmed with the significance of its implications. A woman knowledgeable, powerful, respected, and honored? For the first time, spirituality reflected back a face I recognized. Immediately, I sent copies of the book to my mother, sister, and women friends so they could also share the wonder of this novel concept.

Whatever interests in spirituality the book had awakened were set aside, however, until I returned in the 1980s to graduate school, where I studied rhetoric and composition. There in the academy I found feminist theory transforming standard approaches to teaching and research. In my own research on cognition and writing, I gradually rejected narrow rationalist paradigms of thought processes. I came to see these mechanistic models as by-products of masculinist epistemological assumptions on which is based the dominant academic notion of cognition. Other scholars too were arriving at similar conclusions and offering similar critiques (Grimshaw, 1986; Lloyd, 1984; Longino, 1989). In contrast to these paradigms, nonrationalist forms of cognition, posited as embodied, contextualized, personal, and figurative, were ways of knowing largely absent from the academy.

My interest in investigating this kind of cognition led me again to small groups of women who were working experientially with goddess spirituality, much as they had with sociopolitical issues in the past. This time, however, circles of women were creating rituals to celebrate the seasons, to mark rites of personal passage such as marriage, divorce, and childbirth, or simply to develop an idea, such as sharing the names and memories of those women who most profoundly influenced them. Goddess ritual is grounded experientially by use of incense, candles, singing, drumming, and dancing, thereby enacting a "body-based" knowing. It is rich with image, metaphor, and symbol. Goddesses represent the creative potential of all women; seasons correspond to internal states such as renewal and rebirth or rest and hibernation; the traditional four elements—earth, air, fire, and water—stand for life itself. For an academic steeped in rationalism, ritual was to me a fascinating way of making meaning that was uniquely collaborative, experiential, and metaphorical. As a kind of spirituality, it held special meaning because it centered on concerns of women using positive images of women. It was empowering to have the creation of ritual in our own hands—ritual appealingly imaginative and spontaneous.

As always with women's studies, experience and theory were intertwined. Groups working to develop goddess-based ritual were complemented by research on women's spirituality across many religions, including prepatriarchal goddess traditions. The political had encompassed the spiritual, much to the dismay of a good many feminists. Dubious U.S. feminists, always practical and results-oriented, were initially aghast at this development. Gloria Steinem's immediate response: "After all, how can mythological goddesses from a patriarchal past help us to analyze our current realities or reach an egalitarian future?" (1994, p. ix). Yet by the mid-1980s, thanks in part to the popularity of Alice Walker's (1982) novel *The Color Purple*, in which her heroine's personal development hinged on reconceiving the gender of god, feminine spirituality was starting to be regarded as yet another field to theorize and another aspect of women's personal experience to validate. Theory, then, had to catch up with women's experience, for as Carol Christ (1987) maintains, "The Goddess symbol has emerged spontaneously in the dreams, fantasies, and thoughts of many women in the past several years" (p. 120). My own research developed in this area, as did practical applications that I found in my composition and literature classrooms. It made me question what counts as knowledge, how we make knowledge, and whom we consider legitimate meaning-makers.

GODDESS SPIRITUALITY AS A COMPLEMENT TO RATIONALISM

What actually counts as knowledge-making in the academy? Peter Elbow (1986) responds: "We are in the habit—in academic culture anyway—of assuming that thinking is not thinking unless it is wholly logical or critically aware of itself at every stop" (p. 57). The way of knowing suggested by goddess spirituality exemplifies the sort of cognitive alternative that many feminist scholars have proposed in their critiques of Western rationalism, the system of knowledge-making that undergirds academic research. Rationalist cognition might be said to represent our cultural preference for impersonal disembodied reason (Johnson, 1987; Lloyd, 1984). Mark Johnson explains: "The view of the objective nature of meaning and rationality has been held for centuries by philosophers in the Western tradition, and, in the last several decades, it has come to define *the* dominant research program in a number of related disciplines" (p. xi). Introduced by Aristotle as the "modus operandi" for rhetoric and philosophy and later adapted by Descartes for scientific inquiry, this paradigm for knowledge-making has come to be regarded as synonymous with reason itself. Procedurally, it is based on the belief that we can, metaphorically speaking, hold up a mirror to nature and see reality in it from a "God's eye" or objective view. The results of such inquiry, a piece of objective truth, must then be articulated through literal, orderly, and methodical discourse. However, such an approach to knowledge-making and its verbal expression is not the only way to reason. As Johnson, Genevieve Lloyd, and other feminist scholars pointed out, there are other valid ways to make meaning. In particular, there are contextual, personal, and embodied approaches often associated with women, although, of course, not found exclusively only within this group. Rather than holding up a mirror to nature from a position of detached observation, in these approaches, researchers look into a mirror to see interactively both themselves and the one reality out of many they are attempting to describe.

As a vehicle for reconceiving knowledge-making, goddess spirituality goes about making meaning by using symbol rather than theory. It is not just an alternative Logos, but instead conveys knowledge through metaphor, as do other ways of knowing associated with the holy and sacred (Dooley, 1995;

Wilshire, 1989). Images of goddesses; the seasons; the elements of earth, air, fire, and water; the earth and moon all function as central metaphors of this symbol system. As external symbols, they mirror internal processes, and are used both externally in ritual or internally as objects of contemplation. So, for example, a woman might contemplate the image of the goddess Minerva, who stands metaphorically for the feminine expression of scholarly intelligence. Functioning as a kind of role model, the goddess might emanate such qualities as thoughtfulness, dignity, and depth and might possess an authoritative voice that speaks in measured tones. Her image presumably triggers deep understandings of these qualities, which well up from the unconscious. That is, she is understood not in the rationalist fashion of detachedly assimilating facts from outside oneself, but in the more personal embodied way in which these latent qualities seem to be called up from within. By apprehending the unconscious facet of feminine experience that she represents, one can then begin to incorporate these qualities into one's conscious way of being in the world. Such images provide powerful feminine precursors for knowing and speaking not only individually but collectively throughout the culture: Minerva, the academic woman of intelligence; Aphrodite with her appreciation of art, beauty, and the senses; Artemis, adventurous and athletic; and the Triple Goddess—maiden, mother, and crone representing the life stages of women. As Clifford Geertz (1983) says, myth influences us both individually and culturally at unconscious levels. And we especially need figures suggesting female presence and power. Christ (1987) explains: "The simplest and most basic meaning of the symbol of the Goddess is the acknowledgement of the legitimacy of female power as a beneficent and independent power" (p. 121). Goddess figures can legitimize that power by honoring not only familiar expressions of the feminine such as mothering, but more uncommon ones such as scholarly thought. C. Jan Swearingen and Diane Mowery (1994) observe, "She legitimates woman-as-subject in a phallocracy where the only legitimate subjects have been male" (p. 221).

People who are attracted to goddess spirituality often seem to be reacting to the lack of sacred feminine figures and the limits imposed by rationalist approaches to knowledge-making. They are searching for a way to reclaim the "feminine voice," that voice that honors contextual, personal, and embodied ways of knowing. For many women, the process through which they identify with goddesses is empowering. One woman has remarked: "I find inspiration in the feminine spirituality movement because the Goddess is a deity with whom I can identify. Her body and mine are one; her power and mine are one" (Murdock, 1990, p. 26). Such identification is particularly useful for many women who feel disempowered and alienated by cultural images of god-figures as male. Many have said, no matter what they know or do, somehow they feel "otherized" with their achievements, invalidated because their self-image is so different from the male images of gods that they have previously internalized. They react much as I did first contemplating a feminine god, in feeling astonishment at the resulting sense of empowerment and validation. Goddess figures function, then, not as external entities, but through the identification process, as an inner resource, a symbolic extension of self. As a result, women come to see themselves and their abilities positively—as Ntosake Shange puts it: "i found God in myself & i loved her/ i loved her fiercely" (cited in Sewell, 1991, p. 252). For men, the discovery of goddess figures often activates a latent view of "feminine" self and knowledge, one they may yearn for, but for which they have seen few examples and seldom received any cultural reinforcement.

In embracing goddess spirituality, people embark on what Murdock has called an archetypal "descent to the Goddess." The notion of metaphorical "descent" is important here because in many spiritual traditions, one transcends involvement in worldly or everyday concerns by "ascending." However, in goddess spirituality, one is said to "descend" by grounding oneself in the body and emotions—thus learning to value those sites of knowledge-making by seeing divinity as located there. Such awareness begins to redress limited rationalist notions of what counts as knowledge. As Murdock (1990) says: "We are blind to the rigid, driven, dominating masculine that controls our psyche. Each time we deny our feelings, body, dreams, and intuition we serve this inner tyrant" (p. 158). Participating in ritual—that most ancient rhetorical expression of singing, dancing, chanting, and drumming—becomes a means of recovering this "body-knowledge." Recent cross-cultural studies have identified numerous links between women, speech, and knowledge. For instance, the Indian hymn text, *The Rigueda*, one of four books of Hindu philosophy dating from 1300 BCE, calls the "creative, fecundating power of speech, 'matarah,' or 'mothra'" (Debrida, 1982, p. 138). Greek mythology also recognizes the voice of the Muse, herself a goddess, along with a complete pantheon of vibrant feminine figures. Other knowledgeable feminine precursors can be found in ancient seers, poets, and musicians. In Homeric hymns, a goddess was typically invited into the home to offer a blessing (Bolen, 1984, p. 32). Much as goddesses were once invoked into homes, part of the enterprise of the feminist classroom is to bring the voices of women into the class, "in order to explore women's relationship to language and to make students aware of the rich and varied tradition of female articulation" (Daumer and Runzo, 1987, p. 47). By their presence, these images may reinforce the point that women too are qualified to make meaning.

Although we are increasingly aware of the negative impact on our students of having so few secular female models for speaking and writing, we may not have recognized the lack of sacred models. If being presented with images of women as knowledge-makers does empower women, such an oversight is surely problematic. After all, as numerous studies have shown, the silent woman is still a pervasive cultural archetype (Lakoff, 1975; Olsen, 1978; Spender, 1980). Woman as statue, doll, or mannequin, from the image of the Angel of the House to that of Pat Nixon—these figures personify the suppression of feminine knowledge. Other figures of the vocal but evil woman—the Medusa, Medea, Gorgons, and Furies of Greek mythology—suggest our fear of speaking and knowing women (Debrida, 1982). More recently, the image of

Anita Hill still resonates powerfully in the public consciousness both for remaining silent and for eventually speaking out. Certainly, within our classrooms, the pattern of silent women has been replicated in study after study (Annas, 1987; Kramarae and Treichler, 1990). Women still speak far less than men do there, yet when they do speak, they are often unheard or misunderstood. So too, a "feminine voice" in male students is presumably silenced, for in the typical academic classroom of both male and female teachers, it is only the voice that speaks from a rationalist knowledge-base that is likely to be heard.

In studies of feminist theory, cognition, and cognitive development, however, we still are ambivalent about the need for such alternatives to rationalism. On the one hand, in much of the theory on women and cognition, it is assumed that women, unlike men, automatically retain and are free to express feminine ways of knowing (Chodorow, 1978; Cixous and Clement, 1986; Irigaray, 1985; Ruddick, 1980). Theorizing from a Freudian perspective, some scholars suggest that women never separate psychologically from the "mother" and all the qualities that feminine figure represents. If women, then, always closely identify with the feminine, they are not repressed and can write and speak "from the body" without struggling to recover this ability. In contrast, Mary Belenky and her colleagues (1986), in their landmark study, show many women virtually silenced by rationalist values. Women struggle to emerge from voicelessness by first grounding themselves in a body-based subjective way of knowing. Much like a "descent to the Goddess," they learn to attend to and value their own intuitions. They play a "believing game" rather than a "doubting game" by listening receptively to their own ideas rather than vigorously questioning them (Elbow, 1986). Only after this immersion in feminine self can they cultivate more conventionally masculinist—disembodied and objective— ways of knowing. In most studies of rationalist knowledge-making in males, such alternative conceptions of knowledge never arise as an issue (Kohlberg, 1981; Perry, 1970).

My own sense is that most women and men find themselves, to some extent, assimilating the values of our rationalist and masculinist academic culture. Certainly, in my own case, I needed the experience of goddess spirituality to break out of the rationalist paradigm I had internalized. Diane Stein (1991) observes: "Within the safety and protected space of the cast circle, women [and men] create their idea of what the world would be like to live in under matriarchal/Goddess women's values" (p. 2). With its rich symbolism, it functions for me not just as a way to "rethink" our notion of academic knowledge-making, but rather to "revision" it (Christ, 1987, p. 106). Of course, in drawing parallels between the kinds of knowledge-making and knowledge-makers found in goddess spirituality and secular feminist critiques of rationalism, I do not want to imply that it is the only way to re-envision academic knowledge-making. Certainly, many other spiritual traditions also provide similar correctives. However, from a feminist standpoint, this woman-centered approach has been particularly useful in balancing the masculinist epistemology of the academy with a more feminist one emphasizing connections to self and others (George, 1994). In what follows I detail some of the ways that I apply these spiritual insights in my teaching.

SPIRITUAL KNOWLEDGE-MAKING IN THE ENGLISH CLASSROOM

In women's literature courses, I have begun including selections that focus on spirituality as an issue in women's lives. I am persuaded that these stories are an important way of bringing women's voices on this topic into the classroom. As Carol Christ and Charlene Spretnak (1982) say: "The expression of women's spiritual quest is integrally related to the telling of women's stories. If women's stories are not told, the depth of women's souls will not be known" (p. 327). So I have begun treating spirituality as a valid part of the experience of women, and I have found not only a wealth of selections to choose from, but interest and receptivity on the part of the students. Typically, I pick several examples to comprise a unit on spirituality. Some, like Marion Bradley's novels *The Mists of Avalon* (1983) and *The Firebrand* (1987), are fictionalized accounts of prepatriarchal goddess traditions. The former, a woman's perspective on the Arthurian legend, presents Celtic goddesses and beliefs; the latter, a woman's view of the fall of Troy, covers Greek goddess traditions. These books provide examples of sacred role models—goddesses as women who speak and know. However, I do not just confine the readings to goddess spirituality. Instead, I include a variety of pieces focusing on general spiritual issues for women. Among the best known novels are *The Awakening* by Kate Chopin (1981), *Surfacing* by Margaret Atwood (1972), *The Four-Gated City* by Doris Lessing (1969), *Their Eyes Were Watching God* by Zora Neale Hurston (1985), and *The Temple of My Familiar* (1989) and *The Color Purple* (1982) by Alice Walker. Although not about goddess spirituality in particular, these novels all show women characters on quests that follow a pattern similar to a "descent to the goddess." That is to say, characters recover a feminine voice by immersing themselves in the feminine and forming a new identity.

So, for example, I might focus on a passage in *The Color Purple,* in which the central characters Celie and Shug discuss the nature of a supreme being:

> Here's the thing, say Shug. The thing I believe. God is inside you and inside everybody else. You come into the world with God. But only them that search for it inside find it. And sometimes it just manifest itself even if you not looking, or don't know what you looking for. Trouble do it for most folks, I think. Sorrow, lord. Feeling like shit.
> It? I ast.
> Yeah, It. God ain't a he or a she, but a It. . . .
> She say, My first step from the old white man was trees. Then air. Then birds. Then other people. But one day when I was sitting quiet and feeling

like a motherless child, which I was, it come to me: that feeling of being part of everything, not separate at all. I knew that if I cut a tree, my arm would bleed. And I laughed and cried and I run all around the house. I knew just what it was. In fact, when it happen, you can't miss it. It sort of like you know what, she say, grinning and rubbing high up on my thigh. (pp. 177-78)

The casual unassuming tone of their exchange belies the profundity of the spiritual questions at stake. Can we create our own god or goddess? Does it matter what gender we assign or whether we envision any gender at all? How do we come to "know" this entity—through our minds, our emotions, our bodies? For Celie and Shug, re-envisioning what the culture has taught them is pivotal to their personal development. Only after reconceiving god as less oppositional, that is, less the old White man, and more complementary, as a presence in nature and sexual pleasure, can they incorporate spirituality in their lives. The accessible god they create—"immanent" in the sky, the rich color of flowers, and the sensations of their own bodies—therefore becomes empowering to them.

In coming to understand the meaning of these issues for the characters in the story, I ask the class to play with these notions in their writing journals and class discussions.[1] Have they ever connected god with gender, and does doing so matter in their own lives? Student reflections on this idea typically express a range of views. Some of them declare that they have always thought of god as genderless, and so question the purpose of anthropomorphizing in this way. Yet, ironically, we inevitably notice that even as we try to entertain the idea of a genderless god, somehow in discussion we all keep referring to "It" as "Him." A few students find the entire idea quite threatening: "As far as considering God as genderless I can't. This causes my questioning beliefs and spirituality all together [sic]." Others say that, like Shug and Celie, they have always envisioned god as a mature White man. Because this is the figure most familiar to them, they are comfortable with a male representation. In contrast, many students find the notion of a female representation empowering. As one woman said: "Women, I think, need to visualize the Higher Power in whatever form they can identify with. . . ." Recently, during one of these discussions, an African American woman expressed her own frustration with what she saw as the complete Europeanization of her spiritual tradition, especially the dominant image of the old White man. Celie's experience clearly gave her a voice with which to speak. The variety of responses to these questions is precisely what I am seeking to elicit. Students do not need to agree with me—or Celie and Shug. Rather, I am asking them to engage themselves in spiritually significant issues.

In Alice Ostriker's poem "Everywoman Her Own Theology," a woman is also shown creating her own multiplicitous vision of a supreme being:

---

[1] All information from students was gathered from questionnaires, journals, and papers coming out of two courses in women's literature and advanced expository writing. They have given me permission to cite their work anonymously.

My proposals, or should I say requirements,
Include at least one image of a god,
Virile, beard optional, one of a goddess,
Nubile, breast size approximating mine,

One divine baby, one lion, lamb,
All nude as figs, all dancing wildly,
All shining. . . . (cited in Sewell, 1991, pp. 281-82)[2]

She enacts her own ritual to invoke this pagan vision. Like Martin Luther nailing his theses to the cathedral door, she tacks her descriptions of a deity both

---

[2]The complete text of Ostriker's poem is as follows:
> I am nailing them up to the cathedral door
> Like Martin Luther. Actually, no,
> I don't want to resemble that *Schmutzkopf*
> (See Erik Erikson and N. O. Brown
>
> On the Reformer's anal aberrations,
> Not to mention his hatred of Jews and peasants),
> So I am thumbtacking these ninety-five
> Theses to the bulletin board in my kitchen.
> My proposals, or should I say requirements,
> Include at least one image of a god,
> Virile, breast size approximating mine;
> One divine baby, one lion, one lamb,
> All nude as figs, all dancing wildly,
> All shining. Reproducible
> In marble, metal, in fact any material.
> Ethically I am looking for
> An absolute indorsement of loving-kindness.
> No loopholes except maybe mosquitoes.
> Virtue and sin will henceforth be discouraged,
> Along with suffering and martyrdom.
> There will be no concept of infidels;
> Consequently the faithful must entertain
> Themselves some other way than killing infidels.
> And so forth and so on. I understand
> This piece of paper is going to be
> Spattered with wine one night at a party
> And covered over with newer pieces of paper.
> That is how it goes with bulletin boards.
> Nevertheless it will be there.
> Like an invitation, like a chalk pentangle,
> It will emanate certain occult vibrations.
> If something sacred wants to swoop from the universe
> Through a ceiling, and materialize,
> Folding its silver wings,
> My paper will tell this being where to find me.

kind and peaceful to a bulletin board in her kitchen. By such means, she hopes, somewhat audaciously, to invoke this being and any of its associates who care to join her. Beneath the humorous tone and irreverence of the ritual, some serious spiritual issues are raised. What images of divinity might women create? In a culture in which men still officiate at most spiritual rituals, should women develop their own rites? What would these alternatives look like?

In writing and class discussion we consider these issues by reading the poem through our own spiritual experiences. Both male and female students—but especially women—find the narrator's actions, humor, and sheer temerity inspiring. The outrageousness of this role model empowers them. Typical of student comments: "That's me! I liked this poem because there aren't many other choices for women. I worship in my own way." Often students, having become disillusioned with traditional sites of spiritual observance, are moved that her home was such a special holy place. Invariably, we always talk about a sense of deep contentment many of us feel in our homes or other places of private retreat. So many poems were located domestically, that we labeled these experiences "kitchen spirituality." In a journal entry, one student described her special sanctuary:

> I was able to relate to this poem a great deal. As a child, I designated a certain area of our yard as a place to worship God. The area overlooked a field and in the distance were mountains. I found this particular spot so beautiful that I was sure that I could better get in touch with God (who created beautiful things) and that God could better hear my prayers. So, in that respect, I was sort of doing the same thing as Ostriker does in her kitchen.

Still other students are alienated by the way the character does not align herself with a more traditional religion. Without this mooring, one woman saw the character as lost and confused: "She doesn't know what is right and how to distinguish her beliefs." As with the Walker piece, my objective is not for the class to agree with Ostriker. Instead, I hope that by hearing this feminine voice and contemplating this spiritual issue in their own lives, they will become more aware of their own voices on this subject.

In composition courses, as with literature courses, I encourage writing from both rationalist and spiritual knowledge bases. Many of my assignments call for traditional academic writing grounded in rationalist assumptions. After all, students expect to hone their abilities here, and my intent is not to reject this knowledge base but simply to admit other kinds of knowledge. Through such writing, students appear to "hold a mirror up to nature" by analyzing ideas from a stance of apparent detachment with their personal voices masked. Assignments that demand a kind of pseudo-objectivity are common in college writing. From a standpoint of goddess spirituality, however, this traditional approach asks writers to work from a position of "estrangement" because its essence is that we do not see ourselves as part of the world. We are strangers to nature, to other human beings, to parts of ourselves. We see the world as made up of separate, isolated, nonliving parts that have no inherent value. . . . (Starhawk, 1988, p. 15)

So in contrast to this kind of writing, I also try to include some assignments that, like a "descent to the goddess," ask students instead to ground their knowledge in self—in their bodies, emotions, and experiences. Both male and female students seem to enjoy these assignments, although they are sometimes unsure if what strikes them as such a "creative" approach is really bona fide academic writing. Writing from a stance of immanence rather than one of detachment, "the awareness of the world and everything in it [is] alive, dynamic, interdependent, interacting, and infused with moving energies: a living being, a weaving dance" (Starhawk, 1988, p. 9). Students must see "in the mirror" both themselves and the part of reality that they are trying to describe.

Although not the kind of overt discussion of goddess spirituality included in literature classes, the kind of knowledge-making I integrate into composition classes is actually patterned after that of ancient feminine oracles who spoke ritually through their bodies at the times of "wise blood" in which visions fluctuated and intensified with their menstrual cycles (Grahn, 1993; Wilshire, 1989). Yet, it also has its rhetorical counterpart in the Greek magical tradition. Rhetors made meaning by speaking magically, from the body, when the gods and goddesses they invoked induced a state of "divinely inspired enchantment" (Miller, 1994; de Romilly, 1975). Elbow (1981) explains:

Words were once connected in a more primary way with experience or things. . . . Logic had to be gradually developed and honed out of language. It took a ceaseless overusing of words—words rubbing and rubbing against each other till they gradually get rounded and smoothed and unhooked from things and experience. (pp. 359-60)

In this tradition, immanence rather than detachment was the preferred rhetorical stance.

Over the years I have worked to develop writing assignments that encourage this kind of meaning-making. For example, one that I have often used asks students to recall a meaningful story from their childhood:

Stories that we read or see help us shape our identities and make sense of our world. Think back to a favorite childhood story and consider it from your view as a child, your view as an adult, and from the standpoint of issues raised by some of the theorists we have read. What did the story mean to you as a child? How does it affect you today? Combine all the per-

spectives to explain your story. Consider the images and symbols, and what
it enabled you to imagine as a child that you might not have otherwise.[3]

Through this process of recalling a story that has resonated in their lives, I am
hoping that students can "re-hook" words and experience as Elbow suggests. In
order to recover the memory of its initial impact, I suggest they figure out a "ritual" that will enable them not just to recall the story but to relive it. They must
re-experience not words so much as the images evoked. If the story has truly
reverberated for them, they should discover some long forgotten origins of current attitudes and beliefs.

This assignment is one that students, both male and female, generally
appreciate. As one said, "I think knowing yourself well helps you to get to the
feelings you use in writing." Another commented, "It enabled me to rethink the
issues more thoroughly." The experience of a student whom I call Michael typi-
fies the response. He chose to reflect on what the film *Easy Rider* meant to him
in high school. The film, often considered the quintessential 1960s story, follows the odyssey of two rebellious characters on a road trip. In an effort to
recapture the story's impact, he actually scoured his parents' attic for mementos
from high school. As part of his ritual, he recreated the initial viewing by pin-
ning up his old posters, wearing his old clothes, and watching the film again
alone. It was during this viewing that one character's line, "You do your own
thing in your own time," struck him, as he said, "like a thunderbolt." For the
teenager he had been, it had awakened wild hopes for a life free of duty and
achievement—a life in which he no longer had "to carry around the weight of
an All-American boy persona." From his adult perspective, however, the film
seemed emblematic of his family's values at that time:

> My parents grew up and participated in the struggle for freedom and I grew
> up in the fallout. Nobody was sure of anything anymore, especially what
> freedom was.

Though the film evoked a deep sense of longing for the sort of free life his
parents encouraged, he reaffirmed his own inclinations by concluding, "Utopia is
nice to believe in but reality is more important." Much as ancient feminine oracles spoke from the multiplicitous viewpoint of everchanging blood knowledge,
he had to consider how his meaning-making had changed over time, how his
identity had changed, and how meaning and identity, intertwined with the past,
still formed powerful undercurrents in the present. The ritual he devised for himself seemingly aided him in accessing this fluid kind of inner knowledge.

---

[3]I have further developed this basic assignment by using a composition text by Marjorie
Ford and Jon Ford (1994) entitled *Dreams and Inward Journeys*. This anthology is unique
in the way that it encourages ways of knowing using image, metaphor, and symbol.

For the most part, my efforts to integrate the ways of knowing I associate with goddess spirituality into the English classroom have been successful. I feel I have made some headway in re-envisioning academic knowledge-making by including the sorts of issues, models, and methods that can help both my students and me to recover the feminine voice. In these ways, spiritual belief can surely enhance rather than threaten our traditional ways of making meaning. As I continue trying to teach as much in the tradition of the Egyptian goddess Hathor's temple as of Plato's academy, I hope to keep discovering ways to bring balance to academic learning.

REFERENCES

Annas, Pamela. "Silences: Feminist Language Research and the Teaching of Writing." *Teaching Writing: Pedagogy, Gender, and Equity.* Ed. Cynthia L. Caywood and Gillian R. Overing. Albany: State University of New York Press, 1987. 3-17.

Atwood, Margaret. *Surfacing.* New York: Simon, 1972.

Belenky, Mary Field, Blythe McVicker Clinchy, Nancy Rule Goldberger, Jill Mattuck Tarule. *Women's Ways of Knowing: The Development of Self, Voice, and Mind.* New York: Basic, 1986.

Bolen, Jean Shinoda. *Goddesses in Everywoman.* New York: Harper, 1984.

Bradley, Marion Zimmer. *The Mists of Avalon.* New York: Knopf, 1983.

_____ . *The Firebrand.* New York: Simon, 1987.

Chodorow, Nancy. *The Reproduction of Mothering.* Berkeley: University of California Press, 1978.

Chopin, Kate. *The Awakening and Selected Stories.* New York: Modern Library, 1981.

Christ, Carol P. *Laughter of Aphrodite: Reflections on a Journey to the Goddess.* San Francisco: Harper, 1987.

Christ, Carol P., and Charlene Spretnak. "Images of Spiritual Power in Women's Fiction." *The Politics of Women's Spirituality.* Ed. Charlene Spretnak. New York: Doubleday, 1982. 327-43.

Cixous, Helene, and Catherine Clement. *The Newly Born Woman.* Trans. Betsy Wing. Minneapolis: University of Minnesota Press, 1986.

Daniell, Beth. "Composing as Power/Spiritual Sites of Composing." *College Composition and Communication, 45* (1994): 238-45.

Daumer, Elisabeth, and Sandra Runzo. "Transforming the Composition Classroom." *Teaching Writing: Pedagogy, Gender and Equity.* Ed. Cynthia L. Caywood and Gillian R. Overing. Albany: State University of New York Press, 1987. 45–62.

Debrida, Bella. "Drawing from Mythology in Women's Quest for Selfhood." *The Politics of Women's Spirituality.* Ed. Charlene Spretnak. New York: Doubleday, 1982. 138-151.

Dooley, Deborah. *Plain and Ordinary Things: Reading Women in the Writing Academy.* Albany: State University of New York Press, 1995.

Elbow, Peter. *Writing With Power.* New York: Oxford University Press, 1981.

_____ . *Embracing Contraries.* New York: Oxford University Press, 1986.

Ford, Marjorie, and Jon Ford. *Dreams and Inward Journeys.* New York: HarperCollins, 1994.

Geertz, Clifford. *Local Knowledge*. New York: Basic Books, 1993.

George, Diane. "'How Many of Us Can You Hold to Your Breast?': Mothering in the Academy." *Listening to Silences: New Essays in Feminist Criticism*. Ed. Elaine Hedges and Shelley Fisher Fishkin. New York: Oxford University Press, 1994. 225-44.

Grahn, Judy. *Blood, Bread, and Roses: How Menstruation Created the World*. Boston: Beacon, 1993.

Grimshaw, Jean. *Philosophy and Feminist Thinking*. Minneapolis: University of Minnesota Press, 1986.

Hurston, Zora Neale. *Their Eyes Were Watching God*. San Francisco: Harper Perennial, 1998. (1937).

Irigaray, Luce. *Speculum of the Other Woman*. Trans. Gillian C. Gill. Ithaca, NY: Cornell University Press, 1985.

Johnson, Mark. *The Body in the Mind*. Chicago: University of Chicago Press, 1987.

Kohlberg, Lawrence. *The Philosophy of Moral Development*. New York: Harper, 1981.

Kramarae, Cheris, and Paula A. Treichler. "Power Relationships in the Classroom." *Gender in the Classroom: Power and Pedagogy*. Ed. Susan L Gabriel and Isaiah Smithson. Chicago: University of Illinois Press, 1990. 41-59.

Lakoff, Robin. *Language and Woman's Place*. New York: Harper, 1975.

Lessing, Doris. *The Four-Gated City*. New York: Knopf, 1969.

Lloyd, Genevieve. *The Man of Reason: "Male" and "Female" in Western Philosophy*. Minneapolis: University of Minnesota Press, 1984.

Longino, Helen E. "Can There Be a Feminist Science?" *Feminism and Science*. Ed. Nancy Tuana. Indianapolis: Indiana University Press, 1989. 45-57.

Miller, Hildy. "Sites of Inspiration: Where Writing is Embodied by Image and Emotion." *Presence of Mind: Writing and the Domain Beyond the Cognitive*. Ed. Alice Brand and Richard Graves. Upper Montclair, NJ: Boynton/Cook, 1994. 113-24.

Murdock, Maureen. *The Heroine's Journey*. Boston: Shambala, 1990.

Olsen, Tillie. *Silences*. New York: Delacorte Seymour Lawrence, 1978.

Perry, William. *Forms of Intellectual and Ethical Development in the College Years*. New York: Holt, 1970.

Ruddick, Sarah. "Maternal Thinking." *Feminist Studies* 6 (1980): 342-67.

Romilly de, Jacqueline. *Magic and Rhetoric in Ancient Greece*. Cambridge: Harvard University Press, 1975.

Sewell, Marilyn, ed. *Cries of the Spirit: A Celebration of Women's Spirituality*. Boston: Beacon, 1991.

Spender, Dale. *Man Made Language*. London: Routledge, 1980.

Starhawk. *Dreaming the Dark: Magic, Sex, and Politics*. 2nd ed. Boston: Beacon, 1988.

Stein, Diane, ed. *The Goddess Celebrates: An Anthology of Women's Rituals*. Freedom, CA: Crossing, 1991.

Steinem, Gloria. Foreword. *Goddesses in Everywoman*. By Jean Shinoda Bolen. New York: Harper and Row, 1984. ix-xii.

Stone, Merlin. *When God Was a Woman*. New York: Dial, 1976.

Swearingen, C. Jan, and Diane Mowery. "Ecofeminist Poetics: A Dialogue on Keeping Body and Mind Together." *Composition in Context*. Ed. W. Ross Winterowd and Vincent Gillespie. Carbondale: Southern Illinois University Press, 1994. 219-33.

Walker, Alice. *The Color Purple*. New York: Washington, 1982.

_____ . *The Temple of My Familiar*. San Diego: Harcourt Brace Jovanovich, 1989.

Wilshire, Donna. "The Uses of Myth, Image, and the Female Body in Re-visioning Knowledge." *Gender/Body/Knowledge: Feminist Reconstructions of Being and Knowing.* Ed. Alison M. Jaggar and Susan R. Bordo. New Brunswick: Rutgers University Press, 1989. 92-114.

7

Emunah: The Craft of Faith*

Susan Handelman
University of Maryland

Speaking personally about "the structure of my faith" is something I've never done in an academic setting. In fact, I rarely do it at all. My faith isn't really very structured, and neither is my discipline for that matter. My shyness about discussing such intimate things as one's "faith" in public may be because—to be honest—I'm always struggling with issues of belief. The academy has trained me well in the disciplines of rigorous skepticism about all truth-claims, endless questioning, mistrust of emotional reactions, and a certain fashionable cynicism. What Blake called the "Idiot Questioner" has taken up comfortable residence in my brain, always ready to pop a "Come on, how can you really believe that?"

My reluctance to talk about personal faith in public also has to do with the nature of my religious tradition. For Judaism does not define Jewish identity by what an individual Jew may or may not believe. The definition of a Jew in Jewish law is simply one who is born of a Jewish mother. If you are born of a Jewish mother, you *are* a Jew whether you believe in G-d or not, whether you observe the mitzvot and study the Torah or not. You can proclaim your atheism in ads in the *New York Times* or join the Moonies—but you are still a Jew in the eyes of Jewish Law.

---

*I would like to dedicate this chapter to the extraordinary people who have taught me the Hebrew language over the years. They are all Israelis who have born patiently with me and have given me a most precious gift. Todah Rabbah—"Thank you"—to my Hebrew teachers: Sassona Yovel, Esther Padua, Yocheved Karlin, Chava Yoran, Nurit Sivan, Mira Smolli, Esti Simons, Brachah Weiss, and Dan Sagi.

This chapter was originally published in *Cross Currents*, Fall 1992. Reprinted with permission.

THE PHILOLOGY OF EMUNAH

Let me begin by examining the original Hebrew word for faith, *emunah*. Hebrew bases much of its vocabulary and grammar on root words of three letters. Varying the vowels and adding different endings to these three-letter roots yield an array of words, verbs in different tenses, inflections, and so forth. (This feature, by the way, is the source of many rich puns and ironies in the original biblical text.)

The three root letters of emunah are *aleph*, *mem*, and *nun*. This is a common root in Semitic languages and means "to be strong, firm, diligent." *Emunah* is translated into English as "faith," but more precisely it connotes "confidence, trust." The familiar word *amen* also comes from this root and actually means, "so be it, surely."

Vocalized another way in the verbal root form, *ihmen*, the word comes to mean to "train or educate." From the root *aleph*, *mem*, and *nun*, we also obtain the noun *amahn* which means "artist, expert, master craftsman." In its verbal forms, *amahn* also conjugates to mean "to foster, nurse, bring up." With a different set of vowels and put in the passive form, it signifies "to be found true, trustworthy, firm."

Let me clarify all these connotations with a few citations from the Hebrew Bible. In one of the most famous and poignant phrases of the Pentateuch, Moses is enduring another of the seemingly endless provocations by the people, who are now complaining about the manna of which they are sick and tired. They want meat to eat in the desert, and claim to remember how wonderful it was back in Egypt where they had fish, cucumbers, and melons.

Both G-d and Moshe are very irritated, and Moses says to G-d in Numbers 11:11ff:

> Why have you afflicted your servant? And have I not found favor in your sight that you lay the burden of all this people on me? Have I conceived all this people? Have I begotten them that you should say to me, "Carry them in your bosom, as a *nursing father* [*ha-omen*] carries the sucking child, to the land you have sworn to their fathers?"

This "nursing-father" is a marvelous phrase and the Hebrew word used for it here is *ha-omen*.

In another example, in the Book of Esther 2:7, we are told about Mordechai and his relation to Esther: "And he had *reared* [*omen*] Hadassah, that is, Esther, his uncle's daughter," who was an orphan.

Let me use this brief exercise in philology to reconnect "faith" and the "academy." These examples show us that *emunah*, faith, is connected to education and training in its very root. And education and faith both require much nursing and nurturing. It's a two-way street, of course. We need, in educating our students, to remember not only that we are "rigorously training them in critical thinking, but that we are also "nursing and nurturing them." To nurse or nurture is to affirm, to care for, to have faith in someone.[1]

On the religious level, what can we learn about faith from this philology? That faith, too, is not a sentimental matter; it is a "craft," a "skill," and it needs to be educated, trained, nursed. It is not "blind." It is not something that some people just seem to "have" and others "just don't," as most of my students and colleagues seem to think. To them, faith signifies something wildly irrational, not subject to question, something blind and dogmatic. So naturally, they become uneasy or hostile when discussions about "faith" arise. Alas, there are all too many believers with the same simplistic notion of faith.

The example I gave above of Moses as a "nursing father" is wonderfully relevant here. Moses, after all, directly received a great revelation from G-d, led the people out of Egypt, and then had to deal with them for forty long years in the desert. And Moses had no compunction about complaining to G-d at times, throwing up his hands, even arguing with G-d. But Moses and G-d put up with this infant nation, its temper tantrums, whims and fears—and educated, nurtured, and trained it. In Jewish tradition, we always refer to Moses as *Moshe Rabbenu*—"Moses our Teacher"; we do not refer to him as "Moses our prophet." No: as "our teacher," for the teaching function is higher than the prophetic function in Jewish tradition.

Now the prophets endured a great deal—no doubt about it. But the teacher is the one who always has to pick up the pieces after all the fire and lightning are over, and when the excitement of the original revelation has worn off. The teacher has to trek through the desert with a lot of uncooperative, testy people. And the teacher often doesn't get to see the promised land either. She or he lets go of those students at the end of the semester, and often doesn't know what becomes of them.

In sum, *emunah*—or faith—is a long process of education. There will be times of abject frustration, disbelief, and rebellion. But this comforts me, for it helps me see that my skepticism and my faith are not necessarily opposites. They can accommodate each other, even though the relationship is going to be tempestuous.

Still, I have left G-d out of the equation, haven't I? All the above is very nice for a group of believers, but what difference would any of it make to the skeptical secular academy?

One of my favorite rabbis, Adin Steinsaltz, the great Israeli talmudic scholar, did not grow up as an Orthodox Jew. He was raised on a kibbutz by secular socialist parents. When asked why he became religious, he answered,

---

[1] As the contemporary poet Adrienne Rich put it: "As to trust: I think that simple as it may seem, it's worth saying that a fundamental belief in students is more important than anything else. This fundamental belief is not a sentimental matter: it is a very demanding matter of realistically conceiving the student where he or she is, and at the same time never losing sight of where he or she can be" (*On Lies, Secrets, and Silence* [New York: W.W. Norton, 1979]).

with a twinkle in his eye: "Because I was a skeptic." He questioned the truths told to him as a child. Endless and absolute skepticism, though, are destructive—and that is part of the dilemma of the contemporary academy. It's certainly one of my dilemmas in teaching literary theory. Rabbi Steinsaltz once told a story about this problem of skepticism:

> The story goes that there was a time when King Solomon wrote [in Proverbs] "The fool believes everything." And the fools' world was shocked because they said, "From this time on, everybody will recognize who is a fool, and this is a very dangerous situation." So they made a World Congress of Delegates, and they debated the problem for a long time and came to the conclusion that from that time on the fools should have another maxim: "The fool doesn't believe anything."

Rabbi Steinsaltz then comments,

> This new proclamation shows us nothing has changed. The fact that fools believe everything doesn't show the folly of belief; it shows the folly of being indiscriminate. The same thing goes exactly for the new maxim. So even though the fools who now control the media proclaim everywhere that the less you believe, the wiser you are, basically this is the same formula.

"The less you believe the wiser you are" does seem to be one of the maxims of the contemporary university—at least in my field of literary criticism and theory.

A BRIEF HISTORY OF LITERARY STUDIES

The study of English literature as a formal academic discipline is just about one hundred years old. Prior to that, the Greek and Latin classics were taught, as was rhetoric, but English literature was something a gentleman was expected to pick up on his own. When English literature finally entered the curriculum, it legitimated itself by adopting the dominant model of nineteenth-century historicist scholarship in the classics: historical philology, lower textual criticism, manuscript editing, and so forth.

These very same methodologies, of course, were also being applied to the Bible with devastating results for faith. The "documentary hypothesis" claimed that the biblical text was not an integrated whole, divinely revealed, but rather a rough pastiche, a collection by different authors at different times, put together by a final redactor. And this redactor, in the view of these biblical scholars, seems to have had the same problem as the average freshman in English 101—redundancy, awkward transitions, and unresolved contradictory statements.

The Bible was desacralized by historical and critical scholarship in the nineteenth century, and literature—through the efforts of critics like Matthew Arnold—itself became "sacralized" as a substitute religion. Arnold wrote that since creeds and dogmas had now become questionable and all traditions were dissolving:

> The strongest part of our religion today is its unconscious poetry. . . . More and more mankind will discover that we have to turn to poetry to interpret life for us, to console us, to sustain us. Without poetry, our science will appear incomplete; and philosophy will be replaced by poetry.

It is literary criticism which will now teach us, said Arnold, "the best that is known and thought in the world." These days, the most fashionable literary critics cite Arnold's words with a tone of mockery and contempt. The following brief sketch of the history of literary study in the twentieth century will explain why.

Firstly, literary studies abandoned that older model of philological, historicist scholarship much earlier than biblical studies. The so-called New Critics, whose influence was strongest from about 1940 to 1965, reacted strongly against the previous historicism with an intense formalism. They asserted the "autonomy" of the literary text: the meaning of a literary text, they claimed, could not be determined by examining all the factors external to it—its historical background, or the biography of the author, or even the declared intention of the author. Literature, the New Critics asserted, contained a special kind of knowledge and used a special kind of language embodied in its particular aesthetic forms. To understand, say, Keats's "Ode on a Grecian Urn" what you really needed to know was not—as one of the New Critics said—"what porridge Keats had eaten for breakfast," but the exact words of the poem on the page, their paradoxes, ambiguities, ironies, metaphors, internal structure.[2] The Old Historicists and the New Critics proceeded to battle it out, each accusing the other of destroying literary studies. But the New Criticism eventually won out—especially in the post-World War II university.

I finished college just as the influence of the New Criticism began to wane, but all my teachers had been trained in it, and they proceeded to train me in it. Actually, I had started out as a philosophy major, but since my college philosophy department was run by followers of Wittgenstein, "metaphysics" was a nasty word there. So I switched majors and went over to the religion department where, at last, I could read Kant, Hegel, Kierkegaard, Nietzsche, and others. After reading philosopher after philosopher—each of whom in turn proceeded to critique and undermine the previous great philosopher—I concluded that phi-

---

[2]There was also an implicit theology in the New Criticism. See Lynn Poland's book, *Literary Criticism and Biblical Hermeneutics* (Chico, CA: Scholars Press, 1985). She compares the project of the New Critics to Bultmann's project of demythologizing the Bible.

losophy couldn't provide me with the "absolute truths" I was searching for. Thinking in my innocent way that I might find answers in literature to the Big Questions—the meaning of life, death, and suffering—I was told by my New Critic professors to stuff my heady metaphysical speculations and get down to business by analyzing metaphors, symbols, tone, rhythm.

By the early seventies, a new wave of intense theorizing about the nature of language, meaning, interpretation, and textuality flooded the field: French structuralism, German phenomenology, Saussurean linguistics, deconstruction, poststructuralism, Marxism, psychoanalysis. The new names were Levi-Strauss, Roland Barthes, Wolfgang Iser, Jacques Derrida, Michel Foucault. We became entangled in the thickets of philosophical and linguistic theory. *Everything* was put into question, from the definition of what a "text" is to whether there can ever be any wrong interpretations.

Deconstruction claimed to undermine any notion we might have had of finding some stable structure to literary signification, and proclaimed that textuality was an endless play of slipping signifiers without a center. Feminism then arrived in the academy, energized by its political successes on the streets. We opened our eyes and suddenly realized that the canon of works we had been studying contained suspiciously few by women. What had been claimed to be universal, value-neutral and objective literary judgments were, in fact, pretty clearly expressions of a male point of view. "The damned mob of scribbling women," as our classic author Nathaniel Hawthorne called them (they were his competition in the literary market), might indeed write, read, and interpret quite differently. And, in fact, they should be empowered to do so.

Deconstruction is now on the wane, and the most vigorous movement in literary theory today is called the "New Historicism." Yes, historicism is back. The New Historicists are careful, however, to distinguish themselves from the Old Historicists. Since history, in the wake of poststructuralism, is no longer seen as a continuous narrative, but as a fragmented discourse, New Historicists argue that we have access to the past only through texts; the past is mediated through language, and language and interpretation are never neutral but always affected by issues of power and dominant ideologies. In the mid-nineteenth century, the great historian Leopold von Ranke spoke of knowing "the past as it really was." We can never attain that dream.

As you can infer from this brief description, politics plays a large role in the New Historicism, or as it is sometimes called in one of its variants, "Cultural Materialism." Literary texts are subsumed under the larger category of "social practices." New Historicists want to remind us again and again that literary texts are material artifacts produced in a material culture; since all knowledge is connected to power relations, no one can claim to have a disinterested position. We need, they say, to unmask or demystify hidden ideologies. And we would be hopelessly naive—like the benighted Matthew Arnold—to believe we could set up a neutral objective criticism consisting of the "best that is thought and known in the world." Post-modern literary theorists would also scornfully tell you that Arnold's "best that is thought and known" really reflects the taste of an elite, male, imperialist upper class, and that class's ideologies and self-interests. Because of the relativity of all truth and its connection to social practices and power relations, this argument goes, we can never attain an objective, universal point of view.

Go try and talk about faith to these people.

In fact, one of the worst sins a New Historicist or cultural materialist can accuse you of is "an appeal to transcendence." At conference after professional conference, I've heard one or another lecturer offer as the ultimate putdown: "Why, that's an appeal to transcendence!"

Underlying much postmodern literary theory, and its attempts to unmask and demystify oppressive ideologies, is a deep desire to transform society. Criticism, many in my field now argue, should be overtly political; all this unmasking and demystifying and canon revision should help the marginalized and oppressed, empower the victimized. Here is a sample sentence or two from a colleague's manuscript: ". . . my own teaching is concerned especially with the structures of power in which literary institutions are embedded. And with theories that question universality, canonicity, authorial hegemony, linguistic fixity, coherent subjectivity, and the status of literature itself."

So much for the "structure of my discipline."

Actually, the whole idea of "structure" went out a long time ago. That's why we call ourselves *post*structuralist. Being from Washington, D.C., I can't resist paraphrasing Will Rogers: "I don't belong to any structured field—I am a literary critic."

JUDAISM AND MODERN LITERARY THEORY

Now you can begin to appreciate the difficulty of the task. How *do* I address people in my discipline? What resources from our tradition do I bring to them?—especially when I commit the cardinal sin of appealing to transcendence just about every day of my life! And, conversely, how has my own relation to my tradition been affected by these changes in my field? Let me once again go back to my personal narrative. I hope you will excuse this nonlinear style of discourse, but as one of my students wrote in a wonderful malapropism: "G-d still demands righteousness, but allows for redemption for those who have digressed."

After studying the New Criticism in college, I began graduate school in the mid-seventies, just as all this new literary theory flooded into my field. My background in philosophy was invaluable; these new trends in theory allowed me to fulfill some of my earlier desires to interpret literature in the light of larger philosophical questions. During that same time I was also rediscovering my own religious tradition, and spent time living and learning in Israel, and in a yeshiva for women in New York. Immersed at the yeshiva in traditional Jewish textual study of the Bible, I was amazed at the intricate and sensitive way in which the classical Jewish commentators analyzed every nuance of every word in the Bible. They were impressive literary critics. And conversely,

it seemed to me that literary critics often acted like rabbis in the way they scruti-
nized the minute details of secular literary texts. I attempted to examine this
phenomenon in depth in my first book, *The Slayers of Moses: The Emergence
of Rabbinic Interpretation in Modern Literary Theory.*

Let me briefly summarize the course of my research. In this book, I took
postmodern literary theory head-on by looking at its prehistory and then showing
how the work of some of its most admired writers—Freud, Lacan, Derrida,
Harold Bloom—was inextricably connected to theological issues. In fact, I began
to view much of literary criticism as a kind of substitute theology; I was interested in how rabbinic methods of interpretation and exegesis had subtly resurfaced
in what superficially appeared to be the theological wasteland of modern literary
theory. Conversely, I was interested in how modern literary theory might help
illumine some of the past theological debates about literary interpretation.

In researching this book, I was also trying to work out my own issues of
faith. How could I, a person trained in the skeptical ethos of the university, and
immersed in postmodern theory, which denied any stable meaning or metaphysical center to things, which seemed to reject the logos, or the G-d of Being and
presence—how could I harmonize all that with being a Jew? This, indeed, has
been the historical challenge of modernity to Judaism. How do modern—or now
"postmodern"—Jews address the demands and critiques of the surrounding culture now that we have been accepted and assimilated into that culture?

It didn't seem accidental to me that Derrida and Freud were themselves
Jewish, and only a generation or so away from traditional Judaism. Derrida's
attack on what he calls the "ontotheological" tradition of Western philosophy
was also an attack on its Greek and Christian underpinnings. And perhaps, I
wanted to argue, it was also a return of the "rabbinic repressed."

Indeed, the seed of my first book was a statement I had come across by
the French psychoanalyst (and Catholic) Jacques Lacan—another major figure
in poststructuralist thought, who directly situated Freud within the exegetic tradition of rabbinic midrash:

> For this people who have the Book, alone among all to affirm itself as his-
> torical, in never propagating myth, midrash represents a primary mode of
> which modern historical criticism could well be only the bastardization.

Lacan views the Jews as the interpretive people par excellence, developing their
hermeneutic skills particularly in the crush of exile: "ever since the return from
Babylon, the Jew is he who knows how to read. This means he withdraws from
his literal utterances so as to find an interval which then allows the game of
interpretation."[3] So here, it seemed, was a certificate that my project was
kosher: Lacan, one of the most eminent poststructuralist theorists, had also
made the connection between midrash and contemporary literary theory.

---

[3]Jacques Lacan, "Radiophonie," in *Scilicet, 2/3* (Paris, 1970), quoted in Jeffrey Mehlman,
"The 'Floating Signifier': Levi-Strauss to Lacan," *Yale French Studies, 48* (1972): 33.

MIDRASH AND MEANING

Before I offer some concrete examples, let me first recall the meaning of midrash. For traditional Judaism, the Torah is divided into two parts: Written and oral. Torah, by the way comes from the root *yud, reish, hay* meaning "instruction or teaching." From this root we also get the Hebrew word for parents: *horim*. The translation of the word "Torah" as "Law" is very inaccurate and misleading.

The *Written* Torah is the part commonly known as the Bible—the Five Books of Moses, prophets, psalms, etc. The *Oral* Torah includes traditions, laws, and interpretations that rabbinic tradition considered also to be handed down from Sinai but not explicitly written into the books of Moses. The Oral Torah also contains the rabbis' own interpretation and amplifications of biblical stories and laws, their debates over these interpretations, the commentaries on these debates, the commentaries on the commentaries, and so on. A large mass of this oral material was compiled around the second century C.E. into the *Mishnah*, which was a codification of oral rabbinic law supplementing biblical teaching. The interpretations and debates and commentary on the Mishnah were compiled into what is called the *Gemarah*. And, broadly speaking, Mishnah plus Gemarah constitute the *Talmud*. The word *Talmud* comes from the root *lamed, mem, daled*. Vocalized *talmid*, we have the word which means "student"; vocalized in the verbal form *melamed*, it means teacher. *Talmud*, then, translates as study or learning

Now, finally, to *midrash*. The root of the this word is *drash*, which means to "search, seek out, inquire, demand." Midrash, inquiry into the meaning of Scripture, is often formally dated back to the time of Ezra (fifth century B.C.E.) but it was collected in various works all the way back approximately to the tenth century C.E. The midrash searches Scripture to clarify ambiguities, applies it to contemporary needs, probes for deeper meanings, supplements gaps in the text, speculates about history and philosophy. Many scholars also view midrash as part of the development of Scripture itself—not simply a postbiblical phenomenon. The Book of Deuteronomy, for example, is a kind of midrash on the first four other books.

The sample midrash I have chosen will take us back to my initial discussion of the etymology of the word *emunah*. You will remember that one of the constructions of the root for the word *emunah* was *omen* meaning "nursing-father"; another had to do with being an artisan or workman, and another with training or education. The first midrash from the collection *Bereishit Rabbah*, a commentary on the book of Genesis, is the first comment on the first verse of the Bible, "In the beginning, G-d created the Heavens and the Earth."

Genesis
Chapter I
Bereshith

1. R. Oshaya commenced [his exposition thus]: *Then I was by Him, as a nursling* (amon); *and I was daily all delight* (Prov. VIII, 30). "*Amon*" means tutor; "*amon*" means covered; "*amon*" means hidden, and some say, "*amon*" means great. "*Amon*" is a tutor, as you read, As *an* omen (*nursing-father*) *carrieth the sucking child* (Num. XI, 12). "*Amon*" means covered, as in the verse, Ha'emunium (*they that were clad*—i.e., covered) *in scarlet* (Lam. IV, 5). "*Amon*" means hidden, as in the verse, *And he concealed* (omen) *Hadassah* (Est. II, 7). "*Amon*" means great as in the verse, *Art thou better than No-amon* (Nah. III, 8)? which is rendered, Art thou better than Alexandria the Great, that is situate among the rivers? Another interpretation: "*amon*" is a workman (*uman*). The Torah declares: "I was the working tool of the Holy One, blessed be He." In human practice, when a mortal king builds a palace, he builds it not with his own skill but with the skill of an architect. The architect moreover does not build it out of his head, but employs plans and diagrams to know how to arrange the chambers and the wicket doors. Thus God consulted the Torah and created the world, while the Torah declares, IN THE BEGINNING GOD CREATED (I, I), BEGIN-NING referring to the Torah, as in the verse, *The Lord made me as the beginning of His way* (Prov. VIII, 22).

This midrash is commenting on the word " In the beginning G-d created." The question is: to what does the word "beginning" refer? "In the beginning," R. Oshaya is going to show, means "with the Torah." The Torah is the blueprint for the architecture of creation; "G-d looked into the Torah and created the world." The Torah in this sense is the Wisdom that preexists the world. It's not simply a set of stories *about* the world, or a set of prescriptive laws, but the primordial design of the world. (This notion was translated into Greek in the New Testament and theologically transformed into the notion of Jesus as a pre-existent *logos*: "In the beginning was the Word.")

R. Oshaya begins his explanation by citing a verse from the book of Proverbs, chapter 8, which is a paean to wisdom. In verses 22ff of that chapter, wisdom is personified as the speaker of the verses. Wisdom says: "G-d created me as the *beginning* [*reishit*] of his way, the first of his works of old. . . . " This is the same word used in the first verse of Genesis: *B'reishit*—"In the beginning." Thus, "in the beginning" means "with Wisdom" and Wisdom means Torah.

Proverbs 8 tells us something further about this primordial Torah wisdom through a word play on *amon/uman*—nursling and workman. You remember those words as variations on the root of *emunah*. In 8:30, Proverbs has wisdom describe itself at the beginning of creation as a playful nursling: "Then I was by Him as a nursling [*amon*] and I was daily His delight." R. Oshaya then notes, as we did earlier, the etymology of the word "nursling," and cites some of the verses I also quoted earlier about Moses as a nursing-father and Mordechai as bringing up Esther. He notes that *amon* means "tutor." And he also derives that it means "covered or hidden"—interpreting Mordechai's "bringing up or educating his niece Hadassah as also his "concealing" her.

No-ammon is the name of a Babylon god, and that becomes the source of another word play. And finally, *amon* is a workman, a craftsman. Through this philological play on the word *amon* and its root, the Torah is now shown to have been the "working tool of G-d" in creating the world and a form of cosmic and primordial wisdom.

But first it was with G-d, covered, hidden. This hidden aspect of Torah remains even after the revelation at Sinai which Moses transcribed into writing. Remember, too, that the verses in Proverbs talk about the nursling "playing before G-d" and being "G-d's delight." Perhaps that play and delight and concealment are the divine creative force within the words and letters of the Torah which opens them up to a plenitude of meaning, encompassing all reality. Thus, Torah continuously gives birth to and includes rabbinic interpretation in the Talmud, midrash, legal writings, and so forth

How does this exotic mode of rabbinic interpretation relate to skepticism and to postmodern literary theory? Let me try to answer this by another midrash. It begins with a quotation from the Psalms, "Who is a mighty one like you, O Lord?"

> "Who is a mighty one like you, O Lord" (Psalms 89:9). [Rather one should proclaim]: "Who is like you, mighty in self-restraints?" You heard the blasphemy and insults of that wicked man [Titus] but you kept silent! In the school of Rabbi Ishamel it was taught: "Who is like you, O Lord, among the mighty" (*elim*) (Exodus 15:11)? [Read rather] "Who is like you among the mute" (*illemim*)—since he sees the suffering of His children and remains silent! (B. Gittin 56b; Mikhilta 42b)

This revocalization of *elim* ("mighty" to *illemim* ("mute") seems almost sacrilegious. The original context of the verse from Exodus 15:11 is Moses' song at the sea after G-d has delivered the people from Egypt. It is a song praising God's power. But here it is read as a criticism of G-d's seeming silence and passivity in the face of the Roman oppression of the Jews and the destruction of the Temple: "He sees the suffering of his children and remains silent!"

Here is midrash as a deep search of Scripture trying to answer the pain and catastrophe of that historical moment. Even in this act of what almost seems like blasphemy, the rabbis were able to reopen the text, make it speak and have meaning. I say "almost seems like blasphemy" because in the end this interpretation also embodies their deepest act of faith. In spite of catastrophe and disaster, they turn back to the text, believing that it can speak. It is by no means a message of simple piety—"He sees the suffering of his children and keeps silent"—but a very complex faith that incorporates despair and questioning within itself.

What is fascinating to me is how the rabbis make these twists and turns, in what are very aggressive modes of interpretation. There is no simple literal fundamentalism here. Indeed, to some, these interpretations may appear a bit outrageous. For the rabbis seem to create problems in the simple, literal meanings of the text; they make odd and anachronistic juxtapositions of verses; they break up the flow of the narrative, atomize verses and words, fragment the canon and collapse time. These practices, however, also describe postmodern interpretation. In its critique of modern forms of reason and coherence, postmodernism delights in fragmentation, rupture, and play. These are part of its project to subvert what it considers to be oppressive notions of identity and history.

Were the rabbis postmodernists? No. But the postmodern critique of the Enlightenment form of reason has opened a path for renewed relation with religion. By criticizing the "Dogma of Immaculate Perception"—the idea that there is a neutral, detached, observer who sees things objectively, as they are "in themselves"—it enables us to return to the language of theology and religious texts with a new seriousness—to study how they signify and construct meaning. Postmodern science itself has abandoned the claim to be a description of nature as it is in itself. As the famous physicist Niels Bohr said, "Physics is not about the way nature is, but about what we can say about the way nature is." Whether we are observing atoms or allegorical texts, we are inevitably participants, interpreters who make meaning rather than find facts. Reference is always a matter of the frame of reference we bring to something

Such a position has immense consequences for the academic study of religion and for our approach to reading the Bible where the focus is not on finding the real "text" behind the text. One need no longer privilege the historical "background" as the real referent of the text. Instead, in one of the most interesting developments in academic Bible studies, one can now (once again) approach the text as having the integrity of a whole. We can take it as given to us—as a construct of the communities or editors who put it together. Here is an example of postmodern theory helping us, ironically, to appreciate the premodern view of the Bible as a unity.

What especially intrigues me about rabbinic interpretation, and midrash in particular, is that it is highly self-conscious interpretation. It recognizes—indeed even elicits—gaps, problems, questions; that is, it recognizes our distance from the text. It exemplifies an interpretive battle born of the tension between tradition and innovation, attachment to the text and distance from it. In sum, it is a kind of model for all interpretation because it teaches, as Simon Rawidowicz put it, how to "uproot and stabilize simultaneously, to reject and preserve in one breath."[4]

The rabbis of course, were dealing with a text they believed to be divine, and a G-d who creates the world through speech. So turning it over and

---

[4]"On Interpretation," in Nahum Glatzer, ed., *Studies in Jewish Thought* (Philadelphia: Jewish Publication Society, 1974), 52.

inquiring into the openness of language" was participating in that divine creation.[5] The analogy between postmodernism and rabbinic thought goes only so far; in the modern era, the loss of religious belief also means the loss of the divine guarantee of the ultimate correlation of words and things, language and reality. "Language" with a capital L has taken the place of "God." For literary theory, the openness in language comes from an "otherness," but can this otherness be related to Jewish faith?

LEVINAS AND GOD'S DEBT

I wrote much of my second book, *Fragments of Redemption: Jewish Thought and Literary Theory in Scholem, Benjamin, and Levinas*, to examine that question. In most poststructuralist theory, "otherness" is a term used to signify the notion of a radical rupture which subverts closed identities and systems. What is other is also identified with what has been excluded, marginalized, repressed by philosophy. The key question in trying to relate postmodernism to religion is whether "otherness" is the marker of the limits of our knowledge and thus the fount of endless and irresolvable skepticism—or is it the passage through which the otherness of divine transcendence crosses? Moreover, does the relation to the human other as an individual other person have anything to do with epistemological alterity?

The contemporary French-Jewish philosopher Emmanuel Levinas, though an important source for Derrida's critique of Western metaphysics, has sought to make the alterity—that disruption of identity and ontology—into an ethical binding to the other, and to think a G-d who is "otherwise than being'" yet is still a G-d of ethics and command, though not a G-d of presence in the traditional sense.

Levinas has tried to find the intersection between skepticism and transcendence, other and Other. For me, he is particularly interesting because of his attempt to address Jewish texts philosophically and philosophical texts Jewishly. Despite its seeming negativity, I think that postmodernism can also inadvertently pave the way for a renewed relation of theology and philosophy. Since, after all, it was a only a specific form of Enlightenment reason that came

---

[5]Just what is it about language that makes it a prime medium for relationship with the divine? What is the point of intersection between divine and human language? Perhaps it is the openness of language where words can mean more than they seem to. Literary and theological language share the same paradoxical nature: we can only say what we mean by meaning other than what we say. Yet what is the source of this otherness? If openness is where the Otherness of God can enter into human discourse and existence, then for the same reason, that openness always makes the text elusive, enigmatic—always receding as much as approaching, and escaping ultimate closure. For the rabbis, G-d speaks as much by what is left out of the plain meaning of the text as by what is put in.

into conflict with faith, the postmodern critique of that type of reason can also lead to a new way of thinking about the relation of faith and reason. Or as Levinas puts it, to a "reason less hard on itself—a reason open to the other."

The aim of Levinas's work is to show that reason and freedom are not autonomous but are founded on prior structures. Freedom is justified not of itself *but by and for the other*. Reason is not an autonomous, impersonal form of logic, but bound to the interpersonal relation that language enables. For Levinas, language embodies this ethical form of reason; language is a gift and a vulnerable exposure to the other.

In other words, one of Levinas's key tenets is that language is not merely instrumental or cognitive but coordinates me with another to whom I speak. There is, he claims, a "prophetic dignity of language," which is the ability of language to say more than it says. In theological terms, we might call it revelation, but it is simultaneously that which binds me to the other and that which coincides with the moment of exegesis—of interpretation of this otherness. Furthermore, a "G-d beyond Being" would be defined relationally, not as a "thematized essence," but as G-d in relation to human response and action. And that would be one of the meanings of another extraordinary midrash on a verse from Isaiah 43:10: "You are my witness, says the Lord." According to the midrash this means, "If you are my witnesses, I am G-d, but if you are not my witnesses, I am not G-d."[6]

Perhaps I can sum up some of these themes of Levina's work by discussing one of his commentaries on another famous and striking midrash. In this midrash, G-d says, "So should it be that you would forsake me, but would keep my Torah." Levinas uses this phrase as the title for an essay he wrote about the Holocaust, "To Love the Torah More Than G-d."[7] As postmodern and post-Holocaust Jews we especially need and desperately want to know how to reopen the Book, how to make it speak, how to hear the voice in the silence. Levinas himself endured World War II as a prisoner-of-war in France, but lost most of his family in Russia.

In this essay on the absent G-d of the Holocaust, the G-d who obscures his face paradoxically becomes the very condition of Jewish belief. The loss of a consolatory childish heaven, at the moment when G-d withdraws from the world, is the moment which calls for what Levinas describes as an "adult" faith. In this faith, the adult can triumph only in her or his own conscience and suffering, a suffering that is "no mystic expiation of the sins of the world but the ordeal of an adult responsible person," a "suffering of the just for a justice without triumph which is lived as Judaism." As Levinas puts it, "the moment of atheism [is] necessary for a true monotheism."

---

[6]*Sifre* Deut. 346; Pesikta 102b; Yalkut Shimoni 455.

[7]Emmanuel Levinas, "Aimer la Thora plus que Dieu," *Difficile liberte: Essais sur le judaisme* (Paris: Albin Michel, 1976). Translated as "Loving the Torah More Than God" by Sean Hand in *Difficult Freedom: Essays on Judaism* (Baltimore: Johns Hopkins, 1990).

For Levinas, the intimacy with and immanence of G-d comes to the Jew as "a relation between spirits, through the intermediary of teaching, the Torah. It is precisely a *discourse*, not embodied in G-d, that assures us of a living G-d among us." So even when disappointed by G-d and downtrodden, one keeps the Torah: "Would that they forsake me and keep my Torah." G-d's absence and concealment is a call to humans to be responsible for everything and that is also a great gift to and source of the dignity of the human. As Levinas says, she or he is then "capable of responding, capable of grappling with G-d in the role of creditor and not always a debtor."

The creditor retains faith in the debtor, but will not let the debtor evade his or her debts. That, for Levinas, constitutes an adult faith: love for G-d despite what G-d does. It's a difficult faith, and hard to bear without the hope of some ultimate unveiling of G-d. But, Levinas argues, "only the person who has recognized G-d obscured can demand this unveiling" and in the tension of this relation a mode of equality is established between humanity and G-d. "To love the Torah more than G-d" means "access to a personal G-d against whom one may revolt— for whom one may die."

This notion of G-d's being in debt to humanity, of G-d's having something to answer for, of having an argument with G-d, is one of the most interesting—and for me—most comforting parts of Jewish tradition. The Book of Job, of course, is one of the prime examples in the Bible. One of the great chassidic rabbis, and one of my personal favorites, was R. Levi-Yitzhak of Berditchev [1740-1810]. The story is told of R. Levi-Yitzhak that in the middle of a prayer he said: "Lord of all the world! A time there was when you went around with the Torah of yours and were willing to sell it at a bargain, like apples that have gone bad, yet no one would buy it from you." This refers to a midrash that when G-d was about to give the Torah he took it to various nations of the world to offer it to them—but when they asked what was in it and found out it prohibited things such as adultery, robbery, etc., they wouldn't take it. The Jews finally accepted it. Continued R. Levi Yitzhak, "No one would buy it from you. No one would even look at you! And then we took it. Because of this I want to propose a deal. We have many sins and misdeeds, and you an abundance of forgiveness and atonement. Let us exchange! Perhaps you will say: 'Like for like!' My answer is: Had we no sins, what would you do with your forgiveness? So you must balance the deal by giving us life and children and food beside."

TEACHING AND THE VOICE OF STUDENTS

I have tried to outline how I have been using postmodern literary theory to read rabbinic texts, and how rabbinic texts also provide me with a model of skepticism and questioning for my own struggles with *emunah*—faith. What role does all this play in my teaching? With graduate students, I can share some of these ideas. Undergraduate students are another story. They are looking for clear, uncomplicated, absolute truths. I often find myself in somewhat of a bind when I teach undergraduate courses on the Bible as Literature, or Literature and Ethics. Most of my students are not Jewish, and even those who are have, alas, little familiarity with Jewish tradition. My average class will be a mixture of atheists, agnostics, fundamentalists, indifferents, evangelicals, Jews, Christians, Moslems, and, more recently, Asian students for whom the Western religious tradition is entirely alien. Now how do I conduct a course on the Bible without having a religious war break out?

Some of the born-again students feel it their sacred duty to witness their faith, to show how there are no questions, how all is answered. The atheists and agnostics resent and deplore this and complain that they do not want to be preached to; the mildly curious are put off by the tension between believers and nonbelievers and claim we are digressing. I also confess that despite having given this long, complex, sophisticated account of how I relate my faith to my academic field, I feel downright uncomfortable talking about it to my students.

After all, I teach in a public, state-supported university. The Constitution has mandated the separation of church and state. An English professor paid by the State of Maryland, I am not there to convert anyone or establish any one religion as preferable over another. I am not a cleric. I don't want my classes to get mired in unresolvable arguments over personal belief. Were I to be teaching a course in philosophy of religion, where students would be given sophisticated analytic tools for examining the relation of faith and reason, perhaps that would be something else.

So I tell them at the beginning of the semester of my course on the Bible as Literature that we are going to try to avoid debates about personal belief—for all the above reasons. But twenty-year-old kids are at the stage in life where these are some of the most pressing issues in their lives. What should I believe? Is there a G-d? How should I live? That's where I was when I was their age.

I don't have a solution to this problem except to admit it, and to tell you quite honestly that it is a lot easier to write books and articles for my academic peers . . . but facing my students in the classroom everyday is another matter. Let us listen to the voice of one of my students speak about this:

> The Bible should be read as a "piece of literature," they say. In other words, I should emotionally distance myself and analytically examine the "text" as opposed to reading and experiencing the book. As the class progressed, I tried to read the Bible as literature, but only felt disturbed, uneasy, and distant. It was as if I was asked to detach, empty, and ignore myself. I don't know if I can put my emotions on hold and read something so emotionally charged mechanically. However, most of my English professors advise me to do the same. "Don't get too emotionally wrapped up in the text." I don't understand what the threat is. Why not get emotionally involved? Why dis-

tance myself and apply intelligent theories if the book isn't going to change me? Why am I discouraged [from trying] to experience books? Why do I have to criticize and analyze these "texts?" Why is everyone calling books texts? I've been trying to read the Bible critically. It's difficult because its language demands both an intelligent and a passionate reading. Isn't reading supposed to change us and the world in some way?

This is how I felt one month into the class. Reading was all about identification, emotional responses, interpretations. . . .The class set-up seemed to discourage this type of reading.

The class has become a class about reading and rereading. It has expanded and stretched my narrow reading habits. It takes my emotions, spirit, and intellect to read the Bible. I'm developing a balance. It's not just an emotional or spiritual thing. I come into the class with questions, and I walk out with more questions. Our in-depth readings of certain passages stir feelings but, they also provoke thought.

I was quite amazed by this journal. Very appreciative that the student felt enough trust in me to write it, yet I was also very challenged by it. It was just after the Clarence Thomas-Anita Hill hearings, and I tried to explain to her why so many of her professors stressed analytical responses to texts. The hearings, I said, were a good example of what happens when there is no distancing, no thoughtful analysis, but only highly emotional reactions. The hearings employed no criteria and no experts in the field of sexual harassment; and so there was no common ground for dialogue.

I resorted to the etymology of the Latin word *educare* as the source of the word "education." *Educare*—means "to lead out." I tried to explain critical thinking as a kind of "leading out" from spontaneous emotional responses through a distancing—to see things otherwise, to come out from where one is to positions that can be supported by reasons, to common ground with others. I talked about the difference between the modern secular university and the old medieval university.

I have recently found out that the word "education" has two Latin roots, *educare* and *educere*. The first also means "to bring up, nurture, or rear"; the second "to elicit or evoke reactions." So I think this student is also correct: perhaps we are overdoing it with all our emphasis on "critical thinking." After we undermine all their native beliefs, we do not do a very good job of helping students reintegrate their emotional and religious lives into their newly found sophisticated analytic minds.

Here is another journal entry by a student in my Literature and Ethics class last year after we had read the Book of Job.

This entire unit on God has disturbed me greatly because there are too many answers to choose from and I don't know which one is right. Nobody knows. It frustrates me not to have the correct answers. Some say that there is no correct answer to whether He exists or not; that we have to decide for ourselves. That's a very nice statement but it still doesn't do anything for me. Does He exist or not? and if He does, is He all-powerful? and if He is, how could He let bad things happen to good people? I could ask question after question and never reach an answer.

I pity the people who fervently practice a religion because their parents practiced it. It strikes me whenever I ask people what their faith is and then ask them how they could believe in a religion when that is the only one they know. I have only met one person who has said to me that he has studied most of the religions of the contemporary world and out of those he has chosen one—obviously a wise man.

I am cynical about God and about religion. That is why I have had so much trouble with this unit and why I simply could not force myself to write another journal entry on Job.

I don't know how to solve this problem right now. Perhaps I did what I was supposed to do by exposing this student to the Book of Job, by just raising the issues, by giving her a place to think about them. She was a premed major and she told me she loved this course because it gave her the only opportunity in her college career to study and talk about these issues.

But I'm still not satisfied. I wish I could do more for her. On the other hand, perhaps in these great matters of faith, each of us must go along her or his own path. My answers, my readings of midrash and postmodern theory, may be entirely irrelevant to her at this tender part of her life. Faith, as I said at the outset, is "practice, craft"; it must be nursed and trained. And as we know, it changes as we change. Our notion of God at age ten is not the same as our idea of God at thirty or fifty. Or at least it shouldn't be. For all too many people, though, the problem is that they grow up without their understanding of G-d ever growing up with them. A rabbi I know tried to inspire his congregants to learn more about Judaism by saying to them: "Would you be satisfied if your entire knowledge of sex remained what it was when you were ten years old? What about, then, your understanding of Judaism and G-d?"

So finally, the question of how one actually teaches students is a difficult one, more difficult perhaps than working out one's own problems of faith on an intellectual level. But there are, of course, many other aspects to faith—the part of faith that transcends the intellect and the faith that is actually lived daily, embodied in practice. Another famous chassidic story goes as follows: Reb Leib Saras once said: "I do not go to R. Dov Baer of Mezritch [his great teacher] to learn interpretations of the Torah. I go to observe his way of tying his shoelaces."

THE ACADEMIC ROOSTER

I will conclude with another one of my favorite stories from R. Nachman, another great chassidic rabbi (b.1772). Like all great teachers, R. Nachman understood that you can't ever teach anything directly. A person has to absorb and learn on her or his own terms—in her or his own way. That's why all the great teachers taught in parable. The Bible itself, as I remind my students, is not a theological tract or a set of logical axioms. It's a book of stories. So here is one of the stories of R. Nachman.

> Once there was a prince who fell into the delusion of thinking he was a rooster. He took off all his clothes, sat under the table, and refused to eat any food but corn seeds. The king sent for many doctors and many specialists, but none of them could cure him.
>
> Finally a wise man appeared before the king, and said: "I think that I can cure the prince." The king gave him permission to try.
>
> The wise man took off his clothes, crawled under the table and began to munch on corn seeds. The prince looked at him suspiciously, and said: "Who are you, and what are you doing here?"
>
> The wise man answered: "Who are you, and what are you doing here?"
>
> "I am a rooster," answered the prince belligerently.
>
> "Oh really? So am I," answered the wise man quietly.
>
> The two of them sat together under the table until they became accustomed to each other. When the wise man felt that the prince was used to his presence, he signaled for some clothing. He put on the clothing, and then he said to the prince: "Don't think that roosters can't wear clothing if they want to. A rooster can wear clothes and be a perfectly good rooster just the same."
>
> The prince thought about this for a while, and then he too agreed to put on clothes.
>
> After a time, the wise man signaled to have food put under the table. The prince became alarmed and he said: "What are you doing?" The wise man reassured him. "Don't be upset. A rooster can eat food that human beings eat if he wants to, and still be a good rooster." The prince considered this statement for a time, and then he too signaled for food.
>
> Then the wise man said to the prince: "Do you think that a rooster has to sit under the table all the time? A rooster can get up and walk around if he wants to and still be a good rooster." The prince considered these words for a time, and then he followed the wise man up from the table, and began to walk.
>
> After he began dressing like a person, eating like a person, and walking like a person, he gradually recovered his senses and began to live like a person.

You could interpret this story, if you like, as an allegory about the body and soul. The prince (the soul) forgets who he is (the son of a King, i.e., G-d) and acts like a dumb beast—i.e., dragged down by the body. But the wise man doesn't yell at the prince, or preach at him, or give him a lecture on the history of the human race and why it is superior to that of roosters. Rather a wise man goes and sits under the table with him. Accepts him where he is, becomes his friend. Gradually he weans the prince away from his behavior. The wise man, like Moses, is a kind of *omen*, or nursing-father. He nurses and weans the prince by telling him he can still be a rooster, but can also do things that humans do. He doesn't deny the needs of the body, but reattaches them. Finally, the prince recovers.

Or, we could interpret the parable in another way. The prince acting like a rooster is like the academic believer in the university—who has spent so much time immersed in secular matters that he has forgotten who he is and has started acting like a rooster, scratching around under the table. The wise man teaches the prince—or princess—that he or she can still be a professor and act like a person of faith.

8

At Once the Inspirer and the Condemner: Rorty and Emerson, Antifoundationalism and the Possibility of Belief

Kevin O'Donnell
East Tennessee State University

> So in accepting the leading of the sentiments, it is not what we believe concerning the immortality of the soul or the like, but *the universal impulse to believe*, that is the material circumstance and is the principal fact in the history of the globe.
> —Ralph Waldo Emerson, "Experience"

> Your work is to keep cranking the flywheel that turns the gears that spin the belt in the engine of belief that keeps you and your desk in midair.
> —Annie Dillard (1989)

On late Friday afternoons, after work during semesters, a group of faculty from various departments at my university gathers informally at a tavern near campus, to talk and to gossip, across tables and across disciplines. During these conversations, a colleague of mine, a philosopher who writes about the natural sciences, has become fond of making the observation that "a hypothesis is never proven, only disproved." I've heard him say it a number of times, usually when someone questions a conclusion he is trying to draw from some new research. "How can you be sure of X or Y?" someone will ask, pulling his speculations to earth. In response he'll pull out his trademark observation. "Just remember, no hypothesis is ever proven . . ." The comment is his discursive trump card, but he's not overly smug about it. Or, rather, he usually says it with an odd look on his face, above his mustache of beer, a look that says two things at once, a look that is a mixture of smugness and cynicism on the one hand, and humility on the other.

The look is hard to describe, but in my own mind it serves as an emblem for the understanding that academic knowledge-making is a mixed, double-edged business. After all, the primary model for pursuing knowledge in academic disciplines is still the scientific method. This is true, institutionally and historically, even in the humanities (Connors, 1991). In its idealized form, the scientific method works this way: Hypotheses are proposed, and then they are relentlessly prodded and questioned until disproved, in which case they're either modified or abandoned. A big part of a scholar's job, then, is to adopt a disbelieving stance in order to find holes in hypotheses. Academic culture rewards us for making objections, raising questions, and for generally being skeptical and disbelieving.

And yet, as my colleague points out, the fundamental structure of even scientific knowledge is the hypothesis, a speculative construct of the imagination that does not have any positive grounding. In other words, the hypotheses that make even scientific data meaningful rest on something other than proof. In this sense, academic knowledge is double-edged; the dialectic of knowledge is an interplay between profound skepticism on the one hand, and profound, imaginative belief on the other. Hence, the interplay between smugness and humility in the look on my friend's face.

Yet in U.S. composition studies in the 1990s, as I show in this chapter, the disbelieving half of the process, the skeptical disposition, has been codified and established as a doctrine, *antifoundationalism*. Antifoundationalism is a philosophical position (or rather, some would say it is an "antiphilosophical" position) that has been adopted by many U.S. humanities scholars, and that has been particularly influential in composition studies. Here, I argue that academics who position themselves as antifoundationalist do so only by suppressing or ignoring the other side of the knowledge-making dialectic, the power of belief.

I begin by discussing the widespread popularity of antifoundationalism. Then I show antifoundationalism's contradictions, first as those contradictions have emerged in composition studies and then as they appear in the work of Richard Rorty, who I take as a prominent spokesperson for the antifoundationalist position. Finally, I contrast Rorty's views with Ralph Waldo Emerson's reflections on belief, and show how Emerson celebrated the reality and power of belief, even without returning to the type of unregenerate foundationalism that Rorty and others would like to avoid.

This chapter is not explicitly concerned with religious faith, but rather with what Emerson called "belief" in general. What Emerson called belief is, in its general sense, the capacity to hypothesize, the capacity to intuit the unproven. The antifoundationalist position is unable to account for this capacity. Antifoundationalism leads its adherents to ignore the workings of belief, and thus to dismiss the fact that people live and work every day in the light of what William James (1975) called "living hypotheses" (p. 89).

ANTIFOUNDATIONALISM'S POPULARITY

Antifoundationalism is one of those fuzzy conceptual terms that rose to prominence in American language studies in the 1980s. As with other such terms—*postmodernism* and *theory* also come to mind—the debates surrounding the term have often been concerned mainly with teasing out the meanings and implications of the term itself (see Fish, 1985; also Bizzell, 1986). The general sense of the term is easy enough to grasp, however. James Berlin (1988), a prominent composition theorist, sums it up in a nutshell: "No position can lay claim to absolute, timeless truth, because finally all formulations are historically specific, arising out of the material conditions of a particular time and place" (p. 478). This is a pithy summary of antifoundationalism because it has both the anti ("no position . . .") and the *foundationalism* ("lay claim to absolute, timeless truth"). In general, antifoundationalism always comes down to this: the refusal to accept any version of the absolute, the timeless, or the eternal. Antifoundationalist thinking implies certain attractive corollaries. It implies attention to specific historical and material conditions, and it likewise implies that human perceptions cannot somehow rise above those conditions to become "objective" or "disinterested." As Berlin (1988) puts it, "a rhetoric can never be innocent, can never be a disinterested arbiter of the ideological claims of others because it is always already serving certain ideological claims" (p. 477).

All of this is likely to sound familiar to people in postsecondary language studies because antifoundationalism has become an important part of mainstream humanities. Indeed, it has been said that antifoundationalism is central to the most influential movements in Western academic thought in the past 150 years (Anderson, 1990). Poststructuralism, Marxism, even Darwinism, all have been taken to reject any notion of a realm of the ideal, the unchanging, the absolute. Thus, Berlin cites many of philosophy's biggest names to support his antifoundationalist position—including Foucault, Burke, and Vico.

During the last decade or so, antifoundationalism has become popular in U.S. universities, and many humanities scholars have even adopted it as part of their academic identities. Michael Berube (1991) is a good example. As a young English professor at the University of Illinois, Berube gained attention for his *Village Voice* article defending theory in the humanities against attacks on political correctness. In a later piece (1993), he recounts his intellectual development, concluding with his conversion to antifoundationalism:

> In a word, then, upon reading Bakhtin and Wittgenstein I became an anti-essentialist, and to this day, sure enough, there's a little anti-essentialism in everything I do. In my next close encounter of the mid-1980s, I came up against Thomas Kuhn's *Structure of Scientific Revolutions*, and took a seminar on Martin Heidegger with Richard Rorty, and from that point on I've been an "antifoundationalist" as well. (p. 181)

Of course, not all of the country's young English professors have studied under Rorty. But it is probably safe to say that a good portion of the latest generation of language scholars have, like Berube, staked their professional work on some version of antifoundationalism.

COMPOSITION STUDIES AND THE CONTRADICTIONS OF ANTIFOUNDATIONALISM

In composition studies, antifoundationalism rose to prominence during the 1980s. Since then, it has generated plenty of lively discussion, and it has prompted some significant re-examinations of composition studies discourse. But one of the most notable things about antifoundationalism, now that it has, itself, become part of the mainstream of composition studies discourse, is its inability to shed light on writing practices or the teaching of writing. Indeed, where composition practices are concerned, antifoundationalism appears to be a kind of intellectual cul de sac. It does not open up to any other roads beyond itself.

Take the work of Sharon Crowley (1979), for example. Crowley's article, "Of Gorgias and Grammatology," broke new ground in drawing on deconstruction and poststructuralist philosophy to discuss composition studies. In her article, Crowley argues that the then dominant approach to composition instruction was based on the "metaphysics of presence," that is, based on the idea that there is "a reality, or a truth, which exists outside the perceiving consciousness of man and which is unmoved, essentially unchanged, by his perception of it" (p. 279). Crowley criticized these foundational assumptions. And much of her subsequent work has been concerned with extending the antifoundationalist critique and explicating the antifoundationalist position. In the late 1980s, Crowley was commissioned to write a monograph explaining the connections between her theoretical viewpoint and composition teaching practices. The result was *A Teacher's Introduction to Deconstruction* (Crowley, 1989). Although the book is concerned specifically with deconstruction and the work of Jacques Derrida, it sets out generally to explore how teaching changes when teachers do away with their "foundational" assumptions (p. 2). The book's jacket has a quote from the introduction by W. Ross Winterowd (the book series editor). Winterowd (1979) writes:

most of us would be grateful for assistance in getting the gist of a philosophical position that for at least a decade has been central to discussions of
literature and that, by laws as inexorable as those of plate tectonics, will
influence the teaching of English for decades to come. . . . (p. x)

The book's selling point, then, is that it will explain the connections between
antifoundationalist theory and teaching. However, Crowley admits in the book
that her editors, after reading a draft of the piece, asked her to come up with
more implications for teaching. She still remains reluctant to write about such
implications except in the most general terms. Although she promises in her
preface to "unravel the ramifications of deconstruction for English teaching" (p.
xvi), she ends her book on a diminished note, saying that,

perhaps the best to be hoped for is that a deconstructive critique demonstrates the necessity of continued interrogation of the strategies used to
teach reading and writing. I can only hope that this essay has stimulated a
few of its readers to engage in such a critique. (p. 48)

Her conclusion here does show, in both its tone and its explicit meaning, the
"gist" of the antifoundationalist position. The gist is that antifoundationalism
offers skepticism, "critique," and "continued interrogation," without offering
much hope for any positive formulation of meaningful ways to think about writing and teaching.

Patricia Bizzell is another composition theorist who has diminished
expectations for antifoundationalism. Bizzell helped popularize the notion in
composition studies in the mid-1980s (1986). Since then, however, she has had
serious second thoughts. In "Beyond Anti-Foundationalism to Rhetorical
Authority: Problems Defining 'Cultural Literacy'" (1990), she points out a contradiction inherent in antifoundationalism. She discusses the pedagogy of
Helene Moglen to make the point. Moglen is a feminist who claims to "endorse
only the authority of students' own experiences and judgments," according to
Bizzell (p. 669). Yet this type of thinking presents a problem: "Presumably if
Moglen had a class of wealthy white boys, she would have no choice but to
grant their autonomy and let them avoid literature by women and ethnic minorities if they so desired" (p. 669). That is to say, if Moglen were really antifoundationalist, she would have no positive feminist program to put forward.

Bizzell views the same contradiction in Berlin's pedagogy. She points
to the difficulties Berlin encountered in a composition course he designed.
Berlin's goal was to get students to "deconstruct dominant ideologies." But, in
teaching his course, Berlin found that students held firmly to the ideologies he
wanted them to take apart. Bizzell analyzes the situation this way:

> It seems to me that Berlin, and many of the rest of us who try to make a
> pluralistic study of difference into a curriculum, are calling students to the
> service of some higher good which we do not have the courage to name.
> We exercise authority over them in asking them to give up their foundation-
> al beliefs, but we give them nothing to put in the place of these foundation-
> al beliefs because we deny the validity of all authority, including, presum-
> ably, our own. (p. 670)

Of course, Moglen or anybody else could respond that students should read
diverse literatures, without claiming that such assertion rests on the kind of
absolute, eternally valid truth that antifoundationalists refute. In the broader
scheme of things, none of the failures of antifoundationalism presents any serious problem for the assertion that, as Berlin would have it, we should be wary
of absolute assertions. After all, it is always a good idea to be open to new
ideas, to be aware of the possibility that you might be wrong. Nevertheless, the
fact remains that teachers such as Moglen and Berlin are clearly doing more
than simply calling ideology into question. Bizzell gets to the heart of the matter, then, when she talks about some "higher good." Like the rest of us,
antifoundationalists are putting into play some implicit claim about what is
good, true, or important when they teach. Yet the very idea of "some higher
good" remains incomprehensible in terms of anti-foundationalism.

ANTIFOUNDATIONALISM'S CONTRADICTIONS IN THE WORK OF RORTY

Richard Rorty serves as a fair stand-in for antifoundationalist theory because, as
Berube's remarks suggest, he has become one of its most visible and authoritative spokespersons. Here is Rorty (1990), in an exchange from the pages of the
journal *Critical Inquiry*, explaining his differences with philosopher Hilary
Putnam and, in the process, explaining his own notion of antifoundationalism:

> Putnam is one of those who, like Habermas, wants to develop concepts of
> "reason, truth, and justice, that, while no longer pretending to a God's-eye
> point of view, retain something of their transcendent, regulative, critical
> force" ([Putnam, 1988] 367). I criticize Putnam's treatment of truth on just
> this point. I argue that since Putnam has dropped the notion of a God's-eye
> point of view, a way the world is apart from our descriptions of it in lan-
> guage, he had better give up on the idea of true sentences . . . and give up
> trying to charge the idea of "truth" with what he calls 'normative' meaning.
> (pp. 633-34)

Rorty's criticism of Putnam gives him a chance to state his own position:

> Generalizing from the case of Putnam, I would reply . . . by urging that when we look for regulative ideals, we stick to freedom and forget about truth and rationality. . . . As I have urged elsewhere, if we take care of political and cultural freedom, truth and rationality will take care of themselves. (p. 634)

Here is Rorty's version of antifoundationalism, then. As we might expect, Rorty rejects the idea of universal truth, seeing instead a collective social dynamic, a kind of rhetorical process. In this sense, Rorty's position is similar to Berlin's. Rorty's (1990) version, in addition, has the added coloration of a kind of philosophical Americanism, emphasizing as it does the values of "freedom" and individualism. As long as people are left "alone to dream and think and live as they please" (p. 635), then the collective actions of the community will perform a regulative function. Rorty's political and cultural freedom apparently works in some way like Adam Smith's invisible hand, then. Rorty's position is an epistemological *laissez faire*. For Rorty, the marketplace of ideas and discourse, if left unrestricted, regulates itself.

Thomas McCarthy, as well as Hillary Putnam and others, has criticized Rorty on just this point. In the *Critical Inquiry* exchange, McCarthy says, in so many words, that the marketplace is frightening when left to itself. McCarthy cites Habermas' study of the "public sphere" and how that sphere has become "the public-relations and public-entertainment monstrosity it is" (1990a, p. 653, n.7). Rorty cannot account for the activity of the marketplace, according to McCarthy, precisely because he concentrates on the autonomy of the individual. McCarthy puts it this way:

> He [Rorty] nowhere provides a satisfactory analysis of free *encounters* or *political* freedom, for the simple reason that his account of freedom moves almost exclusively at the level of the isolated individual and scarcely thematizes structures of intersubjectivity or institutional arrangements. (p. 648)

In other words, Rorty's focus on the individual leaves him unable to account for the activities of people in terms of groups. McCarthy calls out this failure by making a well-worn yet deliberately provocative observation: Rorty would have nothing to say to Nazis. That is, if—as in Nazi Germany—an entire community decides to "cling together against the dark" by gathering around someone like Hitler, Rorty has no principled place to stand in order to object. If there is no principle of truth that is seen to lie beyond the consensus of a given community, then how can anyone presume to refute an evil consensus? For that matter, how can anyone define a consensus as evil?

In the *Critical Inquiry* exchange, Rorty gets the last word by arguing cleverly that, in effect, Nazis would never be convinced by epistemological arguments in any case. His response echoes Barbara Herrnstein Smith (1988), who in response to the same question—how does one "answer" a Nazi?—says that "it depends" (p. 154). Presumably it depends on, among other things, whether or not the Nazi has a gun.

Although Rorty's wit and intelligence prevail in this case, the issue is left unsettled. There is, first of all, a nagging contradiction on the surface of things: Like other serious writers, Rorty has a truth he wants to put forth. Now, I realize that I risk begging the question here because the definition of "truth" is the very issue at stake in Rorty's discussion. The debate over truth certainly has a long and complex history, and Rorty (1990) himself "regard[s] modern philosophy as having centered around a discussion of truth" (p. 634). But, even without an airtight definition of truth, we can see here that Rorty puts into play the same general notion of truth that he claims to reject, the notion of truth as a sense of "the way things really are" (1989, p. 8). Rorty continually argues for his version of the way things really are—at the very point where he says that arguments about "the way things are" can no longer make sense. Consider, for example, his closing remarks in an essay on Jacques Derrida. Rorty (1982) shows his agreement with the gist of some of Derrida's thinking by summarizing thusly: "no one can make sense of the notion of a last commentary, a last discussion note, a good piece of writing which is more than the occasion for a better piece" (p. 109). End of essay. Rorty here—that is, the Rorty who speaks through this sentence—is making an unconditional assertion: *"no one can make sense . . ."* (italics added). This is, in fact, Rorty's master argument. He is continually finding new and interesting ways to make this same point. He is convinced that no one can claim to say how things "really are." And that is the way things really are, according to Rorty.

It could be argued that, as with Moglen's position, the apparent contradiction in Rorty's position here is only superficial. On one level, Rorty's position can be understood as the sensible notion that it's a good idea to keep an open mind. After all, Rorty is merely saying that every statement must be subject to revision, and if he himself were faced with some convincing contrary evidence, he would, no doubt, look back on that very statement and revise it.

Yet there is still something important missing from Rorty's account of the way discourse works. For, in the moment he wrote his statement, and likewise in the moment he revised it, he would still have to feel that he were writing about the way things are. Yet that feeling, that sense of the way things are, is something Rorty cannot account for. There is no room for it in his vocabulary. Or, rather, it may be more accurate to say that Rorty has decided that he must not allow himself to talk about it. As he writes at one point, in a discussion of his own views, "the difficulty faced by a philosopher who, like myself, is sympathetic to this suggestion . . . is to avoid hinting that this suggestion gets something right, that my sort of philosophy corresponds to the way things really are" (1989, pp. 7-8). Yes, it must be difficult to avoid "hinting" that he gets things right. For of course he must feel that, at some level, his philosophy *does* get something right. Otherwise he would have nothing to write.

RORTY'S DENIAL OF BELIEF

Indeed, some of the passages in Rorty's work are filled with a sense of rightness that borders on righteousness. Consider this passage, for example, from the opening pages of *Contingency, Irony, and Solidarity* (1989):

> [This book] sketches a figure whom I call the "liberal ironist." I borrow my definition of "liberal" from Judith Shklar, who says that liberals are the people who think that cruelty is the worst thing we do. I use "ironist" to name the sort of person who faces up to the contingency of his or her own most central beliefs and desires—someone sufficiently historicist and nominalist to have abandoned the idea that those central beliefs and desires refer back to something beyond the reach of time and chance. Liberal ironists are people who include among these *ungroundable* desires their own hope that suffering will be diminished, that the humiliation of human beings by other human beings may cease. (p. xv)

Here Rorty goes so far as to argue for the moral superiority of his type of epistemological contingency—as we see in the passage, someone who is "sufficiently historicist and nominalist" is associated with someone who avoids cruelty. Yes, Rorty makes the grand gesture of acknowledging his own contingency, acknowledging that his own desires are "ungroundable." Yet the gesture only strengthens the sense that he has something very right. Indeed, the gesture allows him to claim to occupy a moral high ground that cannot be shared by people who do not share his brand of self-awareness. The following is from a continuation of the above passage:

> The ironist intellectuals who do not believe that there is such an order [an "order beyond time and change"] are far outnumbered (even in the lucky, rich, literate democracies) by people who believe that there *must* be one. Most nonintellectuals are still committed either to some form of religious faith or to some form of Enlightenment rationalism. (p. xv)

It is easy to get the hint here. In Rorty's moral universe, there is a right and a wrong, and an "us" and a "them." The "them" is the mass of nonintellectuals, the "us" is the specially educated reader who has thrown off primitive forms of religion or rationalism. Thus does Rorty's expression of the value of contingency slip into a decidedly noncontingent form.

Rorty's writings generally convey a spirit of good will, and I do not mean rashly to accuse him of moralistic intolerance. But, in respect to antifoundationalism, there is this continuing gulf between what his theory requires him to say and what he actually does. In other words, the same criticism that Bizzell applies to Moglen and Berlin can also be applied to Rorty: Rorty argues that all beliefs are contingent, yet he cannot help but write as if his own beliefs are not contingent. It may be, then, that it's not so easy to do away with the God's-eye point of view, or at the very least it is not so easy to do away with the *possibility* of understanding the way things really are.

ANTIFOUNDATIONALISM IN THE PRAGMATIST TRADITION

In the meantime, however, there is still plenty to be said for the antifoundationalist impulse. In its softer versions, antifoundationalism is simply an appeal against dogmaticism, an appeal to keep an open mind, a reminder that "you might be mistaken," as Rorty (1990, p. 634) said. It seems to me that there is a bit of undeniable good sense in this position. Furthermore, it would be untenable, almost ridiculous, to insist, contra most contemporary antifoundationalists, that historical and material conditions are not worth considering in respect to the world of ideas. It is hard to disagree with the likes of Rorty and Berlin and Crowley at least on this general point, that ideas are often best understood within their historical and material contexts, and that appeals to so-called universal values should be examined critically.

Indeed, this sort of understanding has a venerable history. In U.S. philosophy it goes under the name of pragmatism. One of pragmatism's central figures, for instance, is William James. Regarding the question of truth, James often sounds like a contemporary antifoundationalist. He sees the idea of "truth" not as some idealized epistemological quest for the eternal, but rather as something that takes place in the context of specific historical and material conditions. James (1975) writes that "true ideas are those that we can assimilate, validate, corroborate and verify. . . ." (p. 97). In other words, "truth" only exists in the context of what people do with it. For James, truth is "an event" (p. 97). Truth takes place within a social arena rather than deriving from some eternal realm:

> The possession of truth, so far from being here an end in itself, is only a preliminary means toward other vital satisfactions. . . . True ideas would never have been singled out as such, would never have acquired a class-name, least of all a name suggesting value, unless they had been useful from the outset in this way. (p. 98)

In other words, truth is far from disinterested. It is, to the contrary, something that emerges in specific contexts, in relation to particular human needs.

James popularized the term *pragmatism* as a name for his position in the late 19th century (borrowing the term from Peirce, 1966). But many contemporary commentators see pragmatism's roots in the work of Emerson (e.g., West, 1989). This is because Emerson's insistently antidogmatic posture now seems to prefigure the pragmatist position. One of Emerson's well-known aphorisms comes to mind here: "A foolish consistency is the hobgoblin of little minds, adored by little statesmen and philosophers and divines" ("Self-Reliance," p. 58). Put simply, Emerson, like Rorty, believes it is important for people to keep open minds, to recognize they might be wrong about things. More broadly, Emerson's vision of the moral universe is infused with a sense of contingency. Emerson writes: "There are no fixtures in nature. The universe is fluid and volatile. Permanence is but a word of degrees" ("Circles" p. 282). As Cornel West (1989) observes, one of Emerson's main premises is "that the basic nature of things, the fundamental way the world is, is itself incomplete and in flux" (p. 15). In such a fluid, impermanent world, truth is utterly contingent; or, as Emerson writes, in another aphorism that could almost serve as an antifoundationalist rallying cry: "No truth [is] so sublime but it may be trivial to-morrow in the light of new thoughts" ("Circles," p. 298).

EMERSON'S NOTION OF BELIEF

Given the antifoundationalist drift of pragmatist thought, it should not be surprising that there has been a renewal of interest in pragmatism in recent years. Rorty (1982) claims that all contemporary poststructuralist philosophy is moving in the direction of American pragmatism.

Yet even casual readers will find so much in Emerson that does not sit well with antifoundationalism as Rorty would have it. Here, for instance, is a passage from Emerson's work that at first blush almost seems directly to contradict the passages previously cited. This is from the early, long essay, "Nature," at the beginning of the chapter entitled, significantly, "Idealism." Emerson starts the passage by questioning whether there really is anything "out there." As he says, "A noble doubt perpetually suggests itself . . . whether nature outwardly exists. . . ." His response to this doubt does not sound antifoundationalist:

> Any distrust of the permanence of laws would paralyze the faculties of man. Their permanence is sacredly respected, and his faith therein is perfect. The wheels and springs of man are all set to the hypothesis of the permanence of nature. (p. 53)

The contradiction is striking. A "sacred respect for the permanence of nature's laws" seems irreconcilable with the idea that "the universe is fluid and volatile."

Of course, it may indeed be foolish to read Emerson and expect to find a rigorous consistency. It may be that readers should expect Emerson's thought itself to be fluid and volatile, in light of the vision he embraces. However, on closer reading, the contradiction is not as stark as it first seems. Actually, Emerson's return to "the permanence of laws" is a return with a difference. In the "Nature" essay, Emerson returns to the *hypothesis* of permanent laws, rather than to the laws themselves. The difference is crucial. The universe is still fluid, but that hypothesis, the idea of a permanent, noncontingent realm, is nonetheless for Emerson a fundamental part of "the wheels and springs of man." The hypothesis itself is part of the way people think and act. This, then, is the material fact of belief: The "faculties of man" can only function in relation to the *idea* that there are permanent laws, even as particular laws are continually disproved. This is what Emerson means by referring to belief itself as a "material circumstance," here in the passage from "Experience" cited in the beginning of this chapter: "So in accepting the leading of the sentiments, it is not what we believe concerning the immortality of the soul or the like, but the *universal impulse to believe*, that is the material circumstance and is the principal fact in the history of the globe" (p. 75). Even in the face of the flux—or, rather, especially in the face of the flux—belief is for Emerson as powerfully real as anything.

Antifoundationalists such as Berlin and Rorty might rightly object here that an idea such as "the permanence of laws" should be treated warily because thinkers ranging from Nietzsche to Foucault have indeed convincingly demonstrated how such ideas are often a mask for the self-interested exercise of power. Yet, Emerson does recognize the impossibility of absolute truth. Unlike Rorty, however, Emerson admits at the same time that he will continue to search for such truth, and he affirms the importance of the search. As he writes, again from "Circles," referring to the fact that "there is no end in nature, but every end is a beginning" (p. 281):

> This fact, as far as it symbolizes the moral fact of the Unattainable, the flying Perfect, around which the hands of man can never meet, at once the inspirer and the condemner of every success, may conveniently serve us to connect many illustrations of human power in every department. (pp. 281-82)

Emerson's sense here of contingency is vivid. But, in his view, this sense, the knowledge that there is no end—no final word, if you will—is both "the inspirer and the condemnor" (italics added). The truth is aimed at, the truth is desirable, even as it remains ungraspable, indeed because it remains ungraspable. In this way, human power and human faculties are inevitably linked to the power of belief.

The difference between Rorty and Emerson is actually quite significant, then. It comes down to this: Rorty's version of pragmatism contains only one half of Emerson's equation. Rorty would agree that the contingent, nonfoundational nature of experience is the "condemnor" of every attempt to describe it. But Rorty leaves the "inspirer" part out of the picture. In terms of the scientific method, Rorty leaves out half of the dialectic of knowledge-making. Rorty, along with other contemporary antifoundationalists, declares at the outset of the discussion that the hypothesis is dead. Rorty pretends that the noncontingent is not only unachievable but undesirable, and he tries to suppress the noncontingent nature of his own assertions. Rorty thus equates "truth" with belief only as another way of discrediting truth, that is, as a way of saying that truth is merely belief. Belief is still for Rorty "just belief."

Criticizing Rorty has become something of a cottage industry in its own right—among professional philosophers (Malachowski, 1990), literary critics (B. Smith, 1988), and even composition scholars (Bruffee, 1982). In a collection of responses to Rorty's work, *Reading Rorty*, Alan Malachowski provides a good cross-section of reactions to Rorty. There Rorty is said to be elitist and too focused on aesthetics (Fraser, 1990). He is taken to task for being unintentionally idealist (Heal, 1990) or for being too "anthropomorphic" (Bhaskar, 1990, p. 199). He is scolded for being in too much of a hurry to "abandon the attempt to provide general justification for knowledge claims" (Davidson, 1990, p. 134). Elsewhere, Rorty is criticized for being generally ethnocentric, and for continuously evoking a mindless and ultimately oppressive notion of "community" (B. Smith, 1988, pp. 168-69). From many quarters, Rorty has been criticized for toying with the dangers of "relativism" (McCarthy, 1990b; also, see Rorty, 1990, for his own summary of the charges of relativism that have been leveled against him).

However, no one that I have read has criticized Rorty specifically for being unable to recognize the Emersonian sense of belief. Indeed, in what is probably a related oversight, scholars have not deeply considered Rorty's relationship to Emerson. Rorty has been likened to Emerson—set side-by-side with Emerson as a fellow anti-foundationalist (Berlin, 1987), or likened to Emerson in his de-emphasis of science as a privileged field and his emphasis on poetry and aesthetics as a high human calling (West, 1989). But no one has written on the profound differences between the positions that Emerson and Rorty hold regarding belief.

Rorty does not have much to say about Emerson. He refers to Emerson in *Consequences of Pragmatism* (1982), where he follows Santayana in seeing Emerson as the precursor of an aesthetic attitude towards philosophical vision. (A similar emphasis on aesthetics in Rorty's work is what leads Fraser, 1990, to call Rorty too "aestheticized" [p. 306]). In a more recent essay, Rorty (1994) invokes Emerson while arguing persuasively that Americans should have more national pride. He encourages Americans to take pride in the successes of Emerson, even though those successes are "limited."

It may be that Rorty sees those successes as limited because he doesn't understand them. As I argue here, one of Emerson's successes is that he anticipates the contradictions encountered by Rorty and other contemporary antifoundationalists. Emerson points a way toward moving beyond those contradictions, a way of being "sufficiently historicist and nominalist," as Rorty would have it, while at the same time recognizing and respecting the power of belief. Rorty, Crowley, Berlin, and other antifoundationalists have discussed thoroughly how an understanding of the contingent nature of knowledge can be the "condemnor of every success." Yet we might do well to reconsider Emerson's reminder that such an understanding is also an inspirer. That is, we might do well to remember the power of the hypothesis, even though, as my philosopher friend is so fond of saying, no hypothesis is ever proven.

REFERENCES

Anderson, Walter Truett. *Reality Isn't What It Used to Be: Ready-to-Wear Religion, Global Myths, Primitive Chic, and Other Wonders of the Postmodern World*. New York: Harper Collins, 1990.
Berlin, James A. "Rhetoric and Ideology in the Writing Class." *College English, 50* (September 1988): 477-94.
_____ . *Writing Instruction in Nineteenth-Century American Colleges*. Carbondale: Southern Illinois University Press, 1987.
Berube, Michael. "Public Image Limited—Political Correctness and the Media's Big Lie." *The Village Voice, 18* (June 1991): 31-37.
_____ ."Discipline and Theory." *Wild Orchids and Trotsky: Messages from American Universities*. Ed. Mark Edmundson. New York: Penguin, 1993. 171-92.
Bhaskar, Roy. "Rorty, Realism and the Idea of Freedom." *Reading Rorty: Critical Responses to "Philosophy and the Mirror of Nature" (and Beyond)*. Ed. Alan Malachowski. Oxford: Basil Blackwell, 1990. 198-232.
Bizzell, Patricia. "Foundationalism and Anti-Foundationalism in Composition Studies." *Pre/Text, 7* (1986): 37-56.
_____ . "Beyond Anti-Foundationalism to Rhetorical Authority: Problems Defining 'Cultural Literacy'." *College English, 52* (October 1990): 661-75.
Bruffee, Kenneth. "Liberal Education and the Social Justification of Belief." *Liberal Education, 68* (1982): 95-113.
Connors, Robert J. "Rhetoric in the Modern University: The Creation of an Underclass." *The Politics of Writing Instruction: Postsecondary*. Ed. Richard H. Bullock and John Trimbur. Portsmouth, NH: Boynton/Cook, 1991.
Crowley, Sharon. "Of Gorgias and Grammatology." *College Composition and Communication, 30* (1979): 279-84.
_____ . *A Teacher's Introduction to Deconstruction*. Urbana, IL: National Council of Teachers of English, 1989.
Davidson, Donald. "A Coherence Theory of Truth and Knowledge." *Reading Rorty: Critical Responses to "Philosophy and the Mirror of Nature" (and Beyond)*. Ed. Alan Malachowski. Oxford: Basil Blackwell, 1990. 120-38.
Dillard, Annie. *The Writing Life*. New York: Harper and Row, 1989.
Emerson, Ralph Waldo. *The Complete Works of Ralph Waldo Emerson*. 12 vols. New York: Sully and Kleinteich, 1883.
_____ . "Circles." *Complete Works* II: 281-300.
_____ . "Experience." *Complete Works* III: 47-86.
_____ . "Nature." *Complete Works* I: 13-80.
_____ . "Self-Reliance." *Complete Works* II: 45-88.
Fish, Stanley. "Consequences." *Critical Inquiry 11* (March 1985): 433-58.

Fraser, Nancy. "Solidarity or Singularity? Richard Rorty between Romanticism and Technocracy." *Reading Rorty: Critical Responses to "Philosophy and the Mirror of Nature" (and Beyond)*. Ed. Alan Malachowski. Oxford: Basil Blackwell, 1990. 303-21.

Heal, Jane. "Pragmatism and Choosing to Believe." *Reading Rorty: Critical Responses to "Philosophy and the Mirror of Nature" (and Beyond)*. Ed. Alan Malachowski. Oxford: Basil Blackwell, 1990. 101-16.

James, William. *Pragmatism*. Cambridge: Harvard University Press, 1975.

Malachowski, Alan, ed. *Reading Rorty: Critical Responses to "Philosophy and the Mirror of Nature" (and Beyond)*. Oxford: Basil Blackwell, 1990.

McCarthy, Thomas. "Ironist Theory as a Vocation: A Response to Rorty's Reply." *Critical Inquiry, 16* (Spring 1990a): 644-55.

_____ . "Private Irony and Public Decency: Richard Rorty's New Pragmatism." *Critical Inquiry, 16* (Winter 1990b): 355-70.

Peirce, Charles S. *Charles S. Peirce: Selected Writings (Values in a Universe of Chance)*. Ed. Philip P. Wiener. New York: Dover, 1966.

Putnam, Hilary. *Representation and Reality*. Cambridge, MA: MIT Press, 1988.

Rorty, Richard. *Consequences of Pragmatism*. Minneapolis: University of Minnesota Press, 1982.

_____ . *Contingency, Irony, and Solidarity*. New York: Cambridge University Press, 1989.

_____ . "Truth and Freedom: A Reply to Thomas McCarthy." *Critical Inquiry, 16* (Spring 1990): 633-43.

_____ . "The Unpatriotic Academy." *The New York Times, 13* (February 1994): E15.

Smith, Barbara Herrnstein. *Contingencies of Value: Alternative Perspectives for Critical Theory*. Cambridge, MA: Harvard University Press, 1988.

West, Cornel. *The American Evasion of Philosophy: A Genealogy of Pragmatism*. Madison: University of Wisconsin Press, 1989.

Winterowd, W. Ross. "Introduction." *A Teacher's Introduction to Deconstruction*. Sharon Crowley. Urbana, IL: National Council of Teachers of English, 1989. ix-xiv.

9

Rhetorical Epistemology and Rhetorical Spirituality

Barry Brummett
University of Wisconsin–Milwaukee

The following text is taken from *Treasure Hunt*, the fourth volume in Frederick Buechner's (1990) *The Book of Bebb*. In this text, Gertrude Conover is chastising Babe Bebb for his behavior toward his brother, Leo:

> You always have to get back at your brother, Babe. You always have to go him one better. It is your main trouble. He believes in the Mystery— well, more than believes, he keeps riding it back into the world like Pegasus— and so you believe in saucers, hardware. If he believed in hardware, you would believe in the Mystery, or let on you did. Anything to spite him. You were well named. You are a babe. The Mystery is deep and holy, and you have baby eyes that see only the nasty surfaces of things and the shiny toys in the sky. (p. 516)

Gertrude Conover does not use the word *spirituality*, but that is the basis for the distinction she draws here: Spirituality entails a concern with mystery, as opposed to the material, "nasty surfaces of things." Spirituality is apprehension of the ineffable rather than a fascination with "hardware." Buechner's definition of spirituality here is one that would probably be widely accepted by many people. But it is not the only way to understand spirituality.

What does it mean to be spiritual, and with what is spirituality concerned? I argue here that spirituality may be understood as both epistemic and rhetorical, and that such an understanding ensures a more secure place for spirituality in the academy. I first problematize the term *spirituality*, considering

121

several ways it might be defined. I argue that instability in what spirituality means, and therefore is, entails the particular understanding of spirituality that I eventually offer in this chapter.

DESTABILIZING SPIRITUALITY

Buechner's implied definition of spirituality as a "mysterious" consciousness that is opposed to an engrossment with the material has an a priori appeal. But more careful reflection shows that this meaning does not hold up across all, perhaps even most, uses of the word. For many people, that which they would identify as their spirituality is very much wrapped up in the material. Some people experience no holier moment than when material bread and material wine is transformed into the real body and the real blood of Jesus Christ. Others find the spiritual dimension of life in the "hardware" of candles, menorahs, phylacteries, robes, veils, saints' bones, mandalas, or prayer wheels. It will not do to say that the mystery cannot be immanent in the material.

Can we get a better understanding of what spirituality is by refining this failed distinction? Taking a cue from Christ's reply to Pilate (John 18.36), could we say that the spiritual is not of this world, thus putting it in contrast to the world itself? The problem with this refinement is that spirituality is always an experience in time and space, even if one interprets that experience as being of something beyond time and space, and it is thus an experience in this world. A visitation of spirit is always felt as something by a feeling body. To say "I was lifted up" requires an "I" in this world to be lifted. To say "I saw the heavenly city" implies eyes to see. To attribute that feeling to the Holy Spirit, or to a brief unity with cosmic consciousness, is to construct an explanation for an experience that was nevertheless embodied and thus part of the world.

Perhaps spirituality can be defined in terms of temporal power. Can one say that spirituality entails a disregard for power and privilege in this world, that the spiritual is that which is disempowered and disenfranchised politically, socially, economically? Spirituality could then be seen as an alternative value system grounding alternative communities. Although some spiritualities have certainly fit that description, that definition cannot be maintained across history. Theocracies both East and West attest to the fact that spirituality has often been coupled with a temporally empowered ability to remake this world in its own image.

Other definitions are similarly problematic. We cannot exclusively and universally define spirituality as a faith in things unseen because subatomic physics so often attests to the existence of things for which there can be only the most indirect, and certainly nonvisual, evidence (e.g., quarks, charm, wormholes, etc.). Spirituality cannot be identified as the search for the absolute or the fundamental in the universe because many positivist or behavioral sciences have been self-described as doing the same.

Having raised questions about the stability and universality of several "likely" candidates for defining spirituality, I conclude that spirituality and the spiritual have been defined in different and varying ways throughout history. People use the word *spirituality* with meanings specific to limited times and places, and to their own purposes for acting in those circumstances. Some use the term *spiritual* to mean one thing, whereas others use it to mean another. For everyone who insists that spirituality is an attunement to otherworldly things, some will say that true spirituality means serving others here and now. Universal, even widespread, meanings are difficult or impossible to find.

Instead of pursuing the reductionist or essentialist route of defining spirituality and the spiritual once and for all, I instead make two nonexhaustive claims about how spirituality as a term—as a category of language and meaning—works. First, spirituality functions as epistemology. Spiritualities are systems of explanation. They explain how the world began, why the rain falls, how the human heart is moved, or what will happen when we die. As a system of explanation, a spirituality is also an epistemology: It undergirds a system of knowledge, and tells people how to draw conclusions and truths from certain experiences. Faced with the cruel death of a child, for instance, Hindu spirituality will say that the death means this, whereas Catholic spirituality will say that it means that; but in either case the spirituality offers not just a gloss on that experience but a whole system for understanding cruel deaths. A spirituality is a system for knowing about life, and is thus an epistemology.

Second, spirituality functions as an instrument of rhetoric. In actual practice, spirituality is further defined by systems of signs (rituals, icons, key sacred terms, significant practices). One does not usually say "I am spiritual," but does confess to a Wiccan spirituality or to a Buddhist spirituality, each of which is manifested in a system of signs. These systems of signs carry meanings with suasory impact. But recall that what the signs mean is not stable or universal. Various, conflicting definitions of spirituality show that we are dealing with terms that are charged with the ability to move people. *Spirituality* (and its specific manifestations) is thus a term like *freedom*, or *racism*, in that the very fact of its fluid and unstable meaning allows it to be an instrument in rhetorical, political struggles over meaning. There are not widely differing meanings for carrots or alarm clocks; nobody disagrees much over what it means to be left-handed or mathematical. These are not terms, therefore, with much rhetorical whallop. But to say that spirituality entails this or that, to say that the spiritual is thus or so, is to attempt to manipulate the meanings of a cluster of terms with great social and political impact, and thus rhetorical potency.

Whether one says that spirituality is the most important thing, or that it is a retreat into irrelevancy, or that it has certain properties, is neither right nor wrong. Instead, this is using spirituality (and its different manifestations) as an instrument to praise or condemn the particular people, practices, or beliefs that are for the moment, and in that place, attached to the meaning of the term. The new religious Right may say that spirituality involves enacting traditional

Christianity into law, whereas an order of cloistered monks might say that spirituality involves withdrawing from the world as much as possible. To my mind, neither claim is ultimately right or wrong; each is an attempt to urge others to accept a set of beliefs. Each is an assertion of what life should be like. Each is a rhetorical defense of a political stance—political because each implies how people should order their lives together and manage issues of power.

In summary: *spirituality* and the *spiritual* are not clearly defined, stable "things." Different spiritualities offer different epistemologies, explaining how it is that certain things (exactly what things will vary) can be known and explained. To define and specify the spiritual is a rhetorical act with political impact on power and social relations.

Spirituality and the spiritual do mean something today, particularly in the political struggles of mainstream academia. By the *mainstream academy* I mean most public or nonsectarian schools (e.g., the University of Michigan or Stanford University), but not schools that integrate a particular interpretation of spirituality into the curriculum and social life (e.g., Bob Jones University or George Fox College). I also mean universities with denominational ties, even those with heavy church involvement, that nevertheless recruit and accommodate a spiritually diverse faculty and student body (e.g., the University of Notre Dame and Baylor University). I also define the mainstream academy as the network of professional associations and scholarly journals that embody national or international "disciplines." The disciplines of history, geography, or English, as defined by their infrastructures of scholarly associations and publishing outlets, represent this sense of the mainstream academy. Clearly, it is as difficult to generalize about "academia" as it is "spirituality." The experiences of spirituality vary widely from one academy to the next.

Nonetheless, I step into the trenches of the mainstream academy to present a particular example of how spirituality is treated as something problematic, of how the spiritual becomes the focus of a rhetorical struggle among competing epistemologies. Here, I identify the kind of spirituality that seems to be perceived as a problem within mainstream academia. Specifically, many mainstream academics today construct a sort of spirituality as incommensurate with, and inferior to, the epistemologies underlying their own work. On the other hand, some faculty and students construct their spirituality as equally incommensurate with the academy's epistemology, but as superior and superordinate to it. Both groups abet the isolation of a certain kind of spirituality in the academy, even as they struggle over its relative valuation.

A REPRESENTATIVE ANECDOTE: THE PUBLIC SPEAKING CLASS

The "problem" of spirituality in the academy can be seen in the representative anecdote, as Kenneth Burke (1962) would say of an introductory public speaking class. Here, budding young orators are being asked to give as many as half a dozen prepared speeches in the course of a semester. Within parameters set by the specific skills they are learning for each speech, students are usually free to pick their particular topics. Instructors of these courses in most universities, especially those that are large and public, can expect to hear at least one speech a semester that witnesses to some sort of spirituality. Public Speaking 101, in other words, is a site in which spirituality regularly breaks through into academic visibility.

The symptoms of discomfort with speeches of that particular kind of spirituality are clear and predictable. Fellow students in the audience fall silent, avoid eye contact, and ask few questions at the end. Many instructors roll their eyes inwardly at the first sign of faith in an introduction, and deconstruct those speeches sarcastically, even caustically, with their fellow teachers back in the faculty offices. At the start of the semester, some public speaking instructors go so far as to summarily ban any expressions of religion, just as they sometimes forbid speeches on abortion, on the grounds that they have heard too many of them and do not know how to grade them any longer. Students with religious inclinations are not without resources in this struggle, however. One teaching assistant at a large midwestern university, after banning religious speeches from his 8 a.m. class, found a group of fundamentalists from his class praying pointedly for him at 7:30. Clearly, factions of both the academy and of the spiritually inclined need to change if each is to accommodate the other.

Now, some "religious" speeches are not typically received as problems. In my experience, most instructors and other students would regard a speech that explained Hindu beliefs and customs, or how a local Wiccan coven works, as "interesting." But there is a definite kind of speech on spiritual or religious issues that would not be well received, that would mark the orator as out of place.

What sort of religious speeches are a problem in the public speaking class? Although generalizations are difficult for this subject, the kinds of speeches that seem to provoke the negative reactions described are largely predictable. These are speeches that not only explain or describe the practices and beliefs of a particular spirituality, but attest to its *truth*. These are speeches that not only explain the idea of karma, but say that it is real and that it works in human affairs. These speeches identify the Revelation to St. John not only as an historical document but as a timetable for the year 2000. The speaker who describes the organizational structure of the Roman Catholic Church is received as interesting and informative right up to the point that he or she presents the church as the guardian and repository of God's truth, and then everyone will look away.

In short, spiritual speeches become problems in the public speaking class when they bring to the foreground the epistemological and the rhetorical functions of all spirituality. As soon as spirituality is urged upon others as a path to knowledge, the academy marginalizes it. Spirituality is acceptable in the academy when it is an object, something about which to speak, something to examine as a curiosity. Spirituality becomes problematic when it is subjective, an epistemological perspective from which to speak about objects, about experience, about life. Of course, the most fashionable critical circles in the humanities today make all truth claims subjective. Nevertheless, and ironically, spirituality's claims of subjectivity are likely to be received as scandalous by many of those same humanists. When spirituality explicitly claims to offer a path to knowledge, and when it makes any rhetorical move to bid others to follow that path, it is problematized in the academy.

Reactions to this sort of public speech are, I believe, representative of reactions to similar manifestations of spirituality in most corners of mainstream academia today. Creationism can be examined in history of science courses as a curious system of belief, but cannot be urged (rhetorically) by teacher or student in such a course as a true system of belief (an epistemology; again, I am speaking here of mainstream academia). Anthropologists can hold forth for hours about the structures of myths from all over the world, but students and colleagues would be confounded by a lecture on why a particular myth really means what it says, reveals the truth, and should be accepted as such.

Indeed, the problem of spirituality in the public speaking classroom is a problem that people today confront in many dimensions of life beyond academia. Spirituality is acceptable when viewed as an object in the religion sections of newsmagazines and newspapers. A sidebar story to political troubles in Haiti might explain the role of voodun in the lives of everyday people. But one is not likely to find in *The New York Times* or the *Post* a matter-of-fact explanation of events in Haiti from the epistemological perspective of voodun itself (e.g., seriously attributing a recent crop failure to the intervention of Papa Legba). Spirituality in much of our lives is accepted only as object, not as subjective. When people are actively solicited to accept a spirituality because it is a path to knowledge, spirituality becomes regarded as something strange.

The marginalization of the spiritual in much of U.S. society today is inseparable from the increasing fragmentation of Western culture. I refer to the problem of our fragmented, disconnected, and incommensurable *selves* living through the cultural and economic conditions that have been described as *postmodern*. Our offices call us to be competitive; our children call us to be forgiving; our MTV calls us to be oblivious. We cannot coordinate our careers with our families with our leisure preferences. The spiritual as well has been fragmented and compartmentalized when it is treated as an object to be studied and observed rather than as an epistemology of everyday life, to be rhetorically defended.

Hundreds of years ago, Western culture thoroughly integrated spirituality with most if not all of its other dimensions. In medieval Europe, one's job was truly a calling, sanctioned by its incorporation in an encompassing system of personal and social life anchored in the Church. But today, even traditional Judaeo-Christian spirituality is scarcely seen as "commensurable," as philosophers of science Thomas Kuhn, or Imre Lakatos and Alan Musgrave use the term, with the world of business or entertainment.[1] We tend to bracket our spirituality, leaving it at the door of arenas and clubs, of boardrooms and factories. The recent attempts of the so-called Christian Right to enact what are popularly called "family values" into law are an exception to that isolation of the spiritual. But some will argue, to the contrary, that this is merely the invocation of Christian principles in service of the state, as when moral arguments are mustered in favor of war, illiberal education in the public schools, and so forth. Critics of the religious Right will complain that they appropriate the dead husks of spirituality for political purposes.

Incommensurability is an even worse problem for spiritualities not traditionally grounded in the West, such as pagan, Wiccan, or the many kinds of Asian spiritualities. When the mere trappings of spirituality are used to prop up state or economy, as previously suggested, even real spiritualities that do not share those trappings will be condemned or trivialized. Thus, New Age spirituality is reduced to the comic image of Shirley MacLaine and then managed by agents of the state and the economy in comedy monologues on late night television.

In fact, spiritualities that grow out of the experience of groups that have been marginalized by the state and the economy are especially likely to be seen as incommensurable with the hegemonic epistemologies in command of whole cultures. African, Asian, or feminist spiritualities are treated as marks of the difference of those who embrace them, and then discounted by the dominant culture. Incommensurability, inevitable under postmodern conditions, can become the basis for political action against marginalized spiritualities.

If, as I have claimed, the reception of certain spiritual speeches in the public speaking class is a representative anecdote of the problem of spirituality in the academy, even in Western culture as a whole, then we can understand the specific source of that "problem" by returning to the classroom example. I would not be prepared to argue that any and all spirituality is problematic in the academy. Therefore, I would not be prepared to argue that there is something about spirituality that is necessarily or a priori in conflict with the tenets of academia. Instead, I would treat the "problem" of spirituality in academia or in the larger culture as a rhetorical problem: Specific tenets of a certain kind of spirituality have come to be perceived as inconsistent or incommensurate with specific tenets of the academy. When this kind of spirituality is presented as epistemological and rhetorical, those tenets become problematic.

Another way of posing the question that I address here is: What sort of epistemological claims are rhetorically defended such that the spirituality in

---

[1]One idea, formula, axiom, fact, or principle is commensurable with another, in this usage, if the two can be connected or related in some way. For instance, philosophers of science have often noted the difficulties of making the systems of Newtonian mechanics, relativity, and quantum mechanics commensurable with one another. At many points, these scientific ways of thinking simply do not connect or "talk" to each other. For my purposes, the spiritual idea of "Allah" may be seen by some to have no point of connection or reference to the formulae of chemistry or to tectonic plate theory.

question becomes questionable in the academy? In trying to explore those claims, I return to some of the definitions raised at the start of this chapter, not as essential distinctions but as sources of the rhetorical problem of spirituality. Let me offer this probably incomplete list.

1. Perhaps first and foremost, spirituality is a problem in the academy when it claims that any sort of supernatural being, entity, or dimension, whether God, Allah, or Vishnu, exists and can be known in any way. The mainstream academy will tend to say that such a supernatural force or entity is at best unknowable. Therefore, the issue is epistemological. There is simply no place in the different epistemologies used in physics, or English, or art history, for God or any supreme being as an active and present reality.

    This disagreement is not, I think, structured as a conflict between materialism and nonmaterialism. In fact, many mainstream academics such as critical or literary theorists traffic in concepts such as "meaning" that have no more material tangible reality than does "karma." The problem is simply that mainstream academics have no way to account for how the spiritual might be known within the epistemologies they use in their work. Those epistemologies, which vary widely, are what we call *methods*. Mainstream academia simply has no methods that purport to find God. Thus, a spiritual academic may feel compelled to wander in a wilderness of fragmented and discontinuous epistemologies, with no sure place to rest.

2. Spirituality often, although not always, identifies as a source of knowledge some sacred text, or object, or charismatic figure. A major component of epistemology for some spiritualities, then, is to turn to that text, object, or figure for insight and inspiration. The mainstream academy disagrees in two ways. First, the academy radically historicizes everything. Academics have been taught to disregard any claims of knowledge or truth that go beyond localized circumstances of specific times and places. The truths enunciated in Genesis are therefore identified by academics as truths for or about the ancient Hebrews, but not applicable beyond that original context.

    Second, the academy simply has a different set of texts, objects, or charismatic figures that are perceived to be incommensurable with those of any spirituality. The academy believes those authorities that it has itself sanctioned through the granting of degrees, publisher's imprints, or financial resources. The research studies carried out by seminal researchers or Nobel laureates in a field become an academic gospel. The latest hot critical theorist becomes the Moses of comparative literature.

3. The mainstream academy differs from many spiritualities in evaluat-
    ing the relative epistemic worth of mysticism versus method.
    Mysticism is unmediated knowledge of a supreme being or order.
    Some spiritualities base knowledge on intuition or direct personal
    experience of the object of knowledge (e.g., God, Allah, or Vishnu).
    Spiritualities might very broadly be called *mystic* in the sense that
    they claim the possibility of spiritual knowledge in unmediated ways.

    The mainstream academy, on the other hand, offers nothing other
    than mediated knowledge as its stock in trade, and the name for that
    mediation is *method*. People come to the academy to learn how to
    learn, on the assumption that simple and direct observation of any-
    thing, any dimension of experience, needs to be enhanced by the
    acquisition of method. One essential quality of academic method is
    that it be sharable and replicable. Your article must show me how to
    find the same knowledge that you found, if you claim to use a
    method. Method thus allows for community acquisition and explo-
    ration of knowledge; others can come to know what you know by
    following the same procedures. But although there may certainly be
    communities of people who confess a mystic spirituality, and
    although there are methods and procedures to induce or initiate a
    mystic experience, the experience itself is highly personal. Thus, the
    mainstream academy is discomfited in several ways by one who
    claims direct personal knowledge of anything spiritual.

These, then, are three components of spirituality that are both widespread today
and widely perceived as incommensurable with the mainstream academy. But
the problem of incommensurability is not, I argue, one of principle or definition,
as if mainstream academics and spirituality could not be reconciled. Instead, it
is a rhetorical problem. It is a question of what people believe is or is not
incommensurable. There needs to be a way to think about common ground
between the spiritual and the mainstream academy, to think about how a shared
understanding might be created. Can we think of the epistemologies of the academy and spirituality in ways that restore commensurability? Is there an epistemology that in some way joins different ways of knowing and reintegrates the
spiritual with our lives within and without the university?

RHETORICAL EPISTEMOLOGIES

In answering yes to these last questions, I return to the public speaking classroom. As it was the representative anecdote of our problem, let it contain the
story that will be the solution. Let us think about the example of the public
speaking classroom both in a *disciplinary* and a *pedagogical* sense.

Public speaking courses are taught within the discipline of Communication, but more specifically, within that of rhetoric. Public speaking classes are thus the close cousins of composition courses taught in English departments, but increasingly identified with rhetoric faculty. I argue here that rhetorical studies itself contains the basis for a commensurate epistemology, but first it would be worthwhile thinking about the status of rhetoric within the academy today.

Since the ancient Sophists, rhetoric has occupied an interesting and precarious place in the academy (Backman, 1991). Rhetoric is a Janus discipline. It looks to the world on the one hand, and offers students practical instruction about how to speak and argue effectively in the marketplace and in the courts. The original Sophists were traveling teachers of rhetoric whose success was fueled by a great desire of the ancient Greeks to be instructed in the increasingly important arts of public speaking. The need for practical skill in oratory was created by the rise of democracies in the Greek city-states, and Sophists either filled or exploited that need according to their abilities and morals. But rhetoric also looks to the academy, because there have always been great scholars of rhetoric such as Aristotle who have explicated principles and concepts of persuasion at length. One can spend a whole cloistered lifetime studying techniques of rhetoric without ever stepping outside to give a speech or write an essay. Ideally, rhetoric as applied technique and rhetoric as the learned study of those techniques is carefully balanced, as seen in the person of Cicero, that statesman of the late Roman Republic who spoke so eloquently and wrote so learnedly about speaking.

But precisely because of its dual nature, rhetoric has often been one of the scandals of the academy. Plato (in the *Gorgias* and *Phaedrus*) attacked rhetoric as mere pandering to uninformed audiences. The problem for rhetoric throughout history has been that because it looks to the world, it prepares students to speak about anything and everything. For that reason, it cannot focus its attention on the subject matters that the rhetor would address. Instead, it focuses on tools and techniques that the rhetor would use across those many different subject matters. Rhetoric develops the faculty, as Aristotle said, of "observing the available means of persuasion" in any situation, rather than the study of the knowledge relevant to any given controversy or subject of debate. Rhetorical knowledge is anything but "pure" knowledge; it is even hard-pressed to be specialized knowledge, and often draws widely on studies in psychology, literature, and sociology for principles of persuasion. In an academy in which acquisition of knowledge for its own sake is a cardinal virtue, rhetoric's breadth and unavoidable concern for the mess and mush of real life is an embarrassment. This scandal can be seen reflected in academic politics, in which the rhetoric faculty and curriculum of English departments is often regarded as a little lower than the angels of critical theory and literary analysis, and in which whole disciplines such as Communication may be seen as marginal because of the taint of "performance" classes that may be heavily taught within them.

But, rhetoric itself provides a kind of commensurability between knowing and doing, or between knowing and being. At its best, it is a systematic form of study that follows all the most hallowed "rules" of the academy for method and procedure. Throughout its history, as academic requirements for what counts as knowledge changed, rhetoric has experienced a hypertrophy of categories, whether of stylistic devices, *topoi*, or arguments. If dialectic systems are the academic epistemology of the age, for instance, rhetoric can construct categories and subcategories with the best of them (Murphy, 1974). But at its best, it does so in the service of people who must actually write persuasive letters and essays, who must speak, who must construct advertisements, who must act in the world. The way in which rhetoric makes knowledge and action commensurable has, in fact, been noted throughout history, and is often offered today as a way around our crisis of increasingly specialized knowledge that seems unable to advise us as to what to do with our problems (McKeon, 1987). The public speaking classroom, in other words, is a site of commensurability. It holds the key to this locus of translation among different worlds.

As the parent discipline of public speaking, rhetoric has enabled its scholars to develop another kind of commensurability. Over the last few decades, a tradition of scholarship concerned with "rhetorical epistemology" has been developed by scholars such as Robert L. Scott (1967, 1976, 1990), Alan Gross (1990), Richard Vatz (1973), and Barry Brummett (1976, 1981, 1990). There is space here only to summarize the most general claims that have been defended in that work: Proponents of rhetorical epistemology generally begin by noting the centrality of meaning in human experience. Meaning is integral to experience, indeed, to consciousness itself. By integral, I mean not that first we have experience and then attribute meaning to it; rather, we do not "have" the experience at all unless we make it meaningful in the first place. All questions of epistemology and ontology are therefore referred to the question of what humans can know, and what our reality can be, in a world of meaning.

But meaning, rhetorical epistemologists argue, is essentially malleable and changeable. It is, in fact, arguable. Meanings are usually widely shared by communities, often culturally defined. But people accept those meanings and thus participate in the communities by being exposed to the arguments—to the rhetoric—of daily socialization, of hegemony and revolt, of ongoing interpersonal interaction. What our experience means is something that we are constantly negotiating with others. Some meanings we bracket off as stable or beyond the reach of argument for the moment, but that privileging of certain meanings is always changing and changeable. The rhetoric in which we engage when constructing a particular, focused argument is continuous with the rhetoric that maintains some of our perceptions as stable and unquestioned. Because our experience is shot through with meaning, every dimension of our experience is thus at some level rhetorically constructed, rhetorically maintained, and rhetorically changeable (Brummett, 1991).

Rhetorical epistemologists are by and large relativists, arguing that beliefs and values arise from and are thus relative to communities (Cherwitz, 1990). They would thus appear to step squarely into the problems addressed by this book. Because one way to think about the artificially created gap between

the spiritually inclined and mainstream academics is to think of each as relativists. Indeed, the problem of incommensurability is one of intransigent and
vicious relativism. Neither the stubbornly academic nor the narrowly spiritual
can talk to each other beyond the walls of their own epistemologies. And rhetorical epistemologists might appear to endorse that separation by insisting that the
ultimate grounding of each epistemology is only the rhetoric that created each
epistemology in the first place. In other words, there is no overarching standard
to which the exclusive academic and the isolated spiritualist can refer their
estrangement so as to make their epistemologies commensurable.

But rhetorical epistemologists would nevertheless also argue that a
grounding in rhetorical epistemology bridges gaps among cultures. Rhetoric
itself is the epistemology that provides commensurability. We know because we
have been persuaded to know, and whatever ideas we validate as knowledge we
validate (in this view) because we have been persuaded to do so. This perspective argues that understanding the rhetorical grounding beneath all ideas, values,
and beliefs, including both academic and spiritual epistemologies, avoids
vicious relativism and assures a commensurability founded on rhetoric.
Rhetoric is the flux that merges epistemologies. Argument is the secret passage
connecting ways of knowing. Persuasion is the alembic that can transubstantiate
the academic and the spiritual.

To return explicitly to the problem of the academic and the spiritual: A
rhetorical epistemology would see spirituality as rhetorical, just as it would see
the ways of thinking common in departments of history, psychology, and political science as rhetorical. In other words, people come to accept their particular
spiritually because they have been persuaded to do so, and the ideas and intuitions that come into their heads as a result of spiritual experience are validated,
as knowledge, if they have been persuaded to so validate them. The same is true
for a preference for citation of primary sources in history, for analysis of vari-
ance in psychology, for historicization of literary interpretations in comparative
literature. A rhetorical epistemology would thus encourage spiritual and academic epistemologists to compare their ways of knowing on the common ground
of rhetoric, to see them as different rhetorics and as products of different
rhetorics. The question becomes not which is better or worse in any absolute or
incommensurable way, but rather what is more or less persuasive about the different epistemologies. A rhetorical epistemologist would urge all of us to think
of ourselves, and then of each other, as first and foremost rhetorical beings,
rhetorical agents who have been persuaded differently—but because we have
been persuaded, as beings who can then be persuaded differently, and perhaps
by one another.

Let us also return to the public speaking classroom in a pedagogical
sense. Consider the moment of scandal in which an earnest speaker professes
his or her faith to an audience of bored and cynical fellow students and a
squirming, embarrassed teacher. As noted, this moment mirrors the scandal of
our everyday experience, of our inability to pull together the fragmented and

disparate segments of our postmodern lives. The "embarrassment" (for main-stream academics) of the speech of faith is the scandal within each of us.

The problem is not merely one of encouraging teacher and audience to listen to the student speaker, either. For a legitimate complaint that the teacher often has is that such speeches are usually anything but rhetorical. The speaker simply witnesses, with little effort to be Greek for the Greeks or Jewish for the Jews. The problem is one of speaker, teacher, and classroom audience as vicious relativists, each one cornered in each one's own epistemology. Nobody in this moment of crisis really believes that it is an appropriate moment for rhetoric; that the spiritual insights of the speech need to be argued, nor that they can be defended rhetorically. Nor does the mainstream academic see the episte-mologies underlying her discipline as having the same rhetorical status as does spirituality.

Here is where a rhetorical epistemology can intervene to show the rhetorical nature of both spirituality and the academy. That claim of rhetorically commensurable knowledge changes both the speaker and the audience: It shows the speaker the need to think about how his or her truths are rhetorical, and can thus be argued for an audience—and it shows the audience what connection spiritual claims have with their secular or academic preoccupations.

An introduction to the rhetorical epistemology underlying one's beliefs, whether grounded in spirituality or an academic discipline, can prompt a dramatic reassessment of what one knows. Rhetorical epistemology need not be destructive, although any growing experience must entail at least some conceptual reorganization. Instead of destroying faith in what one knows, it changes the way one thinks about how one knows what one knows.

The rhetorical scholar Scott (1967) argued persuasively that a rhetori-cal epistemology can support a three-part ethics of *toleration, will,* and *respon-sibility.* To teach students that they know what they know because they were persuaded to know it should induce in them—and us—toleration for other belief systems and perspectives. That need not mean that one likes what others believe, but it does encourage one to be tolerant of those who think differently. This is because we are led to see that others think what they think for essentially the same reason that we think what we think: We were all persuaded. A rhetori-cal epistemology is thus a pedagogical tool to discourage the desire to isolate or devalue the different Other, whether that Other is perceived to be spiritual or academic.

Scott's second dimension of a rhetorical ethic is *will.* If an individual realizes that beliefs and insights are shaped through rhetorical interaction, he or she then becomes motivated to share one's important beliefs with others. A rhetorical epistemology is therefore a great goad to invention, for if we do not take to the podium or pen to convince people of this or that, neither human nor supreme being will do it for us. A rhetorical epistemology urges people to examine their own will to persuade, and to consider the importance of approaching others in a rhetorical (rather than proselytical or punitive) stance.

The third dimension of a rhetorical ethic is *responsibility*. The student who is grounded in a rhetorical epistemology cannot defer responsibility for what he or she says or does to another person, to some idea of self-evident truth, to God, or to any transcendent grounding. If the student does a sloppy and half-baked job of defending what he or she takes to be a vital truth in a rhetorical effort, the student has betrayed that truth. If I think you really should change your mind about doing something, but I put off writing the composition that will persuade you to do so until the last moment, I have at least for this moment lost the means for inducing that change in you. I cannot go about wishing that someone else would do so; it was my rhetorical responsibility.

CONCLUSION

One of the senses of the spiritual that I have largely ignored in this chapter is that of connection and connectedness. In pursuing the idea of spiritual episte-mology, I have not looked closely at the dimension of spirituality that is a link among people, that transcends difference, that finds communion. But surely I have ended up with that dimension of spirituality by dissolving epistemology in rhetoric. For when we live rhetorically, we live in connection with others. We live with urgent motivation to reach others and to change them. And if we understand the rhetorical nature of our own convictions, we live with an open-ness to be persuaded differently by others. Should that not also be the essence and the rationale of the academy? To foster an openness and fluidity of thought, a vulnerability of ideas, in ourselves and in others? Epistemology is fundamen-tally rhetorical, just as spirituality is fundamentally rhetorical.

Finally, the profession of teacher itself models the connectedness that comes with a rhetorical commitment to defending one's epistemology. The instructor can make both the spiritual and the academic commensurate by being a model of both openness to change and commitment to rhetorically defend one's beliefs. A "spirited" defense of one's epistemologies, coupled with an understanding that the epistemology itself is open to argument and revision, can and should be modeled in the classroom. The instructor can call his or her stu-dents' attention to the sources of their knowledge, and can inspire an examina-tion of how those epistemologies were formed. In his or her own statements and claims, the instructor can display both a commitment to what he or she "knows" and an awareness that he or she can "know" differently, should he or she be per-suaded to do so. This spirit of balancing commitment and readiness to change commitment is the spirit of rhetorical epistemology.

REFERENCES

Backman, Mark. *Sophistication: Rhetoric and the Rise of Self-Consciousness.* Woodbridge, CT: Ox Bow, 1991.
Brummett, Barry. "Some Implications of 'Process' or 'Intersubjectivity': Postmodern Rhetoric." *Philosophy and Rhetoric, 9* (1976): 21-51.
_____ . "A Defense of Ethical Relativism as Rhetorically Grounded." *Western Journal of Speech Communication, 45* (1981): 286-98.
_____ ."A Eulogy for Epistemic Rhetoric." *Quarterly Journal of Speech, 76* (1990): 69-72.
_____ . *Rhetorical Dimensions of Popular Culture.* Tuscaloosa: University of Alabama Press, 1991.
Buechner, Frederick. *The Book of Bebb.* New York: HarperCollins, 1990.
Burke, Kenneth. *A Grammar of Motives.* Berkeley: University of California Press, 1962.
Cherwitz, Richard, ed. *Rhetoric and Philosophy.* Hillsdale, NJ: Lawrence Erlbaum Associates, 1990.
Gross, Alan G. "Rhetoric of Science is Epistemic Rhetoric." *Quarterly Journal of Speech, 76* (1990): 304-306.
McKeon, Richard. Rhetoric: *Essays in Invention and Discovery.* Woodbridge, CT: Ox Bow, 1987.
Murphy, James J. *Rhetoric in the Middle Ages.* Berkeley: University of California Press, 1974.
Scott, Robert L. "On Viewing Rhetoric as Epistemic." *Central States Speech Journal, 17* (1967): 9-16.
_____ ."On Viewing Rhetoric as Epistemic: Ten Years Later." *Central States Speech Journal, 27* (1976): 258-66.
_____ . "Epistemic Rhetoric and Criticism: Where Barry Brummett Goes Wrong." *Quarterly Journal of Speech, 76* (1990): 300-303.
Vatz, Richard. "The Myth of the Rhetorical Situation." *Philosophy and Rhetoric, 6* (1973): 154-61.

10

The Hermeneutics of Suspicion and Other Doubting Games: Clearing the Way for Simple Leaps of Faith*

Jan Swearingen
University of Texas, Arlington

Reappraisals of the teaching of writing and of the interpretation of written texts brought about by multicultural student populations have revived an ancient philosophical dispute. What beliefs and values are being taught by the modes of thinking, speaking, and writing that are imparted in the college English classroom? The dispute is as old as Plato's defense of Socrates' dialectic, and his proposal that only by working together could the arts of production and sciences of discovery found the curriculum we have come to call the liberal arts. The project of defending the liberal arts in an overly technical rhetorical classroom culture was taken up again by Cicero, who quipped that although the Stoic

---

*Portions of this discussion were developed in a very different context for presentation at the MLA-sponsored conference on Advocacy in the Classroom in June 1995. They appear in "Academic Scepticism and the Contexts of Belief," *Advocacy in the Classroom*, ed. Patricia Meyer Spacks (New York: St. Martins, 1996, 213-224).

Portions of this chapter have been revised and will appear as "The Hermeneutics of Suspicion and Other Doubting Games: Reclaiming Belief in the Writing of Reading and Reading of Writing," *Ethical Issues in the Teaching of College Writing*, ed. Frederic Gale, Philip Sipiora, and James Kinneavy, Peter Lang Publishing (forthcoming).

philosophers are very good at dissecting arguments, they provide no tools for
the construction of proofs and arguments. The Stoic academicians, Cicero
charged, propound a purely negative dialectic. Like today's deconstructionists
and culture wars advocates, the Stoics of Cicero's day were very good at saying
what is not, but not at saying what is, or should be. Augustine found the teachers and teaching of literature and rhetoric in his time so repugnant in their cele-
brations of obscenity, amorality, and dilletantish verbal gymnastics that he
declared his resignation from the profession of teaching rhetoric when he con-
verted to Christianity. In the introduction to the *Metalogicon*, a defense of the
study of grammar, rhetoric, and logic in the 12th century, John of Salisbury
wrote, "I have purposefully incorporated into this treatise some observations
concerning morals, since I am convinced that all things read or written are useless except insofar as they have a good influence on one's manner of life" (p.
13). In the 19th century, the philosopher Søren Kierkegaard chastised his fellow
Danes for practicing mere Christianity, a smug, hypocritical businessman's
comfort that bore little relationship to the social reforms that were the goals of
the earliest Christians. A number of his works challenge the academy and the
churches to revive and teach the ability to feel, to be affected by human suffering, and to address the all too human failings that they professed to care about.

　　We are once again in a "culture of disbelief" (Carter, 1992) both inside
and outside of the academy. As writers and readers, as teachers of writing and
ways of reading, can we better explain, defend, and revise the repertoire of analytic methods and practices that we employ? What changes may be needed to
reform academic methods, pedagogies, and scholarly goals that focus so relentlessly on skepticism and debate? How can we continue to affirm the growing
diversity of student populations, beliefs, and values while at the same time sustaining a common language and common culture in the teaching of writing and
literature? Marxist literary critic Gerald Graff (1990) defends the culture wars,
and propounds "teaching the conflicts." Others have begun to ask: Do recent
critical theories of a hermeneutics of suspicion, deconstruction, postmodernism,
and multicultural studies mean that the discovery and articulation of truth and
meaning is no longer a valid aim of interpretation? (Thurow, 1993). Should criticism and interpretation be devoted entirely to questioning the bases of judg-
ment and to a hermeneutics guided by suspicion of discovered or constructed
meaning, indeed of closure itself?

　　The following discussion presents reappraisals of the perils of abstract,
analytic thought that have been developed in defining alternative pedagogies
and reading strategies for student populations unfamiliar or uncomfortable with
the methods of textual analysis and analytic argumentation commonly
employed in most English classrooms. Critics from very different camps have
converged in issuing a warning: as ends in themselves, outside the goals of criticism and understanding, academic modes of skepticism, debate, and negative
dialectic lead scholars and students alike to become "expressionless, pitiless,

unteachable, . . . incapable of belief" (Wolf, 1984, p. 136). Some go even further, and propose that in an increasingly multicultural academic environment, the goals and tacit traditions of argumentation, dialectic, and criticism are too foreign and too outworn to be sustained as models for thought and language. Feminist criticisms of rationality itself as a masculinist tradition, and non-Western critics of Western philosophical modes have for very different reasons called for the abandonment of traditional Western rationalist genres and patterns of discourse such as exposition and argumentation.

Much recent work in composition pedagogy illustrates how the current multicultural academic setting is a particularly hospitable environment for dialogue and dialogical hermeneutics, for collaborative ways of knowing and ways of learning that have long provided alternatives and complements to skepticism, analytic dialectic, and doctrines of linguistic contingency. Personal voice and personal essays are invited; narrative rather than analytic argument is encouraged in novice writers as they begin to learn the culture of the academy. Teachers at all levels are learning to examine how the home environment fosters or impedes school learning; collaborative writing and group study are supplementing "isolationist," individualist models of writing and knowing. Meaning-making and meaning-building, as distinct from meaning-dissecting modes of discourse have often accompanied one another. Faith—in several senses—is no longer regarded reductively: as superstition, unexamined belief, or the enemy of reason (see Carter, 1992; Ong, 1991). Reading with the eyes of faith is an activity that secular Romantic aesthetics borrowed from Protestant hermeneutics in the late 18th century. The English Romantic poets developed the notion that reading and appreciating poetry require a willing suspension of disbelief, an edifying suspension of skepticism, empathy *with*. Today, we recover the same paradigm as we defend the ability to read *with*, and *as*, a "believing game" (Elbow, 1986). Practicing reading and writing as dialogue, thus understood, has long functioned as a classroom method without diminishing or impeding the complementary merits of skepticism and analysis.

In developing new directions, academia's models of thought, language, and narrative are becoming less hostile to the worlds of belief, conviction, and reasoned action where most people spend most of their time. We can observe this in one of the conversions literary study is undergoing both as an object of interpretation and as a source of models for alternative classroom and scholarly voices. As literary, social, and cultural studies mingle in a multicultural academic environment, reading with the eyes of faith is becoming a more acceptable way of knowing (e.g., Belenky, Clinchy, Goldberger, and Tarule, 1986; Elbow, 1986), and is beginning to generate new canons of self and knowledge.

LITERATURE: OBJECT OF ACADEMIC DISCOURSES, REPERTOIRE OF NEW ACADEMIC VOICES

Literary theory and aesthetics have often emphasized literature's ambiguity, strategic indeterminacy, and status as beguiling fiction. These are very Western and elite designations, however, unfamiliar to those unaccustomed to "high" culture and confused by approaches to literature that emphasize analytic dissection over appreciation and understanding meaning. Literature can also be approached as a vehicle for understanding the making of cultural and personal meanings on the part of both readers and characters. Cultures through their stories and through adult models provide children with "canonical images of selfhood" (Bruner, 1986, p. 130). If approached as a source of images of self, literature and the talk about literature modeled by teachers become more than mere fiction; they assume the roles of supplements to identity, training grounds for thought, and models for language use. Literature and its study then can be seen to provide not only new voices, role models, and ways of speaking, but also new ways of understanding and interpreting. Among the newest methods of interpreting literature are those that re-read traditional literature looking for what it tells about what is not said or not represented. The absence of African Americans from American literature is one subject of recent re-readings of traditional American literature; accompanied now by a growing recovery of African American writers of the last three centuries. These are belief-directed activities in two senses. Only the belief that such authors could be recuperated sustained the difficult work of seeing them back into print. The retrieval of lost writers has been further guided by belief that their presence in the American literary canon would correct narrowness and distortion in the picture of ourselves that is constantly evolving in our literary canon.

Methods developed for rereading women's roles and voices represented in early Biblical and Greek literature exemplify belief-guided interpretive practice at work at two levels of interpretation. Reappraisals of women in Biblical and Greek literature are guided by contemporary revisionist theory (Belenky et al., 1986; Gilligan, 1986; Wolf, 1984): that women's "ways of knowing" (Belenky et al.) and "different voice" (Gilligan) have often been misunderstood as purely emotional, expressive, and thereby without intellectual or rational content. New readings are looking for, and finding, intellectual content within expressive and emotional genres. For example, the keening and mourning sounds that are part of the ritual lament performed by women at burial rituals in many cultures are not always wordless (Alexiou, 1974; Ochs,1993). Although rarely emphasized until recently, women's roles in burial rituals mark a public presence, a religious office, and a tradition of composing songs and laments. In Greek literature, Sappho and Antigone, alongside the biblical Hannah and Deborah, compose and perform ritual songs for the dead (Frymer-Kensky,1992; Trible, 1978) To read women's laments with the eyes of faith means no more, or less, than to look for meanings and to assume a deliberateness of composition instead of taking it for granted that keening is simply an uncontrolled and unrehearsed outpouring of emotion. The belief that women are emotional, and the related belief that their emotional discourses are less reliable, objective, or intellectually substantive is shared across time and cultures. This belief is undergoing revision in rereadings inspired by an alternative belief: We should read for evidence of the theory and practice of "emotional" discourses intended to convey rational, ethical, and philosophical content (Swearingen, 1992).

A number of studies have shown that culturally transmitted beliefs shared by both women and men hold women's ways of knowing in lower regard than those of men because they manifest associative rather than linear structures, because they locate ideas and judgments within narrative and emotional expressive discourse, and because they are not explicitly stated in terms of general principles and abstract rules (Belenky et al., 1986; Gilligan, 1986). Yet, when pressed, many women interviewed as subjects in studies of classroom learning reported that they chose not to conduct rational inquiry apart from conviction and emotion, that to do so was dead, or at least so foreign as to be a violation of their sense of identity as intellectual beings (Belenky et al., 1986). Researchers in this field are extremely cautious to point out that they are making no claims of innate gender natures or differences. Rather, they are observing how by their own self-report women style themselves as "knowers." Developmental and cultural psychologists such as Jerome Bruner and Walter Ong have postulated that for parallel reasons, "story" in many cultures conveys intellectual content that has been invisible to or underrated by educated Westerners who associate intellect with logic.

The revaluation of women's ways of knowing guides two levels of interpretation in Greek and Biblical stories. Reading "story" for intellectual content enables readers to find more than mere ritual or wordless emotion in women's songs, such as Miriam's song of victory in the Biblical account of the Red Sea, or Cassandra's prophecies in Aeschylus' account of her abduction from Troy. Reading as a woman facilitates a recognition scene that is both therapeutic and transformative. By reevaluating their own discourse practices as different but not lesser, women and nontraditional students from numerous cultures are discovering in literary characters more strength, more alternatives, and more intellect than in past readings shaped by 19th-century translators and their 19th-century assumptions. Contemporary interpreters of Biblical representations of women's songs and prophecies are reinstating intellectual content and political agency to genres practiced by women in ancient biblical texts (Meyers, 1988; Trible, 1978). Antigone, Hecuba, Cassandra, and Clytemnestra in Greek Homeric sagas and plays are being reexamined along these lines, as are Miriam, Deborah, and Mary in the Hebrew Scriptures and New Testament. Many of these women character's songs were dismissed as incidental, or as evidence of the restricted roles allotted women as singers and mourners.

Biblical and classical literary reinterpretations have adopted a second, equally controversial critical apparatus and purpose: that of correcting distortions that many now believe were introduced by the original authors as a way of suppressing the validity, power, and strength of women's views and voices in the cultures that produced the texts (Frymer-Kensky, 1992). Readings of the roles and voices of women in ancient texts, then, are openly directed at reclaiming meaning and agency for women and for their voices. Contemporary historical fiction has become an active partner in the rereading and retelling of ancient women's discourses, and of women's self-understandings of their own discourse practices (Brindel, 1982, 1984; Wolf, 1984). In *Cassandra*, a novel refiguring the character of Cassandra that we have long viewed exclusively through Athenian drama, German novelist Christa Wolf (1984) depicts Cassandra's reflections on the nature of her discourse as a seer and priestess, and her understanding of the god Apollo's prophecy that although she speaks the truth no one will believe her. Wolf's novel recounts the story of ancient Troy from the perspective of Cassandra in her roles as a daughter of King Priam, thereby a priestess, and therefore a particularly alluring prisoner for the conquering general Agamemnon to abduct. Wolf's account emphasizes that with the occupation by the Greeks Troy has been invaded by Hellenic understandings of language and religion that are foreign to Trojan experience, belief, and practice. Cassandra reflects on her own practice of language, and considers how it has shaped her belief in herself as a seeress and leader of her people.

Wolf's depiction of Cassandra's role as a priestess and seeress provides illuminating details concerning how a priestly figure understands what it is she does when she speaks as a vehicle for a common view, and as the sensibility and voice of the people.

> Words. Everything I tried to convey about that experience was, and is, paraphrase. We have no name for what spoke out of me. I was its mouth, and not of my own free will. It had to subdue me before I would breathe a word it suggested. It was the enemy who spread the tale that I spoke "the truth" and that you all would not listen to me. For the Greeks there is no alternative but either truth or lies. . . . It is the other alternative that they crush between their clear-cut distinctions, the third alternative which in their view does not exist, the smiling vital force that is able to generate itself from itself over and over: the undivided, spirit in life, life in spirit. (p. 107)

She comes to take refuge in her ceremonial role even after despair about the Greek presence and ways of thinking has eroded her beliefs.

> I taught the young priestesses the difficult skill of speaking in chorus, enjoyed the solemn atmosphere on the high feast days, the detachment of the priests from the mass of the faithful, my guiding role in the great pageant; the pious awe and admiration in the looks of the common people; I needed to be present and at the same time unaffected. For by that time I had stopped believing in the gods. (p. 98)

From the perspective of the Trojans, the gods of the Greeks are self-proclaimed lies, fictions in the theater of Dionysus, mastheads for war, and excuses for murder. The great horse the Greeks have brought—the gift of an "Athena" totally unlike the goddess Cassandra reveres under that name—is accepted in a frenzy by the Trojans.

Finally, there comes a time when Cassandra's voice is no longer heard at all.

> The Trojans laughed at my screeches. I shrieked, pleaded, adjured, and spoke in tongues. Eumelos. I saw the face which you forget from time to time and which for that reason is permanent. Expressionless. Pitiless. Unteachable. Even if he believed me, he would not oppose the Trojans, and maybe get himself killed. He, for one, intended to survive (he said).
>
> Now I understood what the God had ordained. "You will speak the truth, but no one will believe you." Here stood the No One who had to believe me, but he could not because he believed nothing. A No One incapable of belief.
>
> I cursed the god Apollo. (p. 136)

There is no name for what speaks through her, but, Wolf's account emphasizes, it is a *vox populi*, a common voice that is the exponent of an undivided life in spirit, spirit in life. It is for this reason that the priestesses whom Cassandra teaches must learn to speak in chorus, in concert, in harmony.

Remnants of collective choral tradition, fragmentary evidence of its existence and role, survive in the chorus of the Athenian dramas—those fictions in celebration of Dionysus that the Trojans at first found so foreign. A chorus functioning as the voice of the people expressing and affirming common beliefs is a universal characteristic of religious rituals. In chant and song, often led by a priest or cantor, the truth of the group is enacted and reconfirmed. Even secular discourses draw on this tradition and its power, as with Lincoln's assertion at Gettysburg that "we cannot dedicate; we cannot consecrate this ground" for the lives of the dead have already served that function; or, even more pointedly, in the founding assertion, "we hold these truths to be self evident. . . ." Wolf emphasizes Cassandra's ability to perform her role and even to be sustained by the collective voice as independent of her belief in the gods. After she has lost her faith, she knows her performance to be hollow in terms of her own beliefs, but the voice she speaks nonetheless continues to convey the ritual to the people, and she is willing to conduct that sustaining ritual on their behalf. Her voice ceases to "speak," that is, to be heard with understanding, only when the tide of collective belief turns away from traditional Trojan deities and toward the newer Greek gods, the newer Greek understandings of the gods as false idols, as fictions. In Wolf's rendition, it is this shift, and not Cassandra's individual loss of faith, that undermines the sustaining belief, the worldview and values of the Trojan people as a whole. Only within that world, for as long as it is viable, can Cassandra speak and be heard. For as long as she does speak, however, it is as a trained and fully conscious priestess, and not as a raving puppet of ecstatic inspiration and male priests. Wolf's portrait defends a substantial revision of early Greek women in religious ritual. She reads with the eyes of faith, not with a hermeneutics of suspicion that would doubt everything it cannot prove, and reject everything that is not certain. She assumes rationality, and finds it, contributing much to our understanding of women's discourses in early Greek religion.

A line of inquiry parallel to Wolf's rereading of Greek literature has been advanced in recent studies of premonarchic Israel that provide revised accounts not only of its social structure—no central government, no structured politics, no sense of public as distinct from private or domestic domain—but also of roles of women in the tribal political and economic social structures of Exodus and Judges (Meyers, 1988; Murphy, 1993). Elusive remnants of women's discourses appear in these texts of the Hebrew Scriptures. Recent methods of rhetorical biblical criticism add the study of genre, context, social role, and audience to more traditional methods of internal formal analysis. One of the texts that has received active reinterpretation has been the Song at the Sea, the song of victory that is sung after the Egyptians are drowned at the Red Sea by "Moses and the children of Israel" (Exodus 15:1). Since the 1950s, Biblical scholars have increasingly concurred that the Song at the Sea should be attributed to Miriam as much as to Moses (C. Murphy, 1993; Trible, 1978). In a second account of the singing that follows immediately after the first, the Song, it is said, is "sung by the prophet Miriam, Aaron's sister" (Exodus 15:21), the same Miriam who finds the infant Moses in the bulrushes and persuades Pharoah's daughter to raise him as her own. Later, in Numbers, both Miriam and Aaron question Moses' authority: "Has the Lord spoken only through Moses?" While Aaron is not punished for this insubordination, Miriam is afflicted with leprosy and later dies in the wilderness of Zin. What stronger message could be sent to a woman of strong words playing a prophet's role?

In Miriam's story and others, we observe that biblical representations of women as speakers and leaders are obscured by fragmentary preservation—only traces are left of what may have been their greater prominence in the societies of that time (Meyers, 1988). Guesswork is an inevitability in dealing with ancient texts and images (Frymer-Kensky, 1992; Kelber, 1990). Classical and biblical scholars emphasize that in dealing with ancient texts we can never know anything with finality save through our interpretation of the fragmentary traces that are left. We guess, guided as much as possible by informed background material. Cultural reconstruction is an important enterprise in such understanding. Equally important is the knowledge worked at through interpretation, a fundamental goal of the humanist scholar, and one that has been newly provisioned by recent classical and biblical archaeology, as well as by studies in orality, literacy, and culture (Kelber, 1990; Meyers, 1988). Reappraising these oldest stories has in turn revised our idea of story to include truth as well as fiction, and has aided in understanding the complex roles played by story making and story understanding in cultures as well as in the lives of individuals. All of these leaps of interpretive faith, directed at understanding, surmount the hermeneutics of suspicion, and supplement its rigorous questions with the prudent interpretive conjectures that slowly begin to ring true.

All of this is not to say that questions are not asked in revisionist, belief-guided reading. The role played by ritual, and particularly by priestly proclamatory speech, is rendered problematic in Wolf's characterization of Cassandra. She loses her faith but continues to perform. Wolf's depiction of Cassandra's speech, and of her understanding of its powers, exemplifies but also questions more generally the power of priestly, prophetic, and ritual speech. Performers of rituals past and present are often depicted as invoking and evoking superstition rather than as persuading through appeals to changes in beliefs (Kinneavy, 1987). Our understanding of the role played by oracular pronouncements, priestly exhortations, and similar religious discourse rituals within culture can be further amended to include a close look at how belief and ritual are at work in the conventions, and conventional discourses, of academic skepticism as well.

Addressing the fine lines that distinguish religious and secular discourses, and what were in the 1920s termed *primitive* cultures, Cambridge classicist Jane Ellen Harrison (1966) challenged what she charged were rather vague notions of early Greek religion as based on "a sense of the supernatural," as "instinct for mystery," or as "apprehension of an unknown infinite, beyond the visible world" that were being advanced within studies of comparative religion and folklore (p. 488). Instead, she proposed, mystery, the guiding and inspiring spiritual value greater than any individual, is not potent

> because it is unintelligible and calls for explanation, not because it stimulates a baffled understanding, but because it is felt [or is undertaken by contract, vow] as an obligation. The thing greater than man, the 'power not himself that makes righteousness,' is not the mystery of the universe to which as yet he is not awake, but the pressure of that unknown, ever incumbent force, herd instinct, the social conscience. The mysterious dominant feature is not Physis [Nature], but Themis [Society]. (p. 490)

According to Harrison's analysis, it is not a foreign and awesome Nature that Cassandra's "primitive" religion dwells in. Nor is it, from within Cassandra's self-understanding that Wolf sketches for us, a mindless herd instinct that she calls to in her people. Wolf's depiction emphasizes that Cassandra's role is that of sustaining and serving as exponent of a social whole, a unity that Harrison finds represented by Themis and enacted through ritual as the willing undertaking of collective social obligation. Whether this interpretation is couched in feminist or social constructionist terms, the emphasis remains the same: collective, consensual, ethically evaluated language, thought and action are among the highest, not among the lowest, exercises of human art and intellect alike. Women's ways of knowing (Belenky et al., 1986), an ethic of care (Gilligan, 1986) are being reevaluated as among the most conceptually complex, not the intellectually weakest or subjective, forms of human reasoning.

Questioning the late 19th-century enthusiasm for Dionysian and Bacchic rites as ecstatic abandon and even sanctioned violence, Harrison emphasizes the judiciousness, balance, and beauty in what have come down to us as the Greek "mysteries"—rituals that were inculcated and practiced in a range of different modes of consciousness and discourse. Instead of emphasizing that profound break occurred with the emergence of Western philosophy among the Greeks, Harrison reads Plato's depictions of dialogic education, dialectic, and philosophizing as continuations of social collective and ritual traditions, as a "rationalization of the primitive mysticism of initiation, and most of all of that profound and perennial mysticism of the central *rite de passage*: death and a new birth, social, moral, intellectual" (p. 513).

A DOUBLE VISION: BELIEF SEEKING UNDERSTANDING: INQUIRY IN THE SERVICE OF BELIEF

An ancient defense of belief working in accord with intellect that was popular in the Middle Ages posited that intellectual activity is, and should be, faith-seeking understanding: *credo ut intelligam*. The prophetic and priestly functions of a Cassandra, of Miriam's song in *Exodus*, of Hannah's song uplifting the lowly in the Hebrew Scriptures and its echo in Mary's New Testament Magnificat—all express a common voice, repeating and reciting its beliefs through injunctions to a collective. Wolf's Cassandra provides a double vision (Frye, 1991). She exemplifies the negative aspect of belief: It can be manipulated by powerful priestly figures; as well as belief's benign alter ego—a reasoned choice of assent (Carter, 1992). Studies such as Harrison's emphasize social and religious collectivity as both volitional and rational, and not as one of the lower stages in a developmental continuum in which true advancement is marked by the abandonment of belief and superstition. Certainly, collective hierarchical societies can be repressive. Much harm has been done in the name of religion. Is there not in today's academic environment an equally objectionable scene in which compulsory skepticism, negation, and doubt are promoted as ends in themselves? Many novice students, and much of the public, perceive the academy's dogmas, arguments, and intellectual doctrines as mystifying, or repressive (Gates, 1993; M. Murphy, 1993; Phelps, 1992). Restoring some middle ground in the wide gap that divides unthinking repressive forms of religious and social belief and equally doctrinaire modes of academic skepticism is certainly in order. Reprisals of the relationships among belief, collective social values, and the many roles played by literary representation can aid in this process.

Inside of or opposed to, thinking with and thinking against, the collective and the autonomous, the believing game and the doubting game (Elbow, 1986) all have their virtues and shortcomings, their dangers as well as capacities for fostering learning. The most fruitful critical thinking models encourage dialectical views of a variety of intellectual processes and traits, and promote an improved understanding of their dialectical, reciprocal capacities, a double vision. Our critical and interpretive repertoire, unfortunately, is currently replete with a different legacy. In keeping with hermeneutics of suspicion advanced within Freudian theories of identity and Marxian theories of culture, most current developmental models of self and society stress the attainments of moral and intellectual self-sufficiency, and encourage an ongoing questioning of received models of meaning, self, and society. Autonomy is regarded as the epitome of developmental achievement; autonomy as an interpretive aim and model is conceived of as the ultimate objective of both maturity and learning. The academy fosters the creation of "separated knowers" (Belenky et al., 1986). The relation between the intellectual and psychological values of separation and autonomy are presented with incisive clarity by the contemporary literary theorist and practicing analyst Julia Kristeva (1987). "As speaking beings, always potentially on the verge of speech, we have always been divided, separated from nature" (p. 8). Kristeva's goal as an analyst is to effect a transition "from trust to separation" (p. 56). Ongoing self-examination through psychoanalysis "is the modest if tenacious antidote to nihilism in its most courageously and insolently scientific and vitalist forms. It is the superman's shield and protection" (p. 63). Somewhat paradoxically, Kristeva and other postmoderns adopt this Nietzschean defense of skepticism and rationalist autonomy both as a basis for a morality that will be, as in Nietzsche's title, beyond good and evil, and as a corrective to the tendency to dominate. The self-questioning self, they postulate, will not dominate.

In another contradictory assertion, Kristeva asserts that analysis annihilates the self in order to foster relationship. "The analyst takes another view: he looks forward to the ultimate dissolution of desire (whose spring lies in death), to be replaced by relationship with another, from which meaning derives" (p. 63). Movement from trust to separation, removing desire understood as self-annihilation, will ultimately result in the possibility of relationships, which are the home of meaning. In "Who Is Unanalyzable?", the concluding segment of her essay on love, psychoanalysis, and faith, Kristeva (1987) reflects on the receptiveness of different religious and cultural groups to psychoanalysis. Her exposition exemplifies the Freudian preoccupation with sexuality, the hermeneutics of suspicion that fosters self-questioning and skepticism, and the assumption that religion is an illusion.

> Analysis is not less than religion but more—more, especially, than Christianity, which hews so closely to its fundamental fantasies. Protestants *count with* the analyst; they cooperate with their heads more than with their sexuality; Jews *count on* the analyst: they give themselves and attempt to dominate. Catholics *count* only *for themselves*: hostile to the transference, more narcissistic or perverse than other patients, they are relative newcomers to analysis who pose new problems for the analyst as well as new avenues of research. "*Keep on counting*," say Muslims as they get up from

the couch. *"Thank you for allowing yourself to be counted* (accounted)," is
the polite formula employed by Japanese Shintoists, who avoid the crisis of
transference. (p. 53)

In microcosm, Kristeva's litany of selfhoods shaped by religious belief reveals
the limitations in Western secular understandings of how individuals from different religious and cultural traditions enter into participation in Western modes of
analysis and discourse, whether on the analyst's couch or in the classroom chair.

Metacognitive and metalinguistic self-consciousness are tacit and
implicit in many cultures and literatures. The metacognitive reflection, "I think;
therefore I am" has its roots in Descartes and Socrates. The metalinguistic, "I
say" is absent from many priestly and religious discourses. "We have no name
for what spoke out of me" (Wolf, 1984, p. 107). Western philosophy and language theory have made thinking about thinking and speaking about speaking
mandatory vehicles of thought and instruction. The Western separated self is
required to refer explicitly to my identity, my position, my identity, but it is
becoming increasingly clear in cross-cultural studies of identity and intellect
that this self is only one among a number of possible selves and self-images.
Kristeva (1987) posits that trust must be deliberately broken in order to effect
such therapeutic separation. Nonetheless, alternative models of proximal learning, identity formation, belief, and faith underscore a growing awareness, the
product of cross-cultural studies, that selfhood and agency are best—or at least
very successfully—developed from within the circles of community and belief,
contexts that should never be forcibly removed. But what of the academy, and
its uses of these insights drawn from cross-cultural therapeutic and developmental models (Maranhao, 1986)?

A number of writing pedagogies, critical thinking models, and literary
critical theories have become engaged in recent philosophical disputes concerning agency, epistemology, and the nature and value of controversy within the
academy (Graff, 1990; Holmes, 1993; Marino, 1993). I regard this as potentially
refreshing and illuminating because it is a reminder that teaching the conflicts
(Graff, 1990) is hardly new. Certain practices of debate and dialogue foster a
double vision, the ability to see two sides of an issue, rather than armed verbal
warfare. Observing contrasts, differences, and dialectical oppositions has long
been a staple of Western academic traditions, especially in the liberal arts and
philosophy. The common places of ancient rhetoric were regarded as artificial
but useful common grounds for discussing and debating wildly disparate materials, issues, and beliefs. The common places included, however, not just difference and contrast, but similarity and compassion; not just dialectic understood
as opposing propositions but dialectic understood as dialogical truth seeking.
The value of the common places cannot be underestimated in today's academy.
They are ancient, and were at their inception artificial; they have already proven
themselves in the long test of time, shifting cultures and languages within academia. An eminent exponent of the larger dialectic inculcated by rhetorical com-

mon places who directed rigorous attention to the question of the relationship of the life of the mind to the life of faith was Søren Kierkegaard.

NOT SO SIMPLE, THE LEAP OF FAITH

The responsibility to resolve to seek and forge an identity, to make the leap of faith to the conviction that one is a self in the context of beliefs that have been examined and chosen are the enjoinders that lie at the heart of Kierkegaard's (1966) and subsequent existentialist ethics, psychology, and philosophy. Kierkegaard's views of the inevitably unscientific nature of human reason, and of the inevitably flawed human capacities for faith, including faith in humanity, are both expressed and enacted throughout his works. Each of Kierkegaard's works takes its contours from its subject. A study of a divided self struggling to resolve his ethical idealism with his aesthetic hedonism is published in two volumes and entitled *Either/Or*. Kierkegaard's writings are openly confessional as well, providing model after model, discursively, of the acts of contrition, self-effacement, and self-creation that he advocates. How many contemporary ethical philosophers openly employ pseudonyms as a confessional device expressing the belief that they are unable to live out the ethics they propound? Kierkegaard routinely employs pseudonyms for precisely this reason, in order to shear away, through what he depicts as a spiritually therapeutic, self-directed use of literary irony, the festering aspects of himself that impede health and truth. His literary irony is also an irony of selfhood, enacting his philosophical and psychological view that despair is a lack of consciousness of being a self, a spiritual being. Kierkegaard the teacher is at his best in his discussion of achieving spiritual health and of the responsibility each individual has to achieve selfhood and self consciousness. Self-consciousness and selfhood are for Kierkegaard not only states received but states achieved.

> One can be a wizard of introspection, an expert on one's emotional life, and remain totally unselfconscious in the Kierkegaardian sense. Consciousness of the kind Kierkegaard tried to raise requires conviction—the conviction that one is a self. Kierkegaard counselled that self-consciousness is conditioned by our wider system of beliefs: to be awakened in Freudian terms is to be in a slumber according to Marx, and to be conscious according to Marx is to be comatose according to Kierkegaard. (Marino, 1993, p. 112)

Had Kierkegaard's polyvocal, multigenre modes of seamlessly interwoven literary and philosophical discourses come to guide literary practice and theory we might have ended up with a slightly less suspicious hermeneutic tradition. There is a fine line between acting in bad faith or during a loss of faith, as for example Cassandra is shown to in Wolf's depiction of her priestly performances, and anti-

cally undermining faith, as do the ancient Cynics, Nietzsche, and some of the more flamboyant dada deconstructionists and postmodern theorists. In his warning against similarly wanton destructiveness, Kierkegaard implicates literary and philosophical authors, and along with them all individuals as authors of themselves. It takes only a small leap of interpretive faith to see parallels between his academic and cultural environment, and today's. In a double rebuke of the academy and the religion of his day he assigns to them joint responsibility for a cultural malaise that found its most graphic expressions in limp practices of religion, and philosophical methods and movements bent on undermining conviction. He offers remedies as well as rebukes—a helpful antidote to his more stentorian voices. Psychology, we often forget in a post-Freudian and clinically therapeutic era, is an art of studying and healing the spirit that has close ties in earlier eras to art, philosophy, and religion (Maranhao, 1986). Admittedly, an overly therapeutic approach to philosophizing, or to pedagogy, for that matter, can lead to a reductive, feel-good, self-esteem approach (e.g, Gates, 1992). However, can we not attend more closely to the intellectual capacities and duties of the spirit—as in mind, faith—to the conviction and belief sustaining aspects of knowledge (Kinneavy, 1987). Even dispassionate analysis, Kierkegaard and for that matter Plato long ago recognized, is always directed by interests and purposes, passions and beliefs however well masked these may be by claims of objectivity and neutrality that are most often rationalizations and self-denials. The belief that objectivity is impossible and even undesirable may be advanced in either a gleeful or a deeply human spirit. Kierkegaard's deliberately personal forms of philosophizing provide instructive, edifying, examples of a philosophical medium that can sustain multiple genres and foster the development of many varieties of self while still retaining a common language and common goals.

In the hands of diverse practitioners (advocates, reformers, and adversaries), skepticism, criticism, and debate, regardless of the value assigned to them, remain distinctively Western, secular philosophical and academic models. In this "liberal" and "humane" tradition, debate has been sanctioned primarily for and by those in positions of power (e.g., Holmes, 1993). Women and minorities have traditionally not been permitted to dispute, to debate, or even to speak on the public platform (Peaden, 1995). Through similar rules of enfranchisement, particularly in the United States where church and state are so rigorously segregated, religion has often been excluded from the debate and indeed has been cast as an enemy and not as the ally of education, liberal humanism, and the pursuit of knowledge (Carter, 1992; Wills, 1990). Among the many cultures of today's multicultural academy are the cultures of religion and spiritual values whose insistent voices are beginning to be heard. We ignore these self-understandings, these convictions, and their intellect at very great peril to us all.

REFERENCES

Alexiou, M. *The Ritual Lament in Greek Tradition*. New York: Cambridge University Press, 1974.

Belenky, Mary Field, Blythe McVicker Clinchy, Nancy Rule Goldberger, and Jill Mattuck Tarule. *Women's Ways of Knowing*. New York: Basic Books, 1986.

Brindel, June. *Ariadne*. New York: St. Martins, 1982.

_____ . *Phaedra*. New York: St. Martins, 1984.

Bruner, Jerome. *Actual Minds, Possible Worlds*. Cambridge: Harvard University Press, 1986.

Carter, Stephen L. *The Culture of Disbelief*. New York: Basic Books, 1992.

Elbow, Peter. *Embracing Contraries in the Teaching Process*. New York: Oxford University Press, 1986.

Frye, Northrup. *The Double Vision. Language and Meaning in Religion*. Toronto: University of Toronto Press, 1991.

Frymer-Kensky, Tikva. *In the Wake of the Goddesses. Women, Culture, and the Biblical Transformation of Pagan Myth*. New York: The Free Press, 1992.

Gates, Henry Louis. "Pluralism and Its Discontents." *Profession 92*. New York: MLA, 35-38.

_____ . "Beyond the Culture Wars: Identities in Dialogue." *Profession 93*. New York: MLA, 1993, 6-11.

Geertz, Clifford. *The Anthropologist as Author*. Palo Alto: Stanford University Press, 1988.

Gilligan, Carol. *In a Different Voice*. Cambridge: Harvard University Press, 1986.

Graff, Gerald. *Beyond the Culture Wars: How Teaching the Conflicts Can Revitalize American Education*. New York: Norton, 1990.

Harrison, Jane Ellen. *Epilegomena to the Study of Greek Religion* [1921] and *Themis, a Study of the Social Origins of Greek Religion* [2nd edition 1927]. New Hyde Park: University Books, 1966.

Holmes, Stephen. *The Anatomy of Antiliberalism*. Cambridge: Harvard University Press, 1993.

Kelber, Werner H. "Narrative as Interpretation and Interpretation of Narrative: Hermeneutical Reflections on the Gospels." *The Interpretation of Dialogue*. Tullio Maranhao, ed. Chicago: University of Chicago Press, 1990.

Kierkegaard, Søren. *The Concept of Irony, With Constant Reference to Socrates*. New York: Harper and Row, 1966.

Kinneavy, James L. *Greek Rhetorical Origins of Christian Faith*. New York: Oxford University Press, 1987.

Kristeva, Julia. *In the Beginning Was Love: Psychoanalysis and Faith*. Trans. Arthur Goldhammer. New York: Columbia University Press, 1987.

Maranháo, Tullio. *Therapeutic Discourse and Socratic Dialogue: A Cultural Critique*. Madison: University of Wisconsin Press, 1986.

Marino, Gordon, D. "Making Faith Possible, Kierkegaard's Writings." *Atlantic Monthly*, 272:1 (1993): 109-13.

Meyers, Carol. *Discovering Eve: Ancient Israelite Women in Context*. New York: Oxford University Press, 1988.

Murphy, Cullen. "Women and the Bible." *Atlantic Monthly*, 272:2 (1993): 39-65.

Murphy, Michael. "After Progressivism: Modern Composition, Institutional Service, and Cultural Studies." *Journal of Advanced Composition 13*:2 (1993): 345-64.

Ochs, Donovan. *Consolatory Rhetoric: Grief, Symbol, and Ritual in the Greco-Roman Era*. Columbia: South Carolina University Press, 1993.

Ong, Walter, J. S. J. *Faith in Contexts* (Vols. 1 & 2). Thomas J. Farrell and Paul Soukup, eds. Newbury Park, CA: Sage, 1990.

_____. "God's Known Universe." *Thought, 66*:262 (1991): 241-58.

Peaden, Catherine Hobbs, ed. *Nineteenth-Century Women Learn to Write: Past Cultures and Practices of Literacy*. Charlottesville: University Press of Virginia, 1995.

Phelps, Louis Wetherbee. "A Constrained Version of the Writing Classroom." *ADE Bulletin, 103* (1992): 13–20.

Swearingen, C. Jan. "Pistis, Expression, and Belief: Toward a Feminist Rhetoric of Motives." *A Rhetoric of Doing, Essays on Written Discourse in Honor of James L. Kinneavy*. Eds. Stephen P. Witte, Neil Nakadate, and Roger D. Cherry. Carbondale: Southern Illinois University Press, 1992. 123-44.

Thurow, Sarah Baumgartner. "Illusory Compromise. Review of Gerald Graff. *Beyond the Culture Wars: How Teaching the Conflicts Can Revitalize American Education. First Things* (1993): 50-52.

Trible, Phyllis. *God and the Rhetoric of Sexuality*. Philadelphia: Fortress Press, 1978.

Wills, Gary. *Under God: Religion and American Life*. New York: Simon and Schuster, 1990.

Wolf, Christa. *Cassandra*. Trans. Jean Van Huerck. New York: Farrar Strauss Giroux, 1984.

11

Storm in the Academy: Community Conflict and Spirituality in the Research University

Robert L. Brown, Jr.
Michael Jon Olson
University of Minnesota

So what are we? We asked ourselves this question early on in this exploration of the place of spirituality in the research university.[1] Our answer may seem dissonant. Initially, we had difficulty finding the right keywords, because although spirituality in an extended sense does play a part in our lives, religion in the usual denominational senses does not. So why were we writing about ways to secure students' rights to use their spiritual practices in their academic work? "We're materialist theorists, with a syndicalist slant," we said, cringing at the jargon. "We're radical pedagogues," we proposed, laughing over the word *pedagogues*. Probably, too, we're atheists—although both of us would immediately resist the agonal, combative relationships the word calls up. Finally, we realized that none of this defining activity was germane to what we had to offer about the conflicted place of all varieties of spirituality and the various discourses that mediate them in the disciplined, narrow, and often rarefied atmosphere of the research university. It was our work that mattered first, what we did. That work places us in the center of a revealing, we think representative, conflict among discourses and among the selves or subject positions those discourses allow.

---

[1]This project began when Lillian Bridwell-Bowles, chair of the 1992 Conference on College Composition and Communication, suggested we propose a session on the place of spirituality in the discipline because there was much professional interest in the topic.

So we discovered ourselves to be cultural theorists, doctrinally uncommitted, writing about our fierce attempts to defend students' right to their committed, religious explorations—strikingly aware of the irony that we are often lonely voices calling for tolerance and charity in a cacophony seeking to privilege particular practices and languages. As we see it, the central issue is a conflict between what we call *disciplinarity* as a shorthand term for all of the institutional forces at work to form and confirm the citizens of the academy, and *spirituality*, another shorthand term for issues of religious belief and values, morality, purpose, and ultimate meaning—and maybe for just the humbly personal in the sense that Jane Tompkins (1989) has spoken for it.[2]

We *work* as teacher-trainers, members of a departmental team responsible for bringing new teachers into the community of the composition faculty at the University of Minnesota. The teachers joining our faculty are sometimes actual beginners—graduate students teaching autonomously for the first time. But just as often they are former public school teachers or graduate students with considerable teaching experience in their disciplines. "Beginners" in our program, they nevertheless come with considerable scholarly or practical experience. Typically, in seminar discussions and in our training groups, we find ourselves repeatedly defending students' rights to their own experience of the spiritual: their family beliefs, their practices, their views of the spiritual realm. In our view, and that of the composition program for which we work, students have an absolute right to explore their experiences—personal and academic—in whatever discourse they wish, our job being to help them discover the various histories, interests, rhetorical possibilities, hidden tropes and *topoi*, consequences, and so on of their choices.[3] We regard spiritual discourses, including specific denominational/religious articulations, as significant ways of exploring and clarifying experience. This view has an impeccable progressive pedigree, deriving from the work of Paolo Freire and his various U.S. disciples, who insist, practically and theoretically, on allowing students' interests to determine the course of their education. The practical motivation is obvious: Coercion seldom works, as various theories of resistance amply demonstrate (see e.g., Giroux, 1983, for a representative postmarxist account and an excellent bibliography; Heath, 1983, for an account of cultural and family dynamics; and Rose, 1988, for a reading from the intimately personal). The theoretical motivation is more complex, but for us it can be reduced to something like the Golden Rule: Don't force your students in a way you yourself would hate being forced.

---

[2]*Discipline* and *disciplinarity* are usefully ambiguous keywords. We intend them in both the Foucauldian historical sense: a complex system of occulted, subtle, discursive devices deployed to direct our behavior; and in the common sense: ways of talking and writing associated with our academic lives.

[3]For an account of this program and the management structure that disciplines it, see Anson and Brown (1991). In 1996 the University of Minnesota abolished this program, substituting a traditional, hierarchically managed "freshman English" curriculum. An account of this disciplinary change is detailed in Anson and Ruiz (1998).

So why, we asked ourselves, do we regularly hear, every year during our training seminar: "I never let my students write about Jesus. There's just no way they can do a good job"? Often it is a first-year teacher talking about assignment design, but it is just as typically a senior colleague talking about how he or she tries to foreclose writing that takes poetry as a site for meditation or links novels to Biblical teachings. "Jesus," of course, is synechdochic for many religious practices, many ways of writing and talking. So common is the attitude, that we take it as our point of departure for an institutional analysis that we feel promises to help us understand invisible hands determining our teaching lives.[4]

In this chapter, we describe a broad, institutional, dual economy—narrowly material and broadly psycho- and sociodynamic—that explains suppression of the spiritual by examining the complex production of academic identity. Often, even typically, this system of production is mystified, hidden by protective, masking texts. The sign-value of membership in the community, and the systems of power into which such signs enter, often work only if their operations are occulted. So if spirituality—whatever forms it takes—is silenced in the university, we should look to the dynamics of institutional power as an explanation. It is never, we suggest, a matter of the spiritual, narrowly defined. At base may be the cultural and material conditions of academics' personal and working lives, the operations of a complex economy that produces both knowledge, and disciplined selves or subjects. Our reading begins with the material: the complex system of rewards and sanctions that tell us, through the subtle and not-so-subtle practices in our everyday work lives, what can and cannot be said (or done) if we expect to flourish materially in academia.

The material, however, always arrives back at the self. The ferocity with which many of us argue over theory, over classroom practice, over whether we can "let them write about Jesus," tells us that the final question is why any of this matters so much—personally, spiritually, intimately. So the more interesting and more basic aspect of this dual economy is the complex economy of the self. The academic community that supports us exacts payment for the power and solidarity it confers. The exclusion of spirituality from the academy, we claim, has everything to do with how the research university operates as a modernist institution that legitimates and validates knowledge while it constructs disciplinary subjects who do academic work. For academics in (post)modern America, economic selves (livelihood), and psychic selves (identity) are fundamentally linked to a formal organization—the research universities where we are trained, and where many of us continue our academic vocations. The relation between the economic self and the psychic self is dialectical; the two are, in fact, inseparable.

---

[4]Our site, emphatically, is the "research university." Mark Schwehn (1993) makes an eloquent case for its primacy in setting disciplinary rules and for dominating the American academy—at the expense of the liberal arts college and the church-supported institutions with their explicit spiritual-education agendas.

In this chapter, we work from readings of our place in the research university, interpreting actual events from our work lives, and master texts from our professional literature, to try to see the unseen hand of institutional power. We begin with a story of one of our best new instructors, Debby, and a brief examination of the unseen forces that resulted in her acting as a discourse "boundary officer"—despite her best intentions, her intuitions, and our explicit suggestions to the contrary. We also reflect on our inherently conflicted roles as teacher-trainers—"boundary officers" ourselves, in spite of our best intentions. Graduate student/instructors (as academic apprentices) and the mentors who bring them into the academy are a good site to study how academic discourses and ideologies operate to exclude the spiritual. Especially because graduate students are vulnerable and unprotected by positions and tenure, their academic lives and selves depend on their ability to get the codes and conventions of the prospective community right. Often, in this striving for disciplinary belonging, new instructors will privilege the discourse of their prospective communities. More accurately, these individuals may privilege what they assume to be the discourse of these communities. And these assumptions are telling.

Mentors, often tenured faculty in secure positions, are not exempt from these institutional forces. In order to remain members in good standing within the disciplinary community, they must also work to police discourse boundaries and continue to act as good academic subjects. As much as we might try to make professing a discipline simply a "job," it is always more than that. In a powerful way, our communities support and maintain us in a complex psychic economy that is as motivating as the material economy that gives us our daily bread. We will always—although perhaps not consciously—seek to protect and legitimate that supporting "hearth and home," and our protective, legitimating acts will often work to exclude those who do not belong.

DEBBY'S STORY

As we began this project, we asked our faculty members if they had encountered problems with students' writing about the spiritual. Debby, a creative writer with considerable experience in writing workshops, professional writing situations, and teaching writing in international settings, described an encounter that exactly illustrated our disciplinary and personal conflict. Debby met with us several times to discuss this experience, to clarify our understanding of what occurred, and finally, to approve our accounts of the experience.

Many of our instructors simply circumvent students' writing about spiritual issues by creating courses with tightly defined writing assignments that do not invite discussions of the spiritual (or the personal). Some instructors, however, and Debby is among them, create courses with more open-ended assignments that students use as opportunities to explore issues of great importance in their lives. These issues are often spiritual in nature. Debby set up her freshman composition course as a "publications workshop" in which students selected topics of interest to use as themes for class-generated magazines. During her winter class, religion and spirituality were particularly popular and one group of students put together a magazine addressing those issues. Curiously, the writing in the completed publication, *Religious Rendezvous*, does not seem very "spiritual" to us. Even though questions of the spiritual were important to these students, none wrote from a personal point of view; none struggled with questions of ethics, purpose, or meaning; and none treated their topics as anything other than objects of skeptical examination.

How and why did this happen? First, we suspect that students come to the university already somewhat socialized into the codes and conventions of academics, already knowing they need to write about any issue from a detached, skeptical, "objective" (or academic) point of view. With few exceptions, this is the main type of school writing for which they have been trained prior to coming to the university. Second, because by university standards, these students are not particularly skilled in constructing skeptical discourse (despite their socialization in this direction), the freshman composition course exists to further their training. We had, in fact, urged our new instructors to treat freshman students as young scholars and to view their academic writing as a process of "making knowledge."

In her winter quarter class, one of Debby's students began writing a theological exploration entitled "Do We All Worship the Same God?" This exploration speculated that the supreme beings described in the sacred texts of Islam, Hinduism, Christianity, and Judaism were one and the same. Debby's interaction with this student and her essay clearly illuminate Debby's conflicted role as a socializing agent for the academy as she constructed it. Debby was comfortable with those aspects of the paper that were more academic, but she was uncomfortable with the theological nature of the paper as a whole. Debby felt her end comment on the first draft illustrated her perplexity, and shared it with us during one of our meetings:

> Your article is making me think a lot. I like learning the similarities between visions of God. *Your theological musings made me very uncomfortable. I think because they wouldn't be appropriate for an academic paper.* They might be fine for *Religious Rendezvous*. Ask them. I would be better able to follow your point if you took each attribute of God—good, all-powerful, creator—and put them in separate paragraphs with evidence from all the religions. This is very interesting. (italics added)

Debby remarked to us that she thought the first draft of the paper was "too flaky," and did not demonstrate "critical thinking." It reminded her of freshmen sitting around a dorm room wondering about religion. Dorm room talk, she noted, is different from classroom discourse. For academic papers, Debby argued, students must construct arguments with evidence from texts and must anticipate counterarguments. In other words, in the classroom, students must enter into the academic construction of knowledge, the world of "objectivism" and dueling discourses. The organizational scheme that Debby suggested for a later draft of the paper—"Take each attribute of God . . . separate paragraphs with evidence . . ." —is a classically academic and modernist way to organize knowledge of the world (in separate categories, with supporting evidence).

Here we should recall the modernist notion of the autonomous subject and the image of the lone academic "making knowledge" by skeptically examining a series of texts, preferably authoritative texts, and authoring another text. We can (and should) read this image against that of a community of dorm students engaged in a conversation about religion. Which of these produces "truth"? Which produces legitimate, valid knowledge? It is significant that all of Debby's temperamental biases, her training as a creative writer, and her preferred relationships with her students naturally direct her toward the personal, the communal, and the spiritual. The fact that she felt inchoate, disciplinary pressures toward the objective and the academic is compelling evidence of the strength of those unseen, institutional hands.

Debby felt uncertain about how to respond to this student. On the one hand, she suggested that the paper might be acceptable to the peer editors putting together *Religious Rendezvous*. On the other hand, she cautioned that it "wouldn't be appropriate for an academic paper." However, Debby knew, as well as we do, that given the dynamics of power in the university classroom, her authority as instructor would probably overshadow the potentially validating viewpoint of a community of peers. Debby's uncertainty about how to respond led her to bring up the issue with a group of fellow instructors, who, as it turned out, had all attended small, religiously affiliated liberal arts colleges. They offered her a different possibility for how to interact with the student and her text, suggesting that a freshman writing a theological paper was not necessarily nonacademic. After meeting with this group, Debby told the student to "go for it" and retain the "theological musings." But a double message had been sent; it was too late. The student was already in the process of completing a more impersonal and skeptical essay in line with Debby's initial comments.

Acting on behalf of what she assumed to be disciplinary standards, Debby challenged her freshman student's forms of knowledge and ways of knowing, and attempted to shape her as a good modern subject. In her construction of her role as a disciplinary teacher, Debby assumed she should lead her students to rid themselves of "limiting" home language and beliefs, or at least not speak of them in the academy. We, of course, find troubling our role as teacher-trainers in these events. How did we enable this construction of the academy and our new teachers' roles in it? If anything, our training materials and explicit advice go to exactly the opposite end.

Yet in the classroom, as trainers and as teachers, we all are occasionally impervious to our own best advice. Body language? A slight ironic intonation?

Some signs of uncertainty? Surely we often wear our disciplinary selves in our very bodies and broadcast them in our actions, unrecognized. So we worry about what harm we might be doing to our students in our recommendations—both conscious and unrecognized—to their instructors. Undergraduate students compelled to "lose" or at least to provisionally surrender their faith may be giving up something more concrete than a particular theology; they may be losing their connection to family, home, community. If their faith is cast as alien in the academic world, they may lose their most apparent and concrete source of psychic solidarity. To explain further what compels us to limit or exclude the spiritual, we need to look more closely at how the research university operates as an economic and psychic community. Part of this is a matter of the history of the academy in America. And underlying that history are powerful and masked cultural dynamics.

FROM SPIRITUAL EDUCATION TO *WISSENSCHAFT*

It is important to remember that the history of the U.S. academy is the history of a journey from spiritual education to modernist knowledge production. The most acute account of that journey is Mark Schwehn's (1993) compelling history of U.S. academe: *Exiles from Eden*. Schwehn provides the words to understand our history, how the institutions that bore us and support us were transformed from sites of spiritual values-centered teaching to production shops for *wissenschaft*, what we call *knowledge-making*. *Exiles from Eden* is an elegant history of U.S. academe from its roots in the Harvard College model of spiritual education-for-citizenship through its conversion to the Germanic model of the research university. The mere facts of Schwehn's narrative are familiar from other works, notably Gerald Graff's (1987) *Professing Literature*. But what is striking about Schwehn's story is that it is told from the personal (we might say "spiritual") viewpoint of a committed teacher who shares his struggles as he leaves Chicago for Valparaiso—precisely to find a community of spiritual learners. Organizing the book is a personal narrative, and Schwehn is unremittingly present in the entire story, even when he is relating well-documented history. He began his academic career at the University of Chicago—tenured, and from all external evidence, successful. But his response to the academic atmosphere at Chicago—the "Eden" of his title—exactly mirrors the spiritual paradox facing many of our young academic apprentices. Schwehn discloses that he entered academe to engage in a collective search for spiritual knowing. Both the content (spiritual issues and the language to express them) and the formation (a community of spiritual scholars) were central for him. But like many of our colleagues, he found himself isolated from, and in competition with, his peers and encouraged only to write of the narrowly rational.

   The substrate of Schwehn's work is a material reading of academic history. Although writers like Graff have chronicled the sequence of events

(typically publishing and curricular events) that mark the movement from values-centered colleges to *wissenschaft* production sites, Schwehn shows how
these changes are always related to the economic and social history that sur-
rounds them, a material integument giving shape to writing, teaching, and academic management. As the research university takes shape, its contours are
defined by the growing relation between the academy and the industrial/profes-
sional institutions supporting its research and using its practical and discursive
products. Schwehn is equally clear in pointing out, as Graff does not, that colleges centered on (variously) spiritual values have maintained a solid copres-
ence throughout this history. However, the disciplinary center has shifted to the
research university, where graduate training is based. This shift has created conflict within all parts academe. It is this conflict we see everywhere reproduced
in the dissonant behavior of our ourselves and our new teachers.

Schwehn recalls his personal journey and maps it elegantly onto the
events and structures in U.S. academe. He returns our history to us—a valuable
gift. In the following sections, we add to his account a view of the systems
informing the way the spiritual is written and erased in our institutions.

LEARNING TO PROFESS: CYCLES OF CREDIT AND DISCIPLINARY CREDIBILITY

Whatever else an institution produces, it always produces its members. Perhaps
the most acute account of the way academic culture depends on complex
processes of identity negotiation is Bruno Latour and Steve Woolgar's (1979)
Laboratory Life. Latour and Woolgar tease out the complex processes by which
scientific investigation produces the uncontested, "every-researcher-knows
facts." They are ethnographers as well as materialist theorists, so the book is
meticulous as it details the complex day-to-day life in a neuroscience laboratory. Organizing that life of fact production are the systems active in the research
institutions central in both Schwehn's and our accounts. Compressing their long
and subtle story, we can say that facts are the products of power—power to
secure grant funding, hire graduate assistants, buy the complex equipment necessary to "read" cellular structures and functions and "inscribe" the findings.
And along with facts, these operations of power produce academic citizens.

The by-products of successful academic work, as Latour and Woolgar
view it, are *credit* and *credibility*. Credit is public and material; credibility is
personal and discursive. A scholar's credit can be redeemed, in a fairly direct
economic interchange, for funding. Although their term is a trope, it has a solid,
literal basis. An academic worker with credit in the disciplinary community can
redeem that credit for appointments, funding, staffing, travel, conference slots,
and publication opportunities. Disciplinary stars have deep academic pockets
and credit lines at the disciplinary bank.

Credibility, for our purposes, is more powerfully explanatory. Although difficult to sever from credit (credibility is necessary for credit, because the discipline won't "advance" hard-won disciplinary capital to strangers), credibility is central in the construction of academic identities. We have credibility when we are believed at once, when we are known, when our word is good. The credible academic is cited as an authority, whereas those who have not achieved credibility must "support" or "defend" their claims. Latour and Woolgar illustrate credibility with meticulous citation studies. In the early stages of the struggle for credibility, a researcher publishes heavily under his or her own name, and is cited infrequently; once credibility is achieved, the researcher ceases to publish on that particular disciplinary topic, but is then frequently cited by other writers. This movement from publication to citation around a topic marks the gradual building of credibility.

It is critical to note that Latour and Woolgar are not faulting scholars for behaving as though their work were controlled by issues of power and visibility; indeed, they treat cycles of credit as an inevitable aspect of scholarly life. Certainly, neuroscientists are not merely working to aggrandize themselves; they are advancing knowledge in their field. But the work they do depends on processes by which all of us produce our disciplinary selves.

For our purposes, it is critical to understand the cycles of credit driving the research university and its members. Our view, simply said, is that we make *wissenschaft*. Here we recognize that many private colleges—the values- and community-centered institutions—may well participate in a different cycle, one whose product is the educated, self-aware, and satisfied customer—a graduate who will be admitted to graduate or professional school, secure a position he or she likes, eventually recruit other students, and contribute to his or her alma mater.

Credit-cycle economics elegantly demonstrates that we operate within institutional systems that produce us as subject-members, but it does not help us understand the personal dynamics that make such systems so powerful. Finally, it does not detail the operations of the institution on, and in, us. At this level, the issue shifts form institutional dynamics to the dynamics of the self.

WHY IT MATTERS SO MUCH

Composition theorist David Bartholomae (1985) has shown that classrooms are often sites where many discourses compete. In his view, students are engaged in "re-inventing the university" as they enter each of their disciplinary classes and must try to master its particular discourse. In his account, competing discourses are evidence of institutional and disciplinary battles between the epistemological rhetorics of social science and *belles lettres*, for example. We suggest that many students face another deeper and more personal discursive conflict when they first enter the university or any of its classrooms. Every student brings a set of discursive practices with him or her: the discourses of home, family, community. These discursive practices construct and determine the student. Indeed, in many theories, they are the students because they contain the student's history and position the student in relation to the world (Hebdidge, 1979; Hoggart, 1958; or, for a venerable psychodynamic account, Erickson, 1963). French language and culture theorist Pierre Bourdieu (1991) provides a compelling account of this attachment of language and self. At the center of his analysis is his concept of the *habitus*, a term he borrows from classical rhetoric to refer to our complex dispositions to act in particular ways in particular situations. Beyond simple styles of speaking or preferences for particular discourses, Bourdieu's *habitus* is somatic, literally a part of us. After a lifetime of inculcation from every aspect of our everyday lives, our habitus, our ways of being, our everyday practices become us. Such practices were there, embodied in the language of hearth and home, before any of us encountered a classroom. Recent composition research is rich in discussion of the (in)compatibilities of home language and school language (Heath, 1983; Lunsford, Moglen, and Slevin, 1990). But there is little on the way discourse constructs us—the personal, affective, spiritual, psychic "us" always at stake. By way of illustration, let us read a "master text," the writings of one of our disciplinary mentors and the watershed event those writings surround. In the collision of ideology and teaching practice we discuss, there is a parallel to our training experiences, and an antitype to Debbie's "academic apprenticeship" in the composition classroom.

In a sense, James Moffett is disciplinary mentor to many composition scholars and teachers. Credible after many years of scholarship in composition studies, he speaks for a familiar disciplinary position, one associated with his name: *The Student-Centered Language Arts Curriculum, Grades K–12* (1968) described in that landmark process-writing text for teachers. We take Moffett's work as emblematic for a familiar sort of humane liberal humanism. So when Moffett (through his integrated K–12 *Interaction* curriculum) was attacked by the committed, fundamentalist and occasionally violent citizens of Kanawha County, West Virginia, more than his textbook series was at stake.

The West Virginia censorship controversy that made national news of the hitherto rather academic and professional issue of textbook selection and religious belief is detailed in *Storm in the Mountains* (Moffett, 1988; hereafter *Storm*), an eloquent and detailed study of the Kanawha County censorship battle that began with contentious school board meetings and ended with book burnings, school bus bombings, and a highly publicized legal battle that brought the strong legal armament of the formally organized religious right into play. In a later article on the same topic, "Censorship and Spiritual Education" (hereafter "Censorship"), Moffett (1990) reprises some of the issues detailed in his book. Although *Storm* is meticulously documented—probably the most complete ethnographic/investigative account of censorship in the United States—"Censorship" has an interesting further dimension of spiritual work. Here, we feel Moffett is wrestling with pain over the violent rejection of his books, and by implication, of him. He calls *Interaction* "a work of love" (Moffett, 1988, p. 4). Nothing in his writing suggests otherwise. But we hear an intense argumentative edge in both of these pieces: a need to put the Kanawha protesters "in their place," in order to preserve his (and our) place. Although to do so simplifies a complex event and complex writing, we might take the storm in Kanawha County as a battle between discourses. And the discourse of the academy wins—at least in the book, at least in the later article, at least within the academy.

In Moffett's account, for the citizens of Kanawha County to accept *Interaction* they would have had to place themselves in a relationship to language, and to the intersubjectivities it generates, that would have disrupted their core identities. Moffett writes: "As we identify, so we know. As we know, so we identify." This is contentious and powerful writing; his sentence echoes the periodicity of the Biblical or prayer style of his attackers, and in so doing, places him between their ostensible beliefs and their actions. He writes knowingly; he knows their style and their prayer language. He then discusses discourse and identity in a compellingly clear passage:

> Our self and our very life depend, we feel, on identification with family, neighborhood, ethnic group, church, nation, and language. We have an investment in not knowing anything that will disturb such identification. So we tend to limit what we are willing to know to what is known and accepted in our reference group. (1990, p. 117)

He calls this fear of examining the unfamiliar *agnosia*. And, as have writers who have followed him, he uses the term *agnosia* as a way to account for and neutralize what other theorists would call "resistance" to his humanistic, pluralistic, and relativistic agenda. For us, some of the conflict in these positions seems to come from a troubling doubleness of purpose, one tempting to us as well. A closer look at Moffett's rhetorical forms in "Censorship" reveals a pattern everywhere present in *Storm* as well. Because this is an academic text, we are not surprised that it manifests a rhetoric of authority and domination. As humane and self-reflexive as Moffett's writing is—and it is—it seeks to dominate that alien other, those rigid fundamentalist parents and preachers who will not abandon their deontological rhetoric and the view of humanity, God and nature that supports it. Members of a graduate seminar who read *Storm* said that Moffett came to the Kanawha fundamentalists with an "explainer's attitude," not a "learner's attitude."[5] He listened to their words, but could not hear. Finally, many of us felt, he admired them. But he did not like them.

It is tempting to dismiss the Kanawha fundamentalists. As *Storm* so clearly proves, they and their agenda are tied to some well-known figures and forces of the national Christian Right (e.g., to the well-financed military/political alliances behind the Olin Foundation, the Heritage Foundation, and to Pat Robertson's Christian Coalition who, under their current "stealth" tactics, are seeking to place

---

[5]Our thanks to the members of *Ethnography as Cultural Critique*, at the University of Minnesota, 1993.

members in local government while hiding their religious/political alliances). For us, these are not easy people to like. Whatever we feel about their spiritual positions, their political and economic positions are openly hostile to open inquiry, and backed by a well-defined political apparatus (Messer-Davidow, 1993). We can easily write the Kanawha protesters and their allies as "backwoods fundamentalists," and see our academic spiritual issues as somehow different in kind. Our disciplinary bias in favor of rational analysis encourages this move, because it is clear they subscribe to, and act from a very different ontology. But it is better, we think, to treat the entire Kanawha saga—the events, Moffett's reading of the events, and our responses—as a representative case, clearer for being extreme. It is, we think, a struggle over narratives about the world and our places in it.

Finally, the Kanawha parents and the preachers are not humanistic pluralists. The ontology that supports them is absolute, hierarchical, orderly. Firmly anchored in such an ontology, and in a metaphysics of revelation and inspired, infallible Scripture, these antagonists to Moffett's *Interaction* see no point in "gnostic," skeptical, investigative, empowering education. They seem simply not to understand why anyone would want it, and pressed, convert their incomprehension into anger. Such competing ideologies are at the center of the dilemma in academic identity and behavior that troubles and engages us.

In her book, *Cities on a Hill*, journalist Frances FitzGerald (1986) strikingly articulates this conflict of ideology and charity in a chapter on the community around Jerry Falwell's Lynchburg Christian Academy. FitzGerald's book examines alternative communities in America, and finds Falwell's parishioners and teachers tellingly representative of the evolving religious right. In the chapter, she interviews Jackie Gould, a parent from Lynchburg Christian Academy. A pluralist like many of us, FitzGerald asks, "Would [you] consider sending [your] children to something other than a Bible college?" "No," the parent replies, "because our eternal destiny is all-important, so you can't take a chance. College so often throws kids into confusion" (p. 136). It is hard to refute this logic. Indeed, one cannot refute it, except by attacking its premises. And if the premises are so central in our identities that our *habitus*, our self and our very life depend on them, we are likely to be fierce in their defense.

In "Censorship," Moffett (1990) defines spirituality as "the perception of oneness behind the plurality of things, peoples, and other forms . . . ." Religion, on the other hand, he defines as aiming "to tie individuals back to some less apparent reality from which they have been diverted by, presumably, people and other attractive hazards in the environment" (p. 113). This *bifurcatio*, a powerful, authoritative, rhetorical move, captures the spiritual for the academy—and disparages the fundamentalists for their rejection of its worlds of ideas. Comforting as we may find it, this version of the spiritual strips away the irrational and mystical elements at the center of the Kanawha citizens' religious practices. Finally, they are dismissed, written out of the academic discourse with which we construct ourselves. We have made them other, not of our world, not part of our discursive "reference group."

Why the urgency? Why the energy? And what would count as an explanation of that energy? To call the fundamentalists (in Kanawha County or in our classes) sufferers of *agnosis* labels them—and rules them out of bounds by a quick, authoritative act of writing. Yet, in that passage about "identity," Moffett is close, we think, to a powerful explanation—if we took it very seriously. And it is this explanation—of the ways discourse can serve as the center of an economy of self and identity—we offer as an explanation of the energy that can lead both to burned school buses and to good, balanced graduate student teachers "outlawing" papers on Jesus.

It is hard to articulate the power of the unseen institutional forces we discovered in our own professional lives as we talked about teaching with Debby, and as we read about teaching and spirituality through the theoretical lens developed for this project. We are not, we come to see, as free as we thought. Indeed, when our sense of selves and our livelihoods are in danger, we are immensely vulnerable. A beginning graduate teacher, especially one coming to the university for the first time, is also a vulnerable creature, perhaps a disciplinary neonate. Losing the familiar support of friends, school relationships, even the comfortable topography of home, places our self constructs in jeopardy. As the "object-relations" psychologists would say, we lose our (secondary) *self-objects*: the things that reflect back an image of ourselves, coherent, competent, valued, and whole. The new disciplinary community and the departmental structures that inscribe it offer a new way of being. These self-constructs are important to members of communities. We defend them fiercely, as if they were us. Which, if Pierre Bourdieu's (1991) notion of the *habitus* is correct, they are.

And so to a brief proposal for an account that might explain the irrational power of our need for homes and our need to protect them. Underlying our analysis throughout this chapter is an appreciation of the powerful concept of *self-objects*, as psychoanalysts Heinz Kohut, D. W. Winnicott, and Alice Miller articulate them.[6] At base, the primal self-objects are the folks who raised us, who gave us our view of the world—not objects at all, but people. Fathers and mothers, of course, but beyond them, all the members of our community

---

[6]The central appeal of object-relations theory is the elegance with which it allows us to read current behavior as a trope of childhood experience. Although most of its proponents consider (or once considered) themselves psychoanalysts, they have all abandoned the rigidity of classical drive-and-stage theory for a view much less essentializing and more amenable of cross-cultural application. All, with Lacan, would see the unconscious as structured like a language, but they would seek the structure of this language in the cultural matrix that supports us. Thus, there is an easy articulation of the psychodynamic and the socio/political. The best overview is Kohut and Wolf's (1978) "The Disorders of the Self and their Treatment: An Outline." Kohut's two major books, *The Analysis of the Self* (1971) and *The Restoration of the Self* (1977), are complex, but entirely accessible. But most interesting for our work is Miller's eloquent body of work tracing the consequences of German ideology through centuries of childrearing (and abusing) practices. Her method is unremittingly hermeneutic, revealing the meanings of social and personal

who tell us, discursively, how to be. Powerfully central in object-relations theory is the idea that the primal self-objects are everywhere repeated in our symbolic, cultural productions. We make things (physical things, discursive things) that repeat our primal scenes, individually and as a culture. Read this way, all cultural production becomes a text of the political and the spiritual: We create our world in our own (occulted, perhaps fetishized) images. So it seems natural and human for us to seek those things and people that serve to mirror back and support our image of coherent selves. We surround ourselves with stand-ins, substitutions for our familiar, primal objects. Discourse, too, can serve as a self-object—and not just for beginning students. In fact, discourse may be the most powerful of self-objects. It always sets relationships among its participants: roles, formations, a place to be. Discourse invokes a world and a history and locates its users in that world.

Kohut (1971), focusing on the transference operations where our early experience reproduces itself in allegorical enactments of our primal scenes, discusses two basic formations structuring object relations: The *mirroring* relation is the site of security, support, coherence, trust. It is hard not to see the mother as the mirror, slipping into a gendered reading that does some violence to the elegance of Kohut's conception; "mothers" in his theory can be caregivers of either gender. The mother/the mirror reflects back to the young child a sense of being loved, accepted, and valued. Particularly critical in this transaction are the relationships that assure us that we are accepted and loved even when we act aggressively on the world around us. When we enter theoretical, disciplinary discourse as initiates, we re-enter a world mirroring primal wholeness—one for which we worked hard, and one at which we are good. As we hear familiar words, familiar references, familiar names, we are accepted. Perhaps the childhood safety of reading in a quiet corner has transformed itself into a career of reading and writing for a living. In a way, discourse can be the enfolding, supporting place where we feel safe, complete, at home.

The *idealizing* relationship, in Kohut's conception, is the site of power. Our fathers—again, of either gender—may have offered themselves to us as a source of vicarious strength that we seek to recreate later in the relationships we set with the world and its inhabitants. So as we watch our ego ideals (other writers, our mentors, our disciplinary parents) silencing our enemies, we are filled with a sense of the rightness of our beliefs and choices, of our life—protected, defended, whole, coherent. Kohut would say "idealized." Read in this way, both the violent, doggerel ballads that the Kanawha fundamentalists wrote and recorded, and Moffett's eloquent presentation and neutralization of them make deep, affective sense—each for the respective reference group it idealizes, and for its particular, discursive way of relating to the world.

---

behaviors from their roots in early experience. Best known is her first book, The *Drama of the Gifted Child* (1979), but more useful is *For Your Own Good* (1983), in which she shows how charity and understanding come from understanding the social and psychic sources of "dissonant" behavior.

Disciplinary discourse is a world of hard-working words. Choices of theoretical discourses within the disciplines are always personal. The soul does indeed select its own society, and each society has a way of talking and being that announces which souls are welcome there. Theories allow us to read ourselves into particular relationships with the world, and our own fragile selves are implicated in these disciplinary readings.

SIGNS OF LIFE

As we wrote this chapter, at first we found ourselves constructing a narrative of triumph, a story of ways and places that others had failed, and a masterly reading of those failures. That would be familiar academic discourse, composed by well-trained academic "good subjects." But such a narrative, however familiar in the discipline, would contradict the position we are struggling to take; it would confound our attempts to see writing and teaching as logical consequences of the conditions under which we live and work. So we cannot end by claiming to have found privileged access to truth. What we can do is recommend a path, and try to relate it to other ways of working within and around our discipline. Central here is *charity*, which we define as watchful willingness to allow students (and ourselves) to explore the world and our place in it with whatever discursive means we wish—asking, always, how that discourse operates.

Need one discourse dominate? What if students were encouraged to write and talk from spiritual perspectives without fear of rejection? What if they were asked to explore their concepts instead of being confronted for holding them? What if the historicity, structure, deployment, sources, interested involvement, consequences, and personal relevance of their words (and others' words) were the focus of instruction? What if educational practice centered on constant, fearless examination of the ways we have come to be, culturally, historically, spiritually, discursively? A facile answer is that such an examination is the goal of several different academic projects: cultural studies (as defined, if not as practiced), various ethnographies, various feminisms, experiments in critical pedagogy, and of experiments, variously, in writing.

Clearly, it is not just the Kanawha fundamentalists who suffer from *agnosia*. Theirs is obvious to us because it looks so different from ours. But ours is just as powerfully constitutive, just as basic, just as local and invented. Indeed, it is the most naive romanticism that entertains notions of a utopian space where no discourse configures us, where no ideology operates. Moffett (1990) warns us not to "castigate those bigots over there if we're doing our own version of the same thing" (p. 118). What we wrote ourselves into recognizing is that we are necessarily, always "those bigots over there" when we are observed from over there. Our project is to figure out how we might see our own behaviors, charitably, as a prelude to beginning to change them.

REFERENCES

Anson, Chris, and Robert L. Brown, Jr. "Large-Scale Portfolio Assessment: Ideological Sensitivity and Institutional Change." *Portfolios: New Ways to Evaluate Student Writing.* Ed. Pat Belanoff and Marcia Dickson. New York: Boynton-Cook, 1991. 248-70.

Anson, Chris M., and Carol Ruiz. "Graduate Students, Writing Programs, and Consensus-Based Management: Collaboration in the Face of Disciplinary Ideology." *WPA Journal 21* (Spring 1998): 106-20.

Bartholomae, David. "Inventing the University." *When a Writer Can't Write: Studies in Writers' Block and Other Composition Problems.* Ed. Mike Rose. New York: Guilford, 1985. 134-65.

Bourdieu, Pierre. *Language and Symbolic Power.* Ed. John B. Thompson. Trans. Gino Raymond and Matthew Adamson. Cambridge, MA: Harvard University Press. 1991.

Erickson, Eric. *Childhood and Society.* New York: Norton, 1963.

FitzGerald, Frances. *Cities on a Hill: A Journey through Contemporary American Culture.* New York: Simon and Schuster, 1986.

Giroux, Henry A. *Theory and Resistance in Education: A Pedagogy for the Opposition.* Boston: Bergin and Garvey, 1983.

Graff, Gerald. *Professing Literature: An Institutional History.* Chicago: University of Chicago Press, 1987.

Heath, Shirley Brice. *Ways With Words; Language, Life, and Work in Communities and Classrooms.* Cambridge, U.K.: Cambridge University Press, 1983.

Hebdidge, Dick. *Subculture: The Meaning of Style.* London: Methuen, 1979.

Hoggart, Richard. *The Uses of Literacy.* London: Pelican, 1958.

Kohut, Heinz. *The Analysis of the Self.* New York: International University Press, 1971.

_____ . *The Restoration of the Self.* New York: International University Press, 1977.

_____ , and Ernest S. Wolf. "The Disorders of the Self and their Treatment: An Outline." *International Journal of Psychoanalysis, 59* (1978): 413-25.

Latour, Bruno, and Steve Woolgar. *Laboratory Life: The Construction of Scientific Facts.* Princeton, NJ: Princeton University Press, 1986 (1979).

Lunsford, Andrea, Helene Moglen, and James Slevin, eds. *The Right To Literacy.* New York: MLA, 1990.

Messer-Davidow, Ellen. "Manufacturing the Attack on Liberalized Higher Education." *Social Text, 36* (1993): 40-80.

Miller, Alice. *The Drama of the Gifted Child.* New York: Basic Books, 1981 (1979).

_____ . *For Your Own Good: Hidden Roots of Cruelty in Child-rearing and the Roots of Violence.* New York: Farrar, Straus, Giroux, 1983.

Moffett, James. *A Student-Centered Language Arts Curriculum, Grades K-13: A Handbook for Teachers.* Boston: Houghton Mifflin, 1968.

_____ . *Storm in the Mountains: A Case Study in Censorship, Conflict, and Consciousness.* Carbondale: Southern Illinois University Press, 1988.

_____ . *"Censorship and Spiritual Education."* The Right to Literacy. Ed. Andrea Lunsford, Helene Moglen, and James Slevin. New York: MLA, 1990. 113-19.

Rose, Mike. *Lives on the Boundary: A Moving Account of the Struggles and Achievements of America's Educational Underclass.* New York: Macmillan, 1988.

Schwehn, Mark R. *Exiles from Eden: Religion and the Academic Vocation in America.* New York: Oxford University Press. 1993.

Tompkins, Jane. "Me and my Shadow." *Gender and Theory: Dialogues on Feminist Criticism.* Ed. Linda Kaufman. Oxford: Basil Blackwell, 1989. 121-39.

12

The Arts of Compassion and the Instruments of Oppression: James Agee, Lionel Trilling, and the Semiotic Turn

Kurt Spellmeyer
Rutgers University

> *"Education" as it stands is tied in with every bondage I can conceive of, and is the chief cause of these bondages, including acceptance and respect, which are the worst bondages of all. "Education," if it is anything short of crime, is a recognition of these bondages . . . and a deadly enemy of all of them.*
> —Agee and Evans (1941/1988, p. 308)

This chapter is about experience, but not my experience; about teaching, but not my teaching; about religious belief, but once again, not my own beliefs. In a collection of essays whose authors are convinced that experience, teaching, and religious belief should somehow be reconciled, I instead want to ask why such an argument needs to be made at all. For an answer, one might turn somewhat predictably to Reformation England or 17th-century France, but I will begin much closer to home, with a book about the United States in the 1930s. The book is *Let Us Now Praise Famous Men*—half journalistic expose, half spiritual autobiography—and its author was James Agee, an enigmatic critic of modernity who posed many of the questions that we are posing here.[1]

---

[1]Given Agee's complexity, we should hardly be surprised that his own religious commitments are rather hard to define—and for some critics, hard to credence, as well. But as

With the status of "belief" even less secure today than when Agee wrote in 1936, it seems especially important to know that *someone* has preceded us and that we are not speaking here only for ourselves. At a time when intellectuals commonly reject everyday experience as a source of truth—to say nothing of experience when it transcends the categories that our culture makes available—we should try to remember as often as we can that people in other places and other times have fashioned lives less shallow, imitative, and austere than we in "postmodernity" have managed to make. Reading Agee now may help us see that the rise of semiotic philosophy and the reduction of experience to "system" and "code" can never eclipse what lies beyond the text, which the self-styled human sciences have suppressed at an enormous cost. When we choose to confront what lies beyond the text, we may find that more than texts will be transformed—not only our knowledge but the uses of knowledge as well; not only what we read and write but also our most intimate relations to the world. Agee, I feel sure, would have understood; he was there at the moment in our history when experience and formal knowledge became official enemies, and when learning was exiled from the often empty ritual that we refer to as *public education*.

Ostensibly, *Let Us Now Praise Famous Men* is a book about the rural poor, but Agee's real subject, or so I am convinced, is the human cost of social order in our time. Only a distrust of that order can explain why Agee looks so ruefully on so many hallowed institutions—the government, the media, the arts. But the schools occupy an especially crucial place in Agee's anatomy of the modern world. Schooling, Agee knew, is "tied in with every bondage" because schooling brings about the fatal substitution of obedience and credulity for the wonder—and the work—of genuine learning. And "learning" itself Agee understood as an experience so important and so rare that it cannot be produced en masse by eager educationists. I can watch or listen inattentively, and I can read or write with indifference or care, but *learning*, Agee tells us, has not happened until an act of recognition takes place: until I can awaken from the sleep of my routine to experience the world as an open space, a presence beyond the boundaries of my self. Although Agee knew that the achievements of the past—poetry, painting, philosophy, music, science—could potentially renew this awareness of the world, he also knew that by design or accident, education in our society often serves to make the world, potentially open and welcoming, disappear into banality. For Agee, education is the "chief" of "bondages," and he set out, as I do here, to ask why this should be so.

Mark Doty (1981) observes in his study *Tell Me Who I Am*, when surviving "friends or family members attempt to describe Agee, no one fails to address the centrality of religion in his life and works" (131).

Another critic, Victor Kramer (1990), sees in Agee's work "a continuing attempt to accommodate natural and supernational impulses" (p. 8). This distinction, in my view, does not quite capture the spirit of Agee's natural supernaturalism, but it comes closer than have many other critics. The most direct of Agee's own statements on the subject may appear in "Religion and the Intellectuals" (Agee, 1950).

AGEE'S REDISCOVERY OF THE REAL

In the sweltering months of July and August 1936, two journalists on the payroll of *Fortune* magazine—a promising young writer born in Tennessee and a Chicago-raised photographer of modest but growing reputation—arrived in central Alabama to do a story on the Cotton Belt's 9 million tenant farmers. The photographer, Walker Evans, made a darkroom in his Birmingham hotel, but the writer, James Agee, took up residence on the scene, living alongside a tenant family, renamed "the Gudgers" in the book he later wrote (Bergreen, 1984). That Evans and Agee should have gone to Alabama—hardly the kind of place where "the news" gets made—says something about just how unsettled things had become, so unsettled that *Fortune* was lurching visibly to the left with stories on women slaving in the factories, on the abuses of the prairie soil that created the Dust Bowl, and on the all-American childhoods of FDR's socialist deputies. At no other moment in its history did *Fortune* send a message so mixed, with pictures of seamstresses darkly bent over their work, while advertisements on the opposing page might show brighter, slimmer, younger women lounging at the beach or reclining against the shoulders of handsome men in fast new cars (Bergreen, 1984). No one, just then, could tell which way of life the future would bring—more of the Satanic mills or the open road of infinite wealth.

But despite the atmosphere of uncertainty, the editors commissioned Evans and Agee to turn out a story that must have seemed already as good as written. That story was the familiar one about progress and poverty: Without good food, without new clothes, without a decent place to live or a proper education, life would be nasty, brutish, and short. Whatever the differences might have been between the people who hated Roosevelt and the ones who were prepared to redistribute the nation's wealth, they were united in the value of progress and the sordidness of any world without it. To tell this distinctly American story for the millionth time was the task these two journalists assumed, yet it was ultimately one they never got to complete, not for *Fortune* at any rate. Back in New York with sheaves of notes and rolls of gelatin silver negatives, they discovered that their progress-minded editor Ralph Ingersoll had fallen from the grace of the magazine's Republican owner, Henry Booth Luce (Bergreen, 1984). Depression or not, Luce resolved that *Fortune* would celebrate the romance of big capital, and so its pages did forever afterward in the bright, upbeat spirit that has since become that publication's hallmark. But even if their story had survived the purge, Agee and Evans were poorly disposed to tell it in the standard fashion: If they were not Republicans by anybody's definition, neither were they New Deal Democrats, and the final product of their months among the cotton tenants—the book *Let Us Now Praise Famous Men*—might be read as an attempt to show that these supposed antagonists, the defenders of big money and the saviors of the little guys, were really the most intimate of co-conspirators.

Exploiters and improvers were allied, Agee believed, in a basic disre-
spect for the tenant farmers and their way of life; for what we, in our more
anthropologically minded time, might refer to as their "cultural" legacy. Despite
the enormous odds against it, Agee—a country boy uneasily civilized by a
string of private schools—quickly learned to admire that legacy. No one, I
think, has described lives like theirs with greater honesty and feeling than this
sometime-poet. Coming from Harvard, and from the small but enchanted circle
of New York intellectuals, Agee should have found in his profoundly disadvantaged subjects a decisive vindication of everything he possessed: education,
taste, relative wealth, and the mobility of the modern urban professional. But
Agee actually saw himself as more impoverished than his subjects, a person
who had paid an unfair price in self-denial for every one of his "advantages."

The irony of Agee's life lay in this painful contradiction: Each advance in
his own education and career had been accompanied by a growing panic at his
state of worldlessness—his sense of belonging to no one and to nothing. An alcoholic at 28, Agee had already begun to suspect that the problems of America went
deeper than the financial pages could explain and would not be repaired with a rise
of the median annual income or a Bolshevik revolution (Bergreen, 1984). In some
way that took him years to clarify, the sharecroppers embodied everything he
feared about himself, the self he had learned at school to keep concealed. What he
wanted to rediscover 1,000 miles south of his adopted metropolis was precisely
what he wanted to rediscover in his own past: some trace of a basic dignity that
everyone had overlooked. And he pursued this dignity to the point of exhaustion,
convinced that if he could unveil it in the cotton tenants, men and women who
were all but universally despised, then others might acknowledge it in him.

As a journalist, Agee was supposed to fashion the conventional documentary. His subjects—men and women living abjectly on the land—had
become quite familiar to most middle-class readers through the accounts of
backwoods degeneration that had filled the pages of both popular and scholarly
publications for almost twenty years (Pickens, 1968; Rafter, 1988). Even by the
late 1930s, many readers might still have associated people like "the Gudgers"
with the slogans of eugenicists and social engineers, although everyone in those
Depression years had learned to look with greater "toleration" on the urban job-
less and the honest rural poor. The staff at *Fortune* may not have wanted cold
statistics, but they expected their man in the field to furnish as dispassionately
as he could an image of lives emptied out in a cycle of endless work, and
robbed of meaning by a lack of contact with the higher things: good books, ele-
vated company, the fine arts, and great ideas—the amenities that money alone
could buy. As the readers of *Fortune* knew, it was culture that made people
everything they were; it was education, knowledge, manners, poise.

If Agee did not see matters quite that way, he certainly understood what
the toil of the farmers had cost them, growing others people's crops on other people's land only to remain perpetually in debt. And he found their predicament, like
so many other things, "awful" beyond his capacity to describe:

On the day you are married, at about sixteen if you are a girl, at about twenty if you are a man, a key is turned, with a sound not easily audible, and you are locked between the stale earth and the sky; the key turns in the lock behind you, and your full life's work begins, and there is nothing conceivable for which it can afford to stop short of your death, which is a long way off. It is perhaps at its best during the first two years or so, when you are young and perhaps are still enjoying one another or have not yet lost all hope, and when there are not yet so many children as to weigh on you. It is perhaps at its worst during the next ten to twelve years, when there are more and more children, but none of them old enough, yet, to be much help. (pp. 322-23)

What the tenant farmers felt most immediately, as Agee described them anyway, was not a loss of nobility or an absence of refinement, but their own, very tangible powerlessness. For them, living was the experience of an unalterable fate, a cycle of perpetual debt (Mahridge and Williamson, 1989). Yet Agee saw something else besides their oppression. The same labors that made a prison of their hours and days seemed to him nothing less than a "dance"—"slow, gradual, grand, tremendously and quietly weighted" (p. 323):

Annie Mae at twenty-seven, in her angular sweeping, every motion a wonder to watch; George, in his sunday clothes with his cuffs short. . . . Mrs. Ricketts, in that time of morning when from the corn she reels into the green roaring glooms of her home, falls into a chair with gaspings which are almost groaning sobs. . . . Miss-Molly, chopping wood as if in each blow of the axe she captured in focus the vengeance of all time. (p. 324)

In this brief passage, Agee shows us two very different kinds of work, one servile, the other free and inexhaustibly creative. There is, first, the work of people who are forced to fight, quite literally, for their survival, who labor for others until their bodies give out and who have at the end of their lives nothing for their efforts. But Agee shows a second kind of work, for which the English language has no native word: the work of connecting with the world, breathing into the routine of tending corn or chopping wood the animating force of emotions and desires, whether noble or crude, beatifically calm or suffused with "the vengeance of all time." The Greeks might have described this second, animating kind of work as *hermeneutikos*, after Hermes the messenger who mediates between the gods and humankind. Because we today could scarcely be less like the Greeks of antiquity, we might discount the emotions and desires of the tenants as human in the least consequential sense, but it is Agee's intention to teach us otherwise. He wants his readers to see with him the hermeneutic work that lifted people beyond themselves into an existence indestructibly alive.

And for Agee, the discovery of this other, hermeneutic work—by means of which the self and the world are drawn together into the here and now—reassured him that the doors of his own perception were not yet closed, when he had every reason to suppose they had been shut and locked. His "education" had taught him, after all, to believe that the hunger for connection with the world—for a sense of presence, of participation—was a hunger for something that never would be found. Agee knew his Freud and his Marx; he knew the modern (and now, postmodern) tenet that "Reality will always remain 'unknowable,'" as Freud (1949/1989) once declared, and that we are condemned, at best, to an endless tinkering with the symbols and structures handed down to us. But once Agee had arrived in the Cotton Belt, where his formal "education" ceased to apply and a new process of learning began, he could no more take his cue from this "Modern Library Giant"—as he called Freud, referring derisively to the popular edition of his works—than he could from the style sheet at *Fortune*. The second of the epigraphs that opens Agee's book, just after a passage from *King Lear*, is Marx and Engle's famous call to arms from the *Communist Manifesto*, "Workers of the world, unite and fight. You have nothing to lose but your chains, and a world to win." But then Agee appends a caveat: "These words are quoted here to mislead those who will be misled by them. They mean, not what the reader may care to think they mean, but what they say" and "it may be well to make the explicit statement that neither these words nor the authors are the property of any political party, faith, or faction." The world to be won was not the Marxist utopia, which might still be 1,000 years in coming, and not the Christian heaven either, but a dimension of experience in this life accessible to every person everywhere, without the cost of confession or conversion.

If nothing in Agee's education had prepared him for the cotton tenants, nothing in the culture of modern America had taught him to value everyday life for its own sake, without reference to anything higher or better. To Americans of his day, few experiences could have made less sense than to lie down willingly, as Agee did, in the moist, chill Alabama night on a bed of unwashed sheets, which he remembered as "coarse and almost slimily or stickily soft":

> The pillow was hard, thin, and noisy, and smelled as of acid and new blood; the pillowcase seemed to crawl at my cheek. . . . There was an odor something like that of old moist stacks of newspaper. I tried to imagine intercourse in this bed; I managed to imagine it fairly well. [And then] I began to feel sharp little piercings and crawlings all along the surface of my body. . . . I struck a match and a half dozen [bedbugs] broke along my pillow: I caught two, killed them, and smelled their queer rankness. They were full of my blood. (p. 425)

Unable to sleep, Agee got up, lit the lamp and searched his body for fleas and lice; checked the bed, where the bugs were waiting, and finally admitted to himself that he would never "beat them" (p. 426). Walking out of the room to the porch, he unintentionally woke the dog, and then, urinating into the dust beside the house, he listened to the sound of a river roaring somewhere in the dark. After watching the stars and "nodding at whatever . . . [he] saw," Agee returned to his bed and put on both his coat and his trousers, the cuffs tucked into his socks as protection against the bugs. "It did not work well," he recalled, and he spent the duration of the early summer night scratching and shifting his posture, covering, uncovering, tucking, and untucking. Yet at that worst possible moment, he unexpectedly felt himself overwhelmed by "the actual"—a sense of presence exceeding all his frustrations and expectations. "I don't exactly know," he wrote, "why anyone should be 'happy' under these circumstances, but there's no use laboring the point: I was: outside the vermin, my senses were taking in nothing but a deep-night, unmeditatable consciousness of a world which was newly touched and beautiful to me" (pp. 427-28).

Precisely because every person is endowed with this capacity for connecting with the world just behind or beyond our representations of it—what Agee calls the "actual" world—the narrative in *Let Us Now Praise Famous Men* does not begin with a "before" and "after" framing some transformative moment when the scales fell from the author's eyes. To be "educated" one must first be ignorant, and it is the existence of something called "ignorance" that Agee wants most of all to deny. At the start of his account, neither he nor his subjects are living in ignorance, and the conditions for the exercise of their hermeneutic power lie around them everywhere. He writes:

> In any house, standing in any one room of it . . . it is possible, by sufficient quiet and passive concentration, to realize all . . . of [it]. . . and to realize this not merely with the counting mind, nor with the imagination of the eye, which is no realization at all, but with the whole of the body and being, and in translations of the senses so that in part at least they become extrahuman, become a part of the nature and being of these rooms. (p. 183)

In reply to the apostles of progress and literacy, who were prepared to believe that the cotton tenants had descended to the level of savages, Agee told his readers that the real savagery was culture itself, once it had become fixed and sacrosanct in the forms of "science" and "art." But deliverance from savagery, as he discovered there in central Alabama, started when his own education no longer told him what counted as real and he was forced to live from the "whole of the body"—a life that began with the failure of knowledge, the failure of the codes and symbol systems at his disposal. This contradiction—between things as they unfold from moment to moment and things as they are "supposed" to be—made it possible for him unlock the prison-house of language, convention, and history, if only momentarily. And in this process of *unlearning*, he experienced a "translation of the senses"—their immersion in a world too concrete and complex, too open in the absence of any systematic coherence, for even the most fluent language to express. With the translation of his senses, which Agee tries to commemorate on every page of *Let Us Now Praise Famous Men*, the "big ideas" that have preoccupied entire generations of scholars and scientists are unveiled to us as the momentary images—the play of shadows on the wall—that everyone knows they are, and that everyone has been schooled to treat reverentially as more solid and real than experience itself.

So well had Agee's readers learned this reverence for big ideas that almost no one of his generation understood what he wanted to say, and his book, when it came out, sold less than 1,200 copies. But the coup de grace was delivered posthumously, twelve years after Agee's death, in an appreciation of his "great" book by the self-proclaimed liberal critic Lionel Trilling, a man committed to preserving the best that has been thought and said for those who could not think or speak half so well. Agee, Trilling (1942) wrote, was an unreformed romantic, idealizing people more deserving of our pity, or perhaps a stern reproof, than of starry-eyed admiration—people, in other words, who needed badly to be lifted up. No one, to my mind, has more cruelly betrayed Agee's intentions than this ostensibly sympathetic critic, but Agee himself would probably have felt very little surprise, given his distrust of the culture-mongering that became Trilling's stock-in-trade.[2] Never for a moment did Agee suppose his subjects to be "innocent," as Trilling alleged, not even when he wrote this of one Black couple: "The least I could have done was to throw myself flat on my face and embrace and kiss their feet" (Agee and Evans, 1941/1988, p. 42). Agee was far too thoroughly "educated" to see his subjects as good in some abstracted moral sense, or as beautiful in some equally abstracted aesthetic one. What he discovered in them, rather, was a creativity that the worst servitude could not take away: the power, we might say, to uncover a world of "actuality" no less resonant, complete, and inspiriting than the creations of the sort of "great artists" that Trilling idolized—Beethoven, Cézanne, Kafka, Blake, Céline. Agee saw the creations of the artists themselves, symphonies and poems, paintings and novels, as the products of this same process of world-disclosure, forgotten by the priests of the cult of "Art," who were more concerned with erecting icons of authority and permanence than with understanding how it could be that such "great" works had come to exist at all. "Official acceptance," Agee wrote, "is the one unmistakable . . . sign of fatal misunderstanding, and is the kiss of Judas" (p. 15). But if Agee saw the worship of "Art" in this way, as a kiss of betrayal, he did so because its cult operated with breathtaking efficiency to conceal those acts of everyday attention that are no less complex and momentous than the *Songs of Innocence and Experience* or "The Bathers." Had he lived to reply to Trilling's critique, Agee might have said that it was in fact men like Trilling who were guilty of idealizing "mere"

[2]Although a close second to Trilling's review would have to be Paul Ashdown's amazingly unperceptive "Introduction" to *James Agee: Selected Journalism* (Agee, 1985), where he writes, "Like George Orwell," Agee "tried to make himself over as a proletarian. But this also was a form of intrusive deception" (p. xxx). Once Agee "got the tenant farmers out of his system, his writing became more controlled and more forceful" (p. xxxv).

human beings. When Trilling charged, in effect, that Agee failed to see the tangible failings of his rural subjects, Agee might have responded that lovers of "Art" had always willfully magnified differences among people while failing to perceive, with the appropriate awe, the marvelous, perpetual renewal of life through those moments of surprise, loss, and connection that happen every day.[3]

But Trilling, I believe, was compelled to misread Agee's work as he did because it laid the axe so unsparingly to the whole edifice of liberalism, with its faith in the cultural leadership of the many by the few: perhaps in Agee's unhappy Ivy League persona Trilling saw an image of himself, but an image naked where Trilling wanted to be clothed, and small where Trilling wanted to loom large. I do not mean simply that Trilling also felt himself to be a person on the "outside," the son of Polish-German-Jewish immigrants determined to make it in the ultra-Anglo-Saxon milieu of English departments at midcentury; I mean, instead, that Trilling continued throughout his career to imagine education, and the discourse of educated people, as distinct from his own experience. To live by experience, in his view, was to be subjective in an irresponsible way—to be partial, provincial, close-minded, as unrepentant as Shakespeare's Shylock.[4] The best hope for a world of tolerance, of fairness and generosity, was the cosmopolitan faith in a cultural tradition that transcended local knowledge and regional loyalties, to say nothing of emotions and the body's appetites. The pursuit of truth as Trilling understood it required that all people surrender equally whatever belonged to them alone; like a great 19th-century novelist or man of science, a Matthew Arnold or a Thomas Henry Huxley, the cosmopolitan of Trilling's liberal imagination always tried to begin with those assumptions and beliefs that everyone could accept unreservedly, and from that basis, Trilling felt, larger commonalities might be pursued.

With the advent of postmodernity, Trilling's liberal confidence in a common tradition has begun to wear thin, whereas Agee's world-embracing skepticism may seem less cynical than powerfully humane. Only ten years after Agee's stay in Alabama, however, it was his provincial way of thinking that seemed ready to disappear. With the Depression over and World War II at an end, Trilling could announce in 1949 something like the end of history. "In the United States today," Trilling (1950) wrote, "liberalism is not only the dominant

---

[3]In a review of Vittorio da Sica's film *Shoeshine*, Agee (1983) deplores the disappearance among intellectuals of what he calls the "humanistic attitude": "Even among those who preserve a living devotion to it . . . few seem to have come by it naturally, as a physical and sensuous fact, as well as a philosophical one; many fewer give any evidence of enjoying or applying it with any of the enormous primordial energy which, one would suppose, the living fact would inevitably liberate in a living being" (p. 278).

[4]Although Trilling began his career writing for the *Menorah Journal*, he wanted, in the words of Mark Krupnick (1986), to be both a Jew and "an English-style gentleman" (p. 28). A few years later, Trilling became even more decisively committed to "a cosmopolitan ideal of culture." As Krupnick observes, any willingness to be "provincial and parochial" seemed "to Trilling in the [1940s] nothing less than a sin against the self" (p. 32).

but even the sole intellectual tradition" (p. ix). Yet even Trilling recognized a danger ahead, arising from contradictions at the heart of the liberal regime. On the one hand, liberalism encouraged a unique respect for freedom and difference—for "contingency and possibility, and [for] those exceptions to the rule which may be the beginning of the end of the rule" (p. xv). But on the other hand, he noted that the preservation of liberal culture required an ever expanding "organization" of experts and administrators to plan, survey, educate, enforce, and punish. Although these two different aspects of liberal culture looked dangerously incompatible, Trilling regarded it as the critic's task to maintain an equilibrium between the need for fixity and the desire for change; between the value of diversity and the imperative of order.

If Agee seemed deeply pessimistic, Trilling seemed hopeful, even smug. But Trilling was also afraid, and in a way that Agee was not. For on the one hand, Trilling saw the great novels of the previous century as the finest expression of liberal culture's universalizing impulse, the one place where crucial questions about "manners"—about classes, culture, and social life—could be freely entertained and decisively adjudicated on everyone's behalf. Trilling argued that in acknowledging the novel's special role "we can understand the pride of profession that moved D. H. Lawrence to [proclaim], 'Being a novelist, I consider myself superior to the saint, the scientist, the philosopher and the poet. The novel is the one bright book of life'" (p. 212). It went without saying that Lawrence's "pride of profession" somehow carried over from novelists to critics of novels. But Trilling on many occasions also remarked that the novel and its solutions looked increasingly irrelevant to an American scene growing more fractious and decentered every day. The novelist might speak for everyone, but who, finally, would be listening?

It seems fair to suppose, from our vantage point now, that Trilling's faith in a single, all-inclusive liberal tradition has ceased to be the common faith, whereas his pretensions to "universality" look more like a covert form of domination. And for many millions of Americans, Trilling's life may seem far less typical—and also far less exemplary—than the life of a woman like the Black journalist Charlise Lyles, who described her education to Studs Terkel (1993) for his book *Race*. I think it matters enormously that in her conversation with Terkel, Lyles employed a language that Trilling as critic was apparently ashamed to use, the vernacular of experience. From her elementary school in a Black community, Lyles had gone on scholarship to a predominately White academy:

> I received a lot of awards when I graduated. It was a very happy time. At the same time it was painful because I was very lonely. I felt estranged from my home. Even though it was a day school, I didn't really go home, because I lived with a teacher. I felt distant from my family because I was changing.

I became very critical of them sometimes: the way they talked, they way they did things, the way they looked at the world. Going to this school gave me an opportunity to really get to know a white person. When that happens, you abandon some of your prejudices and begin to see that fundamentally these people are just like you. [But] I would go home and try to use some of the big words I learned in school, like "perspicacious"—pretty much useless words. I was condescending.

I realize now how much I hurt their feelings. . . . Sometimes to fit in with the white kids, I would lie about what my mother or father did. . . . It was more than shame; I had the fear of being rejected. (p. 175)

Stories like these have become so much a part of our experience of education, whether we happen to be White or Black, that we often forget that people from other societies might question a process of schooling designed to promote isolation, self-concealment, and competitiveness. An undergraduate literary star at Harvard in the 1930s, Agee vacillated between fierce anger at the institution, which he described in his first year as "a mirror maze of fake self-perceptions," and a desire to see himself, and to be seen, reflected on the surfaces of that maze (Bergreen, 1984). But for Lyles, "education" had demanded from the start a regimen of denial even more absorbing and violent than the one that Agee knew.

To explain Lyles' predicament simply as a problem of "race" and "cultural difference"—of being Black in "White America," or of being a woman under "bourgeois patriarchy"—is to overlook the character of education in modernity, where the liberal pursuit of a single great tradition has had the unforeseen and disastrous consequence of impoverishing life at the level of local knowledge and preventing "small" traditions from taking root. Although White and Black students in the classroom may not find themselves equally unwelcome there, or equally accustomed to its regimens and assumptions, the formation of any knowledge that might be granted professional respect today virtually demands a renunciation of the immediate lived world, an abandonment not simply of one's "prejudices" but also of one's sensory life, one's "home." Far from learning to think and live critically, people like Charlise Lyles are subjected to an ordeal of progressive fragmentation, which teaches them to put on and take off worldless selves as easily as they do their clothes (Goffman, 1974).

The way of life that Lyles entered growing up in 1960s Cleveland was already a fragmented "postmodern" one, with the Black Power movement active out on the streets while programs like *Bewitched* filled the television screen. On the night of Martin Luther King's assassination, Lyles sat watching the suburban witch Samantha struggle to conceal her amazing, disruptive powers for the sake of her husband's upward mobility. "I was totally confused," she told Terkel (1993). "My mother was crying, my big sister was crying. All I wanted was for *Bewitched* to come back on" (p. 172). Even if television programs had not yet entered the school itself as they have today, the lessons that Lyles learned in her classroom still reinforced the same disconnection and worldlessness that we take for granted now. Describing her rise from a fifth-grade failure to an honors student, Lyles told Terkel that she had been "trying to escape, because at home—we were still in the old project—it was starting to get ugly. People were getting shot. . . . Filth was accumulating in the incinerators. . . . I needed another world to go to, and I found it in these books" (pp. 173-74). The books themselves were not her education, however. Lyles' father had been a reader able to recite whole passages from Shakespeare, but he lived out his life as a chronically unemployed alcoholic who "stayed uptown" with "some woman" in a low-rent apartment (p. 177). What Lyles learned at school was not knowledge but a way of using knowledge, first to distance herself from the actual world and then to survey that world from a new but strangely arid vantage point—the view, some might say, from nowhere.

In her retreat from the everyday world into books, Lyles had been made to learn the same painful lesson that Trilling taught. She had learned, in other words, to play the game of liberal culture, but that game left her as unfulfilled as it had left Agee disillusioned, and like Agee—who came from a family of Knoxville farmers—she could not altogether forget the past, her past. For Lyles, the recovery of that past took the form of a determination to break through the cultural logic of disconnection by reaffirming her connectedness with others—by acknowledging that "things have," as she told Terkel, "gotten worse for black people" even though her own life had gotten better (p. 176). And with this recognition, she felt obliged to become a "provincial" once again, concerned not with manners or society in the grand European tradition of Stendhal and Tolstoy but with the specific men and women she knew: with doing "a better job of raising our children" (p. 178). Although Trilling might find "doing a better job" too prosaic an answer to the questions of our time, it is exactly this world-embracing and embodied understanding that the "educated" class has for so long held in contempt, as Agee recognized and as we are each condemned to rediscover now. In order to make a choice like the one that Lyles does—in order to act creatively on the events that act on us—people already need to have some sense of a world in which action might be taken coherently. But it is precisely the possession of a world in all its experiential density that the architects of modernity—liberals in the West, Marxists in the East—have worked so hard, and so successfully, to efface.

LOSING THE WORLD: EDUCATION, ADVERTISING, UTOPIAS

> I could not wish of any one of them that they should have had the "advantages" I have had: a Harvard education is by no means an unqualified advantage. (Agee and Evans, 1941/1988, pp. 310-11)

If it would be true to say that Charlise Lyles never altogether lost her sense of belonging to a world, then her condition was far less desperate than Agee's had been thirty years before. The crisis Agee faced in writing his book, although he never quite explained it as I have here, is the crisis of no longer knowing where he might turn when his "education" has succeeded too well and he awakens one day to find that the world has disappeared—as a *world*, an experiential whole. The question that "the Gudgers" ask themselves, and that Agee repeats as a kind of choral refrain, is "How were we caught? How was it we were caught?" (pp. 80-81). But in asking this question at various moments in their lives, the cotton tenants would express a somewhat different sense of quiet desperation than the one familiar to their more fortunate guest. The irony of the question, at least as I am reading Agee here, lies in his awareness that he was caught more completely than they could imagine because he had learned from his own unhappiness that the achievement of "freedom," wealth, and sophistication did not bring an end to his poverty.

Agee knew, of course, the talismanic significance that "education" held for the cotton tenants, who worked slavishly under the large land-holders because the system of cotton tenantry had in fact replaced the last generation of slaves. But unlike slaves, the mostly White tenants—who were "free" men and women, after all—viewed their situation as somehow their own "mistake," the result of a failing or a weakness on their part. And without the time and information to understand the systemic causes of their poverty, they were condemned to awaken every day of their lives as Annie Mae Gudger did, filled with "utter tiredness. . . since she [had been] a young girl" (p. 88). For Annie Mae, living in a decade when the average U.S. citizen had a ninth grade education, the idea of a school, of books and lessons, held the promise of emancipation; the promise of escape into a life so different from her own that she could not imagine what it might be like. In a certain sense, education might have kept that promise, as Alabama's large landowners had foreseen in 1894, when they overturned laws banning child labor and enforcing attendance in the schools. But even if the New Deal made America's schools a showcase for Progressive reform—although not the schools in Alabama—Agee was afraid that change would only reinforce the great divides separating rich from poor and white from black (Maharidge and Williamson, 1989).

Back in New York to complete his manuscript, Agee remembered Annie Mae's daughter, Maggie Louise Gudger, as a girl "fond of school, especially of geography and arithmetic." She wanted, he recalls in his book, "to become a teacher, and quite possibly," he predicted, "she will" (p. 301). But her brother, Junior Gudger, whom we would now identify as "learning disabled," was still struggling to read and write after three years in the first grade, and Agee doubted that most of the local teachers had the training to provide the specialized help he needed. There were other "difficult" cases as well. Another tenant child, Margaret Ricketts, "quit school when she was in the fifth grade because her eyes hurt her so badly every time she studied books," while her sister, Paralee, who could read with ease, also quit shortly after because Margaret's absence made her lonely. And why not leave, when all the children of the Ricketts family were looked upon as "problem children" by authorities at the school? "Their attendance record," Agee writes, was "extremely bad; their conduct . . . not at all good; they [were] always fighting and sassing back"—although not only because their parents were so poor and they lived so far from school. They were, Agee recalls, "much too innocent to understand the profits of docility"—"sensitive, open, trusting, easily hurt, and amazed by meanness and by cruelty" (p. 303).

To say that the purpose of education was to impart a false consciousness, painting over the grossest exploitation for the sake of what we now call *hegemony*, is to oversimplify the complex, conflicted motives of everyone involved. The stories the children read and the subjects they studied in their "progressive" textbooks did not evoke a mystifying fantasy world but overwhelmed them with details that erased any sense of what a world might be. They read poems by Vachel Lindsay and Robert Louis Stevenson, and sanitized versions of Joel Chandler Harris' slyly racist fables—"Brother Rabbit's Cool Air Swing." They studied nature and they studied science. With the help of a mathematics textbook that went on for 500 pages and weighed more than 18 pounds, they learned to solve problems involving various proportions of mixed nuts, which they had never eaten. But the text that Agee turned to as the most eloquent example of modern, liberal education came from their reader in geography:

1. The Great Ball on Which We Live.
The world is our home. It is also the home of many, many other children, some of whom live in far-away lands. They are our world brothers and sisters. . . .

2. Food, Shelter, and Clothing.
What must any part of the world have in order to be a good home for man? What does every person need in order to live in comfort? Let us imagine that we are far out in the fields. The air is bitter cold and the wind is blowing. Snow is falling, and by and by it will turn to rain. We are almost naked. . . . Suddenly the Queen of the Fairies floats down and offers us three wishes.
What shall we choose?
"I shall wish for food, because I am hungry," says Peter.
"I shall choose clothes to keep out the cold," says John.
"And I shall ask for a house to shelter me from the wind, the snow, and the rain," says little Nell with a shiver. (p.lii)

Is this, Agee asks, really what the children would ask for? Do food and clothing and shelter really make a world, together with the expertise to provide these items, or is it not the case that our equating of such items with the world—and the world with a "great ball," the cartographer's ultimate abstraction—is the worst poverty of all? If Agee's observations tell us anything, they tell us that he looked with the keenest attentiveness on the deprivations of his subjects, noting, for example, how difficult it was for the tenants to buy the few books their children owned. But he wanted his readers to understand that a disaster more fundamental than material deprivation had already overtaken everyone, not simply the tenants, and not simply the teachers of their children, but also his fellow Americans in the prosperous Northeast. "It is," Agee wrote, "as harmful to the 'winners' (the well-to-do, or healthful, or extraverted) as to the losers" (p. 311).

The disaster was this: As the price of their ascent, the privileged had lost the capacity to break through the wall of culture into the "actual"—which Agee understood to mean much more things seen "in themselves," which is simply another a symptom of the disaster. Agee meant things seen in the context of the larger openness, a horizon beyond language and culture that could, as Agee wrote, be uncovered "suddenly . . . by any number of *unpredictable* chances: the fracture of sunlight on the facade and traffic of a street; the sleaving up of chimneysmoke; the rich lifting of the voice of a train along the darkness" (p. 227, italics added). What offended Agee most about America's "democratic" education was its active suppression of this openness among the poor, for whom it was the only consolation. The point of public schooling as he witnessed it was to diminish the scope of the students' understanding through the sheer weight of fragmentary information, which did not unveil the world in which they lived and moved but closed it off one detail at a time.

In the refrain, "How did we get caught?" Agee asks a question that addresses his readers far more urgently than it does the subjects of his report. How, he asks, has it happened that people like ourselves—educated, leisured people who should by rights be profoundly happy—live as unhappily as the Gudgers; why do we, who have the benefit of every opportunity, feel as unfree as those who have no opportunities at all? And Agee's answer takes him back to "education" in the broadest sense: We are, he says, schooled into a poverty of experience—a culture of isolation, displacement, and emptiness—that the greatest material affluence can do nothing to assuage. And if we wish to see the very poorest of the poor, we will not find their photographs on the pages of *Let Us Now Praise Famous Men*; we will have to look back at ourselves.

The most basic lesson that *Fortune* taught in those early years of the Great Depression was the existence of two worlds, each carefully juxtaposed page after page: On the one side, subscribers could read stories of drying croplands or the backbreaking harvest of the cotton; on the other, the advertisements. And what the ads evoked for the journal's readers was less a place they actually knew than another and better place—a utopia of capitalism—designed by its creators to stimulate the reader's fear of the world pictured on the other side of the page, where disappointment and privation were the order of the day. Of course, the ads might be selling nothing more ethereal than Buick sedans, but the cars were just the vehicle for the expression of something else—an entire world without Agee's "actualities," a world, we might now say, of signifiers swept along in an endless, playful circulation. For tough-minded manufacturers and nervous market analysts, the ads operated as a soothing counterworld, where everything that could be imagined was evoked exactly as if it were real. Promising an event like the one Agee experienced in a sharecropper's house—an encounter with the "whole of consciousness," moving outward from the body—the ads told their readers to pursue that goal not by turning, as Agee did, toward the strange and the immediate but by retreating to the safe, the distanced, the imaginary. Tacitly but firmly, the words and images assured the reader that "wholeness" always lies *out there*, in that other, better world of pure representation, where a silent Buick races down a dustless road. But from such dreams, Agee warned, we will all wake up unpleasantly. To believe the ad and to buy the car—or the cigarettes or the scotch—is to court the most acute sense of disappointment; to find oneself in a condition even worse than when one started, because then, at least, one had hope. Desired but never possessed, the product must remain an unattainable idea.[5]

The kind of fulfillment that Agee celebrated must begin with a refusal of just this allure; and he kept telling us throughout his book that a sense of the actual can be achieved neither by pursuing the car nor by possessing it, but only by approaching things obliquely, in ways that allow them to escape our intentions. Seen obliquely against a horizon no longer closed off from view by fear and desire, "a street in sunlight can roar in the heart . . . as no symphony can" (p. 11). But here Agee's powerful language may fail to express what understatement could disclose more truthfully. Several years after Agee's death, an Austrian philosopher of a very different temperament would observe in a similar spirit,

> If anyone should think he has solved the problem of life and feel[s] like telling himself that everything is quite easy now, he can see that he is wrong just by recalling that there was a time when this 'solution' had not [yet] been discovered; but it must have been possible to live then too . . . and even at that time people must have known how to live and think. (Wittgenstein, 1980, p. 4e)

This, it seems to me, comes closest to what Agee meant: There has always been something that thinking and acting could not improve on, which is itself the *ground* of thinking and acting. Prior to the advertiser's world-denying imaginary, prior to the engineer's instrumental expertise, there has always been another and more basic form of being in the world, one premised on the notion that, as Wittgenstein insisted, "the place I really have to get to is a place I must already be at [right] now" (p. 7e).

Agee was convinced that each of us exists in such a place, but that the *Fortune* way of life has made its presence hard to see. And for this very rea-

---

[5]For a recent analysis that confirms much of Agee's understanding of modernity and consumerism, see Schor (1991).

son—because the ideology of liberal progress demands that people believe in their own fundamental insufficiency and impoverishment—he was convinced that any search for "the whole of consciousness" must begin with an act very different from the ones most familiar to the scientist who "dissects" or to the artist who "digests." Both the artist and the scientist in modernity cultivate forms of deliberate alienation by suppressing the actual for the sake of the ideal. But the kind of observer that Agee constantly tried to be must *live through* the object of his perception—must allow himself, in other words, to encounter the world compassionately, "suffering with" everything he meets, as the Latin root of the word "compassion" implies. Rather than imposing his will on the world, Agee allowed himself to be transformed in the attempt to see and hear, to taste and touch without the violence of interfering. "In a novel," Agee wrote, "a house or a person has his meaning, his existence, entirely through the writer. Here [in actuality] a house or a person has only the most limited of his meaning through me: his true meaning is much huger." The difference between fiction and the world lies in the fact that George Gudger really "*exists*, in actual being, as you do and I do, and as no character of the imagination can possibly exist" (p. 12). It is this recognition of "actual being" surrounding us everywhere, always *more* than words and *more* than ideas, that canonical art and institutionalized science both conceal, and so the price we have to pay for their one-sided triumph has been our growing alienation from the world and from ourselves.

Yet Agee recognized that this perception of the whole—"this effort," as he put it, "to suspend or destroy imagination" and to open "consciousness" to the world and the people in it—is an *activity*, and not a limp receptiveness like Keats' negative capability. As Agee knew, reaching past the barrier of culture into the world demands the labor of clearing away preconceptions by seeking out again and again exactly those things that resist the explanatory power of words and ideas. Only then does it become possible to refashion our words and ideas in turn. To experience the world as whole and perfect in its presentness is to become a *participant*, to identify with "the other" so intensely that the opposition between self and other disappears. By contrast, the effort to isolate and diminish the object in an aesthetic or analytic spirit is not to "suffer with" it, but to forestall the possibility of any real opening to experience. The point of listening, say, to a piece of music is not to register its constituent parts—to hold oneself at the distance necessary for a detached and analytic understanding; the point, Agee insists, is to get "inside the music" so completely that you are "not only inside it, you are it" (p. 16). Heard in this way, the music becomes a question like *Let Us Now Praise Famous Men* itself, a question addressed to the reader, although not in the sense of something that has to be solved and put away, but as something that demands to be *lived through*. Every musician and every dilettante lives through music in this way. It is only the scholar, the professional "knower," who prevents him or herself from *listening*.

In opposition to the spirit of his age—and ours—Agee refused to choose between knowing and feeling, discipline and spontaneity, order and randomness. Instead, he asked how we can create such things as poems, novels, symphonies, paintings, and cities—how we can create and inhabit culture—without allowing our creations to become burdensome and paralyzing. What he wanted to explore was not a world without culture, a primitive, Edenic condition, but a different and less helplessly dependent relation to the products of human ingenuity. An attention to form, he understood—and at a time when formalism had become every modernist's creed—could not sustain our independence, since formalism set out to fix an ever-changing reality. Only by understanding form as empty in itself, valueless in itself, without an animating experience, could the people for whom he wrote his book overcome the injuries done to them by their schooling.

Today, of course, the apparatus of schooling lies in our hands. But how, exactly, might we follow Agee's lead in our work as teachers and scholars: How we can we place learning, as an experience, at the center of education? It might be profoundly reassuring to think that simply by permitting our students to draw on their own traditions—their own histories, commitments, and beliefs of every kind—we will have solved the problem. But to imagine this congenial scenario is to forget what Agee cautioned us about the university, where the fashioning of knowledge has always begun with the demand that our commitments get left at the door. No matter how "tolerant" a teacher might be, what will happen to the Moslem student who must read *Of Woman Born*, or the Christian fundamentalist we require to discourse on Nietzsche's death of God, or for that matter, the young White feminist who must somehow bring together her sense of self-worth with the Pauline dictum that although man is the glory of God, woman is the glory of man?

Liberalism has preserved the illusion of neutrality by suppressing historical differences and, in the last remove, meaning itself. But what will we do if we actually allow multiple and often conflicting beliefs to be heard in the public space we call the university? It seems to me that Agee pointed toward one solution when he called on us to recognize the conditional nature of all belief, and the potential of every creed and doctrine to obscure what it promises to reveal. In the discord of beliefs that our classrooms will become if we try to restore human meaning there, teachers and students may both have the chance to see knowledge as it really is: always a partial expression of the truth. And the truth itself—it remains beyond words, not because it is transcendent but because "truth" describes the process of connecting with the world. One cannot speak the truth, but one can live in truth. Agee said that this truth is our common human legacy, the hidden core of every faith and discipline. It is also something that we cannot teach unless we are prepared to care less about knowledge for its own sake than about the value of not knowing.

What matters more than knowledge is the openness that this "not-knowing" allows. To us, typically, the not known, the unsaid, is meaningless, but Agee wrote in praise of "bareness" and "space" precisely because they seemed to hold "such greatness" that he could not "even try" to explain their fundamental character (p. 155). In the process of writing *Let Us Now Praise Famous Men*, Agee came to understand that the greatest eloquence, and also the greatest compassion, could never be achieved by filling all the spaces up with words but by leaving a "bareness" for the others who would come later. And is it not this openness that has given value to the things we value the most? Poems and plays, loves and friendships, forests and journeys, each of these creates a space—a hole in our certainties—that enlarges and extends our sense of presence. To know a poem, or anything else, in the way that Agee recommended is to encounter the world as we never have before. And only when the world as we have known it is changed can we say that the poem has found place in our lives.

THE WORLD, THE CRITIC, AND THE TEACHER IN A SEMIOTIC AGE

There can be, I believe, no way of life more deeply antithetical to Agee's experience of the "actual" than our current social order, which derives its nearly irresistible power from its denial of openness—its radical asceticism. Modernity promises plenitude but produces the very opposite, and this fact may explain why Trilling felt himself called on to charge Agee with "a failure of moral realism." Like Freud, whom Trilling praised as the greatest thinker of our century, Trilling himself considered *some* denial of the actual to be the essential underpinning of "culture" in both senses of the word, as Arnold meant it and as anthropologists do. And this conviction makes Trilling, rather than a "romantic" like Agee, our great ancestor in English departments, even at a time when liberalism has become the target of everyone's critique.

Trilling was convinced that we must not get the sort of "wholeness" Agee wanted; what the continuity of liberal culture instead demands is a willingness to accept the next best thing, and that next best thing is the vicarious experience of wholeness through literary art. The arts, and culture generally, must create desires that life itself cannot possibly satisfy, but which spur us on, all the same, to an ethical obligation that stands as a modern, secular substitute for God's covenant with his people: a law to be pursued but never finally, bodily lived through. For Trilling, however, even the idea of a covenant must be reduced to the status of a metaphor. The purpose of art is not to restore what Wordsworth—one of Trilling's inspirations—describes as the "visionary gleam," but to demonstrate again and again that this gleam has "fled," and to teach us a wise forbearance of our inescapable abandonment. It is this conviction at the heart of Trilling's liberalism that allows him to maintain with serene confidence that the real subject of Wordsworth's "Ode on Intimations of Immortality" is not immortality after all, but the value of literature as a path to maturity in a disenchanted world (Trilling, 1950).

Trilling's Wordsworth is not the poet of nature, with or without the capital "N," but of "reality," which means something quite different than Agee's intimations of presence. To clarify the character of this "reality," Trilling (1950) draws on *Civilization and Its Discontents*, where Freud describes the inevitable waning of the child's "oceanic" sensibility, the false and immature impression of "limitless extension and oneness with the universe" (p. 144). Despite his powerful nostalgia for an oceanic "oneness," Trilling's Wordsworth recognizes that "we fulfill ourselves by choosing what is painful and difficult and necessary, and we develop by moving toward death" (p. 148). Although Wordsworth may begin his famous poem by affirming that the "child is father to the man," he knows that if there is one thing a person can never be again without looking like a fool, it is a child; and Trilling goes on to insist, by the same reasoning, that for all its reliance on a "theistical metaphor, the Ode is largely naturalistic in its intention" (p. 149).

Quite apart from Wordsworth's intention, Trilling's version of the "Immortality Ode" teaches us the same lesson conveyed by *Fortune* magazine: in the absence of a world, we have consoling images of a better one. If Trilling differs at all from the casual reader of *Fortune*, he differs in his belief that satisfaction ultimately lies not in breaking through one of Agee's "inconceivable walls," but in wanting the things it is responsible to want; and then, when disappointment follows as it must, in recognizing disappointment as our human lot. Yet this is the lesson that Agee thought of as his deepest injury, and that Wittgenstein rejected when he wrote that philosophic problems could be resolved only by transforming the way of life from which they arose. Like Agee, Wittgenstein knew that the pleasures of art could never substitute for this essential transformation, but even Wittgenstein scarcely seemed to understand how a way of life might be renewed once it has fallen into disrepair.[6] The way back to coherence, Agee believed, lay ready to hand in experience itself. For him, the point of culture was not to manage neurosis, as Trilling held, but to cure it; not to balance contradictions but to dissolve them by returning to the here and now in the conviction that an order will always be there, if we are only patient enough, observant enough, to let that order manifest itself.

As a teacher of English at a university, I seldom read Trilling today without regretting the persistence of the liberal legacy, not only in higher education but in our society as a whole, which endlessly reinstates, in a hundred different venues and a hundred different ways, the logic of worldlessness. But I am also increasingly persuaded that those of us who have followed the avant-garde

---

[6]As Wittgenstein wrote in 1930,

> What Renan calls "the bon sens précoce" of the semitic races. . . is their *unpoetic* mentality, which heads straight for what is concrete. This is characteristic of my philosophy.
>
> Things are placed right in front of our eyes, not covered by any veil.— This is where religion and art part company. (p. 6e)

of our profession in taking its semiotic turn—its turn away from experience to the somber pleasures of "textuality"—may have unknowingly revealed ourselves to be Trilling's most obedient disciples, more obedient than any of his contemporaries. There are certainly alternatives, however, and we may find them in unexpected places. Here, for example, are the words of one critic of Trilling's generation who refused to believe that poetry could offer nothing more than a pale image of emancipation:

> By making forms [the poet] understands the world, grasps the world, imposes himself upon the world. But the "made thing" that the poet produces represents a different kind of form from all the others we know. . . . The form of a [poetic] work represents, not only a manipulation of the world, but an adventure in selfhood. It embodies the experience of a self vis-à-vis the world. . . . The self has been maimed in our society because. . . we [are losing] contact with the world's body, los[ing] any holistic sense of our relation to the world. . . . So in D. H. Lawrence's poem "Cry of the Masses":
> Give us back, Oh give us back
> Our bodies before we die. (pp. 72-73)

The writer here is Robert Penn Warren (1975), a fellow-traveler among the now-reviled New Critics, and he read these lines aloud to a Harvard audience more than twenty years ago. To me, speaking as someone thoroughly convinced that the disappearance of the world is the symptom of a social pathology, the most striking quality about Warren's talk is its consonance with Agee's work. Of course, Warren invested poetry with an importance that Agee would give it only ambivalently—Warren even goes so far, quoting Harry Levin, as to call poetry the "richest and most sensitive of human institutions" (p. 76). Worse yet, Warren celebrated a relation to the world—imposing, assertive, possessive—that Agee found repellent. But Warren demonstrated, all the same, an understanding of the modern situation nowhere evident to me in Trilling's work. "The self," Warren writes, "has been maimed" by its disconnection from the "world's body" (p. 73). Like Agee, Warren recognized that the world's body, in its resistance to our projections and demands, holds the key to the freeing of our own bodies—and that a medium like poetry, apprehended as *experience* rather than as *sign*, can provoke in the reader "a massive re-enactment, both muscular and nervous" of "the rhythms of the universe" (p. 74). However wrong he may have been to claim that poetry is the most fully human of human activities, Warren's ideal poet does what Agee tells us that we all should do, using words, symbols, and ideas to overcome our sense of isolation. Critical dogma may teach otherwise, but poems are never "about" poetry: They are "about" the arbitrary limits of ourselves and the movement beyond those limits.

And what holds true for Warren's ideal poet holds true for his ideal readers of poems. To read a poem, on his account, is to overcome the perception of the poem as a "poem" or of a word as a "word." The act of reading should culminate experientially in a disappearance of the text into world, and with it a disappearance of the reader, if only momentarily—Warren's "adventure in selfhood." But this is seldom the way we speak about poems now, with the rise of semiotics and its post-structuralist successors, for reasons that the following passage makes clear:

> [One] insidious legacy of the New Criticism is the widespread and unques-tioning acceptance of the notion that the critic's job is to interpret literary works. . . . In this critical climate it is therefore important, if only as a means of loosening the grip which interpretation has on critical conscious-ness, to take up a tendentious position and to maintain that, while the *experience of literature* may be an experience of interpreting works, in fact the interpretation of individual works is only tangentially related to the *understanding of literature*. (Culler, 1983, p. 5, italics added)

Here there can be no more talk about such things as the "world's body." What this second critic, Jonathan Culler wants instead of experience "both nervous and muscular" is a distanced, objective study of the signifying systems that pro-duce individual literary works. "At its most basic," Culler writes, "the lesson of contemporary European criticism is this: the New Criticism's dream of [an] encounter between innocent reader and autonomous text is a bizarre fiction. To read is always to read in relation to other texts, in relation to the codes that . . . make up a culture" (pp. 11-12). Although literature can, and probably must, be experienced through acts of interpretation, the proper object of professional study as Culler imagines it is not meaning or "felt life" but the signs and codes that predetermine the nature of meaning and feeling—the systems and struc-tures of signification that make reading possible.

A century from now, historians may ask themselves what disasters must have happened in the brief period that begins with liberalism's ascendan-cy, circa 1950, and concludes with the strident antihumanism of the semiotic "turn." Whatever answer these historians might provide, it will be clear that people living and working during those thirty years were forced to address a major collapse of confidence in some of their society's most fundamental insti-tutions. The semiotic turn marks a moment of social crisis whose causes reach beyond my purview here, but I would like to point out that the turn has not taken us anywhere except back to the dilemmas and disappointments of thirty years ago. When Culler shifted from the isolated text to the "text" of culture, he assumed that this larger text could be known with a precision and completeness never hoped for by the New Critics. But the history of criticism since the rise of the structuralist enterprise has been a history of growing disagreement and dis-array, not of greater concord on the question of method. As each new mode of reading supplants the next—structuralism supplanted by deconstruction, decon-struction by Foucauldian archaeology—it becomes more and more obvious that there will never be a science of meaning or ideology, since the "cultural text," no less than any poem, is subject to an infinite number of inescapably circular readings, each beginning with some root metaphor (words are signs, words are weapons, words are displacements, words are money) and each amenable to extension outward from an individual poem or novel to explicate all notable forms of representation. It is possible to conclude from this trajectory that we are learning more and more about "textuality." But it is also possible to say that the quick succession of critical trends exposes a continuing failure to decide what poems are really for in the absence of a human world.

Our great mistake, Agee might say, was to imagine that the codes and signifying systems, conventions or laws of structural transformation might give us a permanence lacking in our contingent, unpredictable everyday lives. He was convinced, in fact, that it was only a profound experience of contingency that might save us from our own worst impulses by overturning the terrible certainties that make one particular chair just a "chair," one particular tree just a "tree," one particular person just a "tenant farmer." Agee knew that all the things humans do in their everyday lives—preparing food or performing open heart surgery, writing novels or repaving roads—to the degree that these make possible an enlargement of human sympathy, might be understood as acts, as arts, of compassion. But Agee also recognized that the products of those same arts, if they are treated as permanent, obligatory systems, might be fashioned into instruments of our own oppression.

Nowhere did Agee see this transmutation more openly displayed—this negative alchemy by which the gold of human life is turned to lead—than in education. From the Cotton Belt to Harvard, the pedagogy was exactly the same: take the most splendid examples of humankind's encounters with world, which are always achieved in the uncertainties of a moment that will never return, and reduce them to an abstract formula that can be repeated ad infinitum. By this venerable means one can, of course, produce many millions of young men and women with all kinds of advanced degrees, but at the same time one pays a certain price because the construction of such knowledge creates a growing sense of unreality. And the haunting intimation that the real has dropped from sight keeps driving us back, in the most vicious of all vicious circles— because it consumes the best minds generation after generation—to the search for an even better method. On the one hand, institutionalization demands that the production of knowledge be made routine, but on the other, learning of the kind that restores our sense of connection to the world is, as Agee warned, the mortal enemy of routine.

To read Agee now is to understand how completely the academy has chosen education over learning, and how far we have to go if we hope to transform the instruments of oppression into something else. In our discourses today, the discourses of high theory and the semiotic turn, people like Agee have no voice at all. As for Agee himself, he remained throughout the brief span of his alcoholic life a gentle, gregarious revolutionary condemned to a solitary freedom he found unbearable. Praised and then forgotten, he has become the unfortunate subject of psychologizing biographers. Those of us who regret that the messenger arrived too soon should remember the trust he never ceased to demonstrate in the face of his despair about modernity: a trust in himself and in others, as beings capable of living fully in the world—but also a trust in the world as a home, as a body, complete beyond our power to diminish it. Only a decade before *Let Us Now Praise Famous Men* went to press, a professor of English had complained about the recalcitrance of that world. "Life," Joseph Wood Krutch (1932) had written in exasperation, always "baffles and seems almost to mock. It refuses long to remain consistently one thing or another and it seldom puts us in one mood without violating it soon after," reducing every-thing to the "hideous confusion" of nature (p. 50). Krutch thought that art could be better than life because art was more orderly, but Agee told us that "confu-sion" is our saving grace, and he cautions us that order itself has become our labyrinth, our prison. Beyond the labyrinth, at the place where our confusion returns, the world has been waiting for us. It is still waiting.

REFERENCES

Agee, James. "Religion and the Intellectuals." *Partisan Review, 17* (February 1950): 106-13.
_____. *Agee on Film.* Vol. 1. New York: Perigee, 1983. (1941).
_____. *James Agee: Selected Journalism.* Ed. Paul Ashdown. Knoxville: University of Tennessee Press, 1985.
_____, and Walker Evans. *Let Us Now Praise Famous Men.* Boston: Houghton Mifflin, 1988. (1941).
Bergreen, Laurence. *James Agee: A Life.* New York: Dutton, 1984
Culler, Jonathan. *The Pursuit of Signs: Semiotics, Literature, Deconstruction.* Ithaca: Cornell University Press, 1983.
Doty, Mark A. *Tell Me Who I Am: James Agee's Search for Selfhood.* Baton Rouge: Louisiana State University Press, 1981.
Freud, Sigmund. *An Outline of Psycho-Analysis.* Trans. and ed. James Strachey. New York: Norton, 1989. (1949).
Goffman, Erving. *Frame Analysis: An Essay on the Organization of Experience.* New York: Harper and Row, 1974.
Kramer, Victor A. *Agee and Actuality: Artistic Vision in His Work.* Troy, NY: Whitston, 1991.
Krupnick, Mark. *Lionel Trilling and the Fate of Cultural Criticism.* Evanston, IL: Northwestern University Press, 1986.
Krutch, Joseph Wood. *Experience and Art: Some Aspects of the Esthetics of Literature.* New York: Harrison Smith and Robert Haas, 1932.
Maharidge, Dale, and Michael Williamson. *And Their Children After Them: The Legacy of Let Us Now Praise Famous Men: James Agee, Walker Evans, and the Rise and Fall of Cotton in the South.* New York: Pantheon, 1989.
Pickens, Donald K. *Eugenics and the Progressives.* Nashville: Vanderbilt University Press, 1968.

Rafter, Nicole Hahn, ed. *White Trash: The Eugenic Family Studies, 1877-1919*. Boston: Northeastern University Press, 1988.

Schor, Juliet B. *The Overworked American: The Unexpected Decline of Leisure*. New York: Basic, 1991.

Trilling, Lionel. "Greatness with One Fault in It." *Kenyon Review 4* (Winter 1942): 99-102.

_____ . *The Liberal Imagination: Essays on Literature and Society*. New York: Viking, 1950.

Terkel, Studs. *Race: How Blacks and Whites Think and Feel about the American Obsession*. New York: Anchor/Doubleday, 1993.

Warren, Robert Penn. *Democracy and Poetry: The 1974 Jefferson Lecture in the Humanities*. Cambridge, MA:Harvard University Press, 1975.

Wittgenstein, Ludwig. *Culture and Value*. Ed. G. H. Von Wright and Heikki Nyman. Trans. Peter Winch. Chicago: University of Chicago Press; Oxford: Basil Blackwell, 1980.

Author Index

A

Agee, J., 171, 172*n*, 178, 178*n*, 179*n*, 182, *194*
Alexiou, M., 140, *151*
Anderson, C., 7, *11*
Anderson, W. T., 107, *118*
Annas, P., 75, *82*
Anson, C., 154*n*, *168*
Atwan, R., 33, *38*
Atwood, M., 76, *82*

B

Backman, M., 130, *135*
Banks, J. A., x, *xii*
Bartholomae, D., 161, *168*
Battenhouse, R., 5, *11*
Belenky, M. F., 75, *82,* 139, 140, 141, 145, 147, *150*
Bellah, R. N., 41, 46, 47, *52*
Bergreen, L., 173, 174, 181, *194*
Berlin, J. A., 107, 117, *118*
Berling, J. A., 7, *11*
Berube, M., 107, *118*
Bhaskar, R., 117, *118*
Bizzell, P., 107, 109, *118*
Blanchard, F. A., 44*n*, *52*

Bolen, J. S., 74, *82*
Bourdieu, P., 162, 165, *168*
Boyer, E. L., 1, *11*
Bradley, M. Z., 76, *82*
Brereton, V. L., 61, *66*
Brindel, J., 142, *151*
Brown, R. J., Jr., 154*n*, *168*
Bruffee, K., 117, *118*
Brummett, B., 131, *135*
Bruner, J., 140, *151*
Buber, M., 45, 45*n*, *52*
Buckley, M. J., 45, *52*
Buechner, F., 121, *135*
Bunch, C., 56, *66*
Burghardt, W. J., 48, *52*
Burke, K., 124, *135*
Burtchaell, J. T., 5, *11*
Bynum, C. W., 22, *38*

C

Cantor, N., 22, 23, *38*
Carter, S. L., 6, *11,* 138, 139, 146, 150, *151*
Cherwitz, R., 131, *135*
Chodorow, N., 75, *82*
Chopin, K., 76, *82*
Christ, C. P., 70, 72, 73, 75, 76, *82*

197

Subject Index

cosmopolitan, 179-80
in humanity, 176, 188-89
in natural law, 115-16
religious, 1-10, 20-23, 27, 34, 37,
39-40, 48-52, 55-66, 85-104,
113, 125, 132-33, 159
See also academy: relationship of
faith to; community: faith
feminism, 9, 56, 66, 70-76, 82, 90,
109, 127, 139, 145, 167, 188
Forche, Carolyn, 25
formalism, 89, 188
freshman students, 2, 47, 50, 88, 154-
59, 161-62, 166
fundamentalism
religious, 15, 26, 55-56, 61-63,
96, 100, 125-26, 162-67, 188

G

"gassho": Buddhist practice of, 23-24
"Gemarah": rabbinical, 93
Genesis, Book of, 93-95
glossing: textual, 28
"gnosis": cultivation of in monastic
education, 20, 34
Gospel of John, 18
graduate education, 2, 3, 14, 32, 59,
71, 91, 99, 166
See also teaching assistants: graduate
"grammatica": monastic practice of, 28
Great Depression, 173, 174-75, 179,
185
Greek choral tradition, 143
Greek literature: interpretation of,
140-46
Greek religion, 143, 145-46

H

"habitus": Pierre Bourdieu's concept
of, 162, 164-65
Hebrew Scriptures: interpretation of,
85-88, 93-97, 141, 144
hermeneutics, 91-97, 138-50, 165-66,
175-78

Holocaust: Jewish response to, 98-99
humanism, 192, 197

I

"idealizing" relationship: Heinz
Kohut's concept of, 166
intellectual ideas
influenced by antifoundationalism, 105-14, 116-18
influenced by semiotic turn, 171-
72, 179, 189-94
in relationship to spiritual beliefs,
1-10, 15, 17-37, 34-52, 55-66,
69-82, 85-104, 113-18, 146-50
in relationship to women's ways
of knowing, 140-41, 145-46
intellectual skepticism: causes and
effects of, 3, 5, 6, 19, 21, 29-30,
85, 87, 95-99, 106, 109, 138-39,
145, 146-47, 150
intertextuality, 63-64
iterability: in textual interpretation,
63-64

J

Jesuit education, 45-46, 48-49
Job, 99, 101-102
Judaism, 4, 9, 15, 26, 50, 85-88, 91-
99, 102-104, 147-48, 157
Julian of Norwich, 22-23

K

Kempe, Margery, 22-23
knowledge-making
academic, 57, 69-72, 82, 106, 116-
17, 159-60
spiritual, 72-82

L

leap of faith: Kierkegaardian, 149-50
"lectio divina": monastic practice of,
28-29
Let Us Now Praise Famous Men,
James Agee's, 171-80, 182-89,
191, 193-94
Levi-Yitzhak of Berditchev, Rabbi, 99